Marketing Ethics

Foundations of Business Ethics
Series editors: W. Michael Hoffman and Robert E. Frederick

Written by an assembly of the most distinguished figures in business ethics, the Foundations of Business Ethics series aims to explain and assess the fundamental issues that motivate interest in each of the main subjects of contemporary research. In addition to a general introduction to business ethics, individual volumes cover key ethical issues in management, marketing, finance, accounting, and computing. The books, which are complementary yet complete in themselves, allow instructors maximum flexibility in the design and presentation of course materials without sacrificing either depth of coverage or the discipline-based focus of many business courses. The volumes can be used separately or in combination with anthologies and case studies, depending on the needs and interests of the instructors and students.

1 John R. Boatright, *Ethics in Finance*, second edition
2 Ronald F. Duska and Brenda Shay Duska, *Accounting Ethics*
3 Richard T. De George, *The Ethics of Information Technology and Business*
4 Patricia H. Werhane and Tara J. Radin with Norman E. Bowie, *Employment and Employee Rights*
5 Norman E. Bowie with Patricia H. Werhane, *Management Ethics*
6 Lisa H. Newton, *Business Ethics and the Natural Environment*
7 Kenneth E. Goodpaster, *Conscience and Corporate Culture*
8 George G. Brenkert, *Marketing Ethics*

Forthcoming

Robert E. Frederick, *Business Ethics*
Denis Arnold, *Ethics of Global Business*

Marketing Ethics

George G. Brenkert

Blackwell Publishing

© 2008 by George G. Brenkert

BLACKWELL PUBLISHING
350 Main Street, Malden, MA 02148-5020, USA
9600 Garsington Road, Oxford OX4 2DQ, UK
550 Swanston Street, Carlton, Victoria 3053, Australia

The right of George G. Brenkert to be identified as the author of this work has been asserted in accordance with the UK Copyright, Designs, and Patents Act 1988.

First published 2008 by Blackwell Publishing Ltd

2   2009

Library of Congress Cataloging-in-Publication Data

Brenkert, George G.
   Marketing ethics / George G. Brenkert.
      p. cm. — (Foundations of business ethics)
   Includes bibliographical references (p.   ) and index.
   ISBN 978-0-631-21422-9 (hardcover : alk. paper) — ISBN 978-0-631-21423-6
(pbk. : alk. paper)   1. Marketing—Moral and ethical aspects.   2. Marketing—
Social aspects.   3. Business intelligence—Moral and ethical aspects.   4. Business
ethics.   I. Title.

   HF5415.B637 2008
   174′.9381—dc22

                              2007033955

A catalogue record for this title is available from the British Library.

Set in 10.5 on 12.5 pt Minion
by SNP Best-set Typesetter Ltd., Hong Kong
Printed and bound in Singapore
by Fabulous Printers Pte Ltd

The publisher's policy is to use permanent paper from mills that operate a sustainable forestry policy, and which has been manufactured from pulp processed using acid-free and elementary chlorine-free practices. Furthermore, the publisher ensures that the text paper and cover board used have met acceptable environmental accreditation standards.

For further information on
Blackwell Publishing, visit our website at
www.blackwellpublishing.com

Contents

Preface

Skepticism concerning business ethics has given rise to many well-worn jokes. But the skepticism regarding the ethics of marketing is much less humorous. The following complaints are common: Advertisements delude people and encourage them to buy things they do not want or need. Promotional campaigns encourage endless consumption and the acquisition of debt levels people cannot afford. Marketing researchers lie to respondents about the true nature of their research and intrude on their privacy. Direct marketing interrupts dinners and favorite television programs, as well as bringing the activity of the marketplace into one's private residence. Segmentation has targeted vulnerable populations with products that harm them. International marketing may take advantage of Third World populations. These are examples of complaints that are both frequent and widespread.

Unfortunately there is truth to many of these complaints. Marketers do engage in some of these activities. Marketers are sometimes their own worst enemies. But there is also exaggeration, misunderstanding, and misrepresentation of what marketing is about and what marketers do.

Since some form of marketing is unavoidable in modern economies, we are faced with a pressing dilemma. Do we acquiesce in the face of real (as well as mistaken) charges about the ethical nature of marketing, simply letting things go on as they may? Or do we attempt to address the ethical questions that marketing raises by directly responding to them? Despite the large numbers of people who seem to opt for the first alternative, the answer would seem obvious. We must directly address the ethical issues surrounding marketing. In adopting the second option, this book responds to and evaluates a number of the important ethical challenges marketing faces.

Ethical Challenges to Marketing

The basic ethical problem marketing raises is how to design a system for producing, distributing, and monitoring products in an ethical manner when market relations play a central role in this process. Current ethical challenges to marketing arise during a time when marketing, as well as most businesses, face considerable change and stress. The internet and e-commerce have altered the way business operates and the forms that marketing takes. Globalization and the intensified competition it represents have imposed added demands and pressures on marketers. In short, marketing is in considerable flux today. In many businesses, marketing functions are being rearranged. All this places significant moral strains on those in marketing.

This occurs while other changes are taking place in business and society more generally. There is great uncertainty and concern regarding the values and principles by which we work and live. Views on property rights are challenged by the ease of downloading music, software, and videos from the internet. Privacy is endangered by the data storage and mining techniques available to marketers. Employees' well-being is threatened by job insecurity due to outsourcing. Successful marketing techniques are said to lead to obesity and environmental degradation. Business scandals at a host of major corporations (both in the U.S. and around the world) have cast ethical doubts on the accounting, auditing, and investment communities. And marketing remains one of the most regularly and strongly criticized areas of business. Under these circumstances, it is urgent that we address the ethics of marketing.

A major thesis of this book is that marketing is a moral activity in the sense that it falls within the moral arena. Unlike amoral (or non-moral) technical questions concerning, for example, at what angle an all-terrain vehicle will tip over or how to calculate a firm's return on investment, marketing directly raises a host of moral issues. As such, morality is integral to marketing. Accordingly, I seek to explore those moral values and principles which are central to marketing. This is to explore marketing itself, not something peripheral to it.

To do this, I do *not* follow the path of previous books on the ethics of marketing. Typically, they present, first, a number of theories of morality or ethics. Like shoppers at a supermarket for ethics, readers are invited to place one or more items in their marketing ethics shopping basket. These books then proceed to identify various ethical problem areas in marketing and attempt to apply various formulae or schemas drawn from the ethical theories to moral issues within marketing. In doing so, they sometimes, at their weakest, merely ask the reader how he or she feels about that problem, before proceeding to the next problem. At their best, the ethical formulas seem external to the world of marketing.

This well-worn form of applied ethics does not take the reader into the ethical complexities of the problems marketers face. It suggests too readily that morality lies outside marketing and must be applied to it. It implies that values and norms are independent from the facts of marketing, and matters of personal feeling (see Putnam, 1995). These views should be rejected. On the other hand, the abstract general rules that such accounts come up with often offer little or no guidance to a marketing executive. Thus, I agree with Robin and Reidenbach that "the direct application of popular moral philosophies such as deontology or utilitarianism to ethical questions in marketing falls short in providing necessary guidance for marketers" (Robin and Reidenbach, 1993: 97). This kind of approach attempts to turn morality into a technical skill, one using various formulae or schemas. It is a legacy of modern philosophy (beginning with the seventeenth or eighteenth century) which sought to discover (and apply) natural laws of morality to man and society, as the natural sciences had done to nature.

Instead, I believe that moral thought and judgment grow out of a particular way of viewing or understanding moral situations (which include marketing). This involves drawing upon various principles, values, and ideals but cannot be reduced to them. Hence, it is crucial to grasp what it is to view situations morally and the various concepts and tools this involves, if one is to understand the strengths and weaknesses of the formulae and schemas that others present on behalf of morality.

It is natural in the face of moral complexity for people to seek a simple formula or magical moral wand by which they can easily resolve the moral issues they face. Let me state up front, there is no such thing. Or, perhaps more modestly, I should say, I have not found one. Of course, there are those who claim to have found such a magic formula. But one should be wary of such claims. They tend to be the moral equivalent of the "amazing" potions and wonderful "cures" that unscrupulous hucksters have offered to those in need. Moral formulas both simplify and falsify. For example, some have said that you can determine the ethical course of action by asking whether you would want to see that course of action announced in the morning newspaper with your name attached to it (the "Morning Paper" test). Matters are not so simple.

Some people might delight in seeing in the morning paper accounts of their activities which others would consider to be highly immoral. Surely (at least) some bank robbers enjoy seeing accounts of their deeds in the morning paper. On the other hand, if the "Morning Paper" test presupposes that one is, in some sense, "morally normal," then we need a test of "moral normality." Once again, the reader can see that we are off into something far more complex than a person's reaction to the morning paper.

In contrast, I seek to bring out the integral relations of marketing and morality as the basis for a practical (not applied) ethics. Since marketing activities fall within the moral arena, their moral nature is best addressed by simply discussing those marketing activities. Given the length of this book, it is *not* possible to discuss (or even to list) the many ethical issues that arise in marketing. That is not part of its aim. Besides, this would not foster ethical understanding. Instead, I take a few problems from a number of areas and discuss them so as to introduce essential concepts, principles, and theories. If the reader follows these presentations, then he or she can proceed on their own to other issues in marketing.

Accordingly, an objective of this book is to provide a number of illustrative discussions of ethical issues in marketing such that upon finishing this book a person will be better prepared to see and to understand the ethical issues in marketing. In these regards, it is striking that prominent texts in marketing will discuss packaging, but not its environmental implications, and portray product development, but not the effects of those products on children (see Kotler, 2000). They present models of consumer behavior, but omit any consideration of the ethical dimensions of these models. At best, ethics appears in occasional sidebar presentations, set off in a manner that appears designed to quarantine any spread of ethics to the main text on marketing.

In contrast, the present book draws out the ethical aspects of these marketing issues and provides the reader with a number of "ethical tools" which may be used on other occasions and with different issues in marketing. The identification and discussion of these "tools," together with the marketing ethical framework they constitute, is a central feature of this book. At the same time, I seek to raise some of the fundamental ethical questions which underlie major areas or domains of marketing. This involves considering various broader meanings and background assumptions of marketing that (together with their ethical dimensions) are infrequently considered in marketing literature. Among these are the importance of individual choice, freedom and responsibility, desire satisfaction, non-coercive exchanges, and instrumental efficiency. These are important not simply to marketing but to broader social and political views. Such notions suggest reasons why marketing has found expression far beyond its business roots in politics, social issues, and even religion. Such broader meanings and assumptions give meaning and direction to many of the discussions of the various problems in marketing ethics. I believe that this is another distinctive feature of this book.

Teaching Ethics

What about those who object that you can't teach ethics, so that little ethical good can come from these discussions? I agree that a book by itself cannot make people ethical. However, that is to place an unreasonable demand on discussions of marketing (or business) ethics. Through confronting the issues raised in such discussions people can learn more about their own values and moral thinking; they can gain a better idea about the presence and nature of moral issues in marketing; they can acquire a better sense of the nature of morality and of the complexities involved in making moral judgments; and they can come away with an idea of what kinds of things need to be done to enhance the place and role of morality in marketing. When people are better able to see the ethical dimensions of their behavior, they may be more inclined to act morally. When people open themselves up to the consequences of confronting questions of marketing (and business) ethics through books such as the present one, their behavior may change and some ethical good can be promoted. Further, as I note below, they may seek to change the systems within which they (and others) act. This can have an important effect on the ethical level of their behavior.

To this end, then, this book discusses ethical values and principles central to marketing. Among the most basic are those of autonomy, freedom, justice, trust, truth, and well-being. The nature of these principles and values is discussed within the context of various marketing issues. As such I seek directly to engage these moral questions, rather than keep them at arm's length. This contrasts with much of the literature on marketing ethics which is of a descriptive nature – it describes, lists, and categorizes various areas and problems of ethics in marketing (marketing research, distribution, etc.). Knowledge of how things actually work in marketing is important for moral reflection. However, the typical descriptive account of marketing ethics is not offered in the service of ethics or morality so much as on behalf of scientific knowledge. But just as it is mistaken to separate morality and marketing, it is also mistaken sharply to separate morality and descriptive (or scientific) studies (see Baier, 1985; Putnam, 1995). These divisions should be overcome, not deepened.

In so proceeding, this book is aimed at those interested in an introductory (but not elementary) acquaintance with the ethics of marketing. The book does not presuppose prior knowledge of marketing. Hopefully those who know very little of marketing will learn something about it in these pages. And those who are already well familiar with marketing may come to see its moral dimensions and how to address them more clearly. The book is written with the situation of marketing in the U.S. in mind. This is not wholly misdirected, in that marketing has such a free rein in the U.S. However, I have also tried to bring in a number of international dimensions and implications of a marketing ethics, so even those outside the U.S. may feel that they are not merely considering a domestic situation that does not relate to them.

Assumptions of the Book

Lying behind any discussion of these complexities are various assumptions that each author makes. If warning labels are appropriate to various products, warnings of an author's assumptions might be relevant for any book a person is about to read. The problem with this is that many times one's own assumptions are so familiar and close to one that they are difficult to identify.

Among the assumptions that I consciously bring to this book are the following. Ethics is an important and worthy topic of discussion that can be fruitfully and rationally discussed. Ethics or morality is not simply a matter of personal (or subjective) opinion. In this sense, ethics is not merely an individual matter. Some answers in ethics are better than others. We may not know "the" right answer, but we can identify reasons and grounds why some answers are better than others. Ethical closure may never be reached on all (or even most) subjects. This is true, however, of most interesting and important topics of human life. This does not mean that they cannot be fruitfully and rationally discussed. Marketing is one of the crucial areas of business. Finally, morality concerns decisions regarding both individuals and social and political conditions. Thus, I understand morality in a broad sense – it is not simply a matter of individual decisions and actions, but also of their social dimensions and implications. This is sometimes said to be a Greek sense of ethics, inasmuch as it sees morality and social and political philosophy as bound up together. I wholly embrace this view.

Accordingly, particular ethical decisions need to be considered within a larger view of the good life and how one's decisions and actions contribute (or don't contribute) to that overall good end. It may be that a person is effectively trapped and cannot do anything to change the general features of his or her life or job. Still, it is important to recognize such situations and consider how to deal with them. At the same time our account must take into consideration the diversity and pluralism of views held in most contemporary societies.

Finally, it will also be part of the following study that ethical questions cannot ultimately be resolved, in general, simply by individuals making ethical decisions. Individual responsibility is important. Through discussions of the preceding kind, this book seeks to foster that responsibility. However, individuals need the support which only their peers, their organizations, and society can provide. Hence, I do not propose a severely individualistic account of ethics. Instead, I like to think that it is a rather pragmatic account of marketing ethics that recognizes the role of individuals but also the limitations and opportunities they face in translating moral reflection into moral action.

Chapter One

Marketing, Ethics, and Morality

I The Ethical Challenges Marketing Faces

Marketing does not simply surround us, but envelops us, permeating our lives. Television, radio, newspapers, magazines, billboards, clothes with labels, packaging, the internet, posters, the movies, sky writing – virtually wherever anyone turns there is evidence that it has been touched by some marketer intent on promoting, informing, persuading, and/or selling us something.

Marketing is how we get our food, clothes, and the items we use every day. It influences and reflects how we think about the world, though surely marketing is not the sole influence to which we are subjected. In turn, marketing is influenced by what people themselves want and are willing to do. The influences run back and forth. As such, marketing plays a large role in people's lives. It is, in part, how a society defines itself and its treatment of its members.

A person might think that such a pervasive and important activity on which so much time and money are spent would be the object of relatively widespread moral agreement. How else has it achieved such significance in people's lives? Why else do people wear clothes with brand names, seek out brand products, watch commercials, and envision a better life in terms of acquiring more (and larger) products?

However, we are very ambivalent when it comes to marketing. It may satisfy us in many ways, but it infuriates us in others. We rely on it, but there are parts of it we dislike intensely. Marketing speaks to a larger drama in our lives of the conflicts between different sets of values and norms – between those related to the role of competition, identity, desire, greed, and fear in our society, but also those involving certainty, dependable quality, consumer-friendly service, trust, and inexpensive products and services. In short, to talk about marketing is to address an ongoing ethical conflict.

Ethical criticisms

The criticisms of marketing are both well known and widespread. They are raised not simply in North America or Europe, but appear in most countries around the world. Advertising is, of course, a favorite target of moral criticism. Its use of sex and fear to increase sales, not to mention its deceptive practices, are condemned by many. Retailers are often charged with privacy invasion. For example, when customers use their credit cards at retail stores the data from their use not only informs the company of which goods to restock but also is mined as part of a data profile which data processors can develop on individuals and various market segments. The amount and detail of the information can be impressive. Similarly, telemarketers are criticized for intruding on people at home with their telephone calls. When laws are passed regulating this activity, they seek ways around those laws, while insisting on their right to call potential customers.

Marketers are also faulted for how they treat their business customers when, for example, salespeople offer money, bribes, or other "special considerations" to suppliers or retailers to obtain special favors. Large retailers are attacked for exercising their considerable economic power over smaller retailers and suppliers. Some of these methods inhibit open competition by requiring smaller retailers only to stock the products of one marketer rather than those of others. For example, Coca-Cola insists that those who handle its products not handle Pepsi Cola. If they do, then Coke will withdraw its product, as well as other favorable financing arrangements they provide to the handlers. Microsoft has been repeatedly taken to court for the pressure that it has placed on other businesses to use its products. And Wal-Mart is frequently attacked for driving local enterprises out of business while destroying the central business districts of small towns. These criticisms resonate around the world.

If this were not enough, marketing has been criticized more generally as simply being wasteful, expending billions of dollars to persuade people to buy products they don't need. It is accused of bringing about the commercialization of society and human relations. It is reproached for promoting both materialism and consumerism. Marketers are said to foster conditions under which people take their identities from the brands they buy and wear, as opposed to developing their own, non-commercial identities. The current problem of obesity is attributed, at least in part, to the marketing practices of fast-food producers and advertisers.

Finally, an important part of anti-globalization protests relates to marketing. International marketers have been charged with imposing the values of their home countries on the countries in which they do business, destroying local businesses, and manipulating people to want things they cannot afford. The efficiency, rationality, and uniformity brought by international marketers have been attacked under the banner of the "McDonaldization of Society" (Ritzer, 2000).

Ethical defenses

Others, however, point to the benefits that marketing brings, not to mention other marketing feats that some say are morally praiseworthy. Brand marketing is said to provide a guarantee of quality, and a level of trust and security that customers welcome in a diverse and complex marketplace. Marketers have also been commended for helping their suppliers to improve standards and their own quality of production and delivery. For example, Starbucks has worked with coffee bean growers in Central America to improve their farming methods and the quality of the beans produced.

Through the competition marketing promotes, it is said, increasing numbers of people have been provided with more and better-quality goods and services than previous generations have ever experienced. And this has been done more cheaply than prior generations could imagine. Through the information marketing provides, customers can make more knowledgeable decisions than their predecessors about which products they want to meet their needs and desires. It is true that fear is used in some advertisements, but it may also move people to protect themselves and their families in ways they would not otherwise consider. Similarly, much of the information collected on people's purchases is not person-specific, and so does not violate anyone's individual privacy.

Marketing is also praised for contributing to the economies of developing nations. It brings them goods, services, and knowledge of products that they would otherwise not have. And though marketers have been accused of corrupting other societies and imposing on them Western or commercial values, it remains the case that many people in developing countries ardently desire to have such consumer goods available. Long lines of people freely line up at McDonald's restaurants, for instance, when they are available. In addition, some believe that Western marketing multinationals have played a positive role in improving the ethics of their nations (Kavali et al., 2001).

Finally, marketing techniques, when used by social marketers, have addressed social concerns, such as leprosy, AIDS, and forest fires. The results have been rather dramatic in some areas. For example, in Sri Lanka the levels of leprosy have dropped dramatically. In short, marketing is said to bring multiple and important benefits to people in both developed and developing countries.

Overview of this chapter

These ethical criticisms and praise are a small representation of the large number of different kinds of moral challenges marketing faces. The upshot is that we respond to marketing in a very mixed way. Whereas some people see darkness, others perceive considerable brightness surrounding marketing. We harbor, as a society, a deeply divided consciousness over marketing. Marketing reveals something about American – or perhaps modern – society, that is not always attractive. People engage in it and seek it out. Some pay to wear tee-shirts that advertise various marketing companies, such as the Gap, or Marlboro, or will only wear, eat, or use certain brands. But they also criticize and reject many of these companies' actions. How these criticisms and praise are to be handled, how they are ethically to be viewed, is the main topic of this book. It is little wonder that marketers often seem an embattled group.

However, marketers should not be viewed simply as forces of evil imposing themselves on innocent victims. Unless customers and citizens are simply dupes, passively taken in by marketers, we must also consider that they are co-participants in marketing, its successes and even its excesses. They too need to be challenged or questioned when it comes to the ethics of marketing and their views of the good life. In fact, a complete view of marketing ethics would consider marketing to consist of the full set of interrelations between marketers and customers. There is, then, room for self-reflection all the way around – customers, government, citizens, and marketers! Nevertheless, in this book, due to constraints on space and because of the initiating role they play in most marketing relations, I will focus mainly on the role of marketers.

Marketers (as well as the rest of us) need a way to sort through the many different ethical problems and promises attributed to marketing. Developments in technology (the internet, huge databases, ways to track goods, etc.) and globalization only make this situation all the more urgent and difficult, as do new techniques in persuasion and targeting people. To make sense of these ethical challenges and to do so in a way that merits serious consideration, three things must be done at the outset to set the stage for later discussions. Both ethics and marketing are misunderstood in ways that separate them and confound their relation. Hence, the first two tasks of this chapter are to address each of these notions. In doing this, I will work first towards a constructive pluralist view of ethics. I will then examine in some detail the nature of marketing. How we think about marketing and ethics (or morality) directly affects the ways we try to address the kinds of ethical criticisms and defenses noted above.

The third task is to draw out their interconnections. The result will be an initial sketch of a normative marketing ethical framework that, I will claim, is not only available to marketers when confronting moral issues, but is also rooted in marketing itself. We can proceed in subsequent chapters to fill in the details of this framework and how it can be used to address the ethical challenges marketing faces. These issues, the above criticisms should make plain, are not simply marginal, theoretical, or academic matters. They are central to the conduct of twenty-first-century marketing.

II Thinking about Ethics and Morality

Some marketers have responded to the above disputes by asking for moral guidance when it comes to particular marketing practices, or even marketing in general. They expect morality to speak to these situations and to offer directions as to what should be done. This book is an attempt to respond to these requests. However, there is no short answer, or simple formula, that can be given in response. The view that one or two easy formulas (e.g. the "Golden Rule" or the "Morning Paper" test) can answer the ethical issues in marketing is an obstacle that we must get past to think seriously about marketing ethics. Simple answers to complex problems should be viewed with suspicion. They may make us feel good and secure, while misleading us. As H. L. Mencken noted, "There is always an easy solution to every human problem – neat, plausible, and wrong."[1] Instead, this book provides a more complex, and hopefully correct, solution.

A different obstacle marketing ethics faces is the view that morality is unhelpful, because it is simply a matter of personal opinion. Different people have different moral opinions, so turning to morality isn't going to help you solve any problems.

This view, that dismisses the relevance of morality to resolving marketing disputes, needs to be addressed here, since it is widespread. One can imagine that if morality were simply a matter of opinion, it could not, as such, gain any "traction." On such a view, there is nothing outside each person to hold on to. Moral criticisms are simply personal feelings without any greater significance. You have your feelings and beliefs; I have mine. There is nothing "else" to which we can turn to resolve ethical disputes in marketing.

Though this view may be widely held, it is mistaken. It is both too broad and too narrow. It is too broad in that not every opinion or belief is a moral one. Some of our beliefs and values are moral, but others are religious, aesthetic, self-interested, etc. There may be some overlap, but they are distinguishable. One of the dangers of morality arises when it is extended to all realms of life.[2] This "moralization" of life falsely confers on every part of life the special importance and significance of morality. This is dangerous since it dilutes morality's significance.

This view is also too narrow in that morality is not simply an individual affair, or merely a matter of individual feelings and beliefs. Our individual moral beliefs and feelings are part of a moral system that extends far beyond each of us as individuals. It is that set of most important values, character traits, principles, and ideals which people in particular societies (and even globally) have developed to address what others have called the human predicament, i.e. the problems of human relationship and conflict. Some interpret this problem as the tendency of things to go wrong (Warnock, 1971; Robin and Reidenbach, 1993: 100). This is, however, too negative. Rather the point is simply that, within the relations and values which constitute and direct our daily lives, things may go wrong. However, they may also go "right."

Instead, morality refers to those basic and constitutive features of the lives of reason-giving beings that provide action-guidance with regard to the well-being of sentient life and the integrity of their world.[3] Since the resources, knowledge, and sentiments of people involved are all limited, there may also be conflict. But since many of the resources and occasions for solving these related "problems" are alike in all societies, similar outcomes have developed in different areas of the world. Still, there remain many differences among societies, cultures, communities, and individuals.

Accordingly, we are born into these moral systems. We don't simply create them individually. It is true that each of us has his or her own beliefs and feelings about what is moral in any particular situation. But that is simply to say that we interpret more general values and norms as being applied or realized in different ways as a result of other factual beliefs, tolerances for risk, relationships, etc. that we may have. Even in situations where we come to different conclusions in these disputes, we may share the same values and norms. So morality isn't *simply* a matter of personal beliefs and feelings, though it does involve the different experiences, sensitivities, and emotions that people have in similar situations.

But since morality regards the actions, relations, consequences, and character traits that form our lives with others, as well as the contexts in which those are experienced, various facts, logical implications, and empirical theories are relevant to our discussions with other people about our moral beliefs and judgments. We see examples of this appeal to different facts, consequences, and relationships in the above sections on "ethical criticisms" and "ethical defenses." Many of the points made there are parts of much larger arguments regarding the ethics of various marketing practices.

For these reasons, we can discuss the moral dilemmas and problems that people have in our society, as well as in other societies (both past and present). Our understandings may, of course, be limited in various ways. But, again, we are not separated into isolated moral universes of individual moral belief.

The importance of morality, then, lies in the fact that without moral systems in which we agree, at least in general, life would not only be a much less bearable experience, it would also be utterly changed. The relations of parent and child, friend and friend, employer and employee, seller and purchaser, etc. all presuppose various moral expectations, responsibilities, and duties. Without them, our very identities as human beings would be transformed.

The fact that most people behave in accord with large parts of the moral systems of each society means that people are not gratuitously harmed, they can trust at least some other people, they experience love, exhibit courage, expect honest answers, and are outraged when treated unfairly. It would be silly, of course, to hold that all people always act on these values and principles. That is why the principles of morality are normative, which is to say that they tell us what we ought to do or to be. They don't simply describe what we actually do. In this, morality and law are similar. They are both prescriptive, not descriptive. But though what they direct us to do may overlap, morality and law still differ in their justifications, forms of enforcement, penalties, domains of concern, and the types of behavior they cover. The law is something that we identify as bound up with courts, legislatures, and the police. In short, though its influence extends across most of our lives, it is a distinctive area of social life. Morality, on the other hand, cannot be identified with such distinctive, or separate, social organizations or public agents. It does not have courts, buildings, or appointed officials. Morality is how we go about those important and defining parts of our lives, when questions arise regarding the well-being of ourselves and others, and the integrity of our world.

In the preceding I have used both the terms "ethics" and "morals" (or "morality"). In doing so I have followed the practice of those who equate these two terms (one is from Greek and the other from Latin). However, others distinguish between ethics, as the theoretical or reflective study of morality, and morality, as those values, norms, and ideals people live by. Either usage is acceptable, so long as we understand that there are these different activities – theoretical studies, on the one hand, and the primary normative principles and values by which people should live, on the other hand.

Ethics as a reflective study of morality only emerges when people do not simply rely on traditional or conventional rules or principles, but attempt to take the measure of morality in some critical and evaluative manner.

According to some, such ethical reflection only pertains to "general questions about what is good or right and not when it tries to solve particular [moral] problems" (Frankena, 1973: 5). But this is to pose a form of reflection or theorizing about morality that might be carried on without being tested or put to particular uses. This is not how ethics is understood here. Instead, I view ethics as critical reflection or theorizing about morality that must be tested against how well it can help us to solve the particular moral problems we face, such as those raised in marketing.

Regardless of whether we talk about morality in its general or specific features, it is mistaken to hold that morality is irrelevant or unrealistic if everyone doesn't follow it. It would be irrelevant if it set a standard so high that no one could follow it. Then it would be absurdly idealistic. But this need not be the case. Instead, an effective morality will set standards, subject to reason and evidence, by which people can and should behave. The upshot is that morality is neither simply a matter of opinion, nor irrelevant to marketing. Though too many marketers don't always do what they morally ought to do, this does not itself make morality (or the ethics of marketing) irrelevant.

None of what has been said here, so far, suggests which things are ethical or not. I haven't identified any particular moral values, norms, or ideals. I have "merely," but significantly, contended that we cannot simply look to our own beliefs, and that reasons and evidence are relevant to ethical or moral issues. Of course, not everyone will do what reason and evidence imply; they will not all do what they should. Still, because morality is normative and humans fallible, this should not be surprising. In any case, such views are not the basis for skepticism regarding the importance of ethics for marketing. On the contrary, having a clear view of morality is one of the most helpful aids we can have in confronting the kinds of ethical challenges noted above.

Now, just as various views of morality are unhelpful in thinking about the ethical challenges marketing faces, so too are various views that some people have regarding marketing. This includes the views that marketing is simply a scientific, amoral affair, or that all its questions can be solved by appealing to self-interest and the law (see Gaski, 1999). A regrettable consequence of such a view is that it contributes to marketers not seeing moral problems that they face. But first we must refine our views on marketing. Because many marketing books and texts often begin with a simple definition of marketing, they thereby close off some important insights into what marketing is and its relations to ethics. Once we have a better view of marketing we can, then, address these other questionable views of marketing and begin to build a case for the marketing ethics that we can use to address the ethical challenges above.

III Defining Marketing

It might be thought rather simple to say what marketing is. In fact, there are very different views about marketing. In the past half-century, the American Marketing Association (AMA) has championed three different definitions of marketing, each with distinctive implications. And dozens of other definitions of marketing have been offered by others. Since marketing was only identified and defined as a distinctive set of activities at the beginning of the twentieth century, this should not be terribly surprising. Accordingly, the very attempt to define marketing is part of an ongoing process of the self-creation of marketing.

The business concept of marketing

For a large part of the twentieth century, marketing was understood in terms of a number of interrelated business activities whereby a product is transferred from the producer to the customer. So viewed, it involved more than advertising or even retail sales, though these were essential to it. The 1960 definition of marketing by the American Marketing Association captured this view when it defined marketing as "the performance of business activities that direct the flow of goods and services from producer to consumer or user" (AMA, 1960: 15).[4] As such, marketing includes "All of those activities involved in the distribution of goods from producers to consumers and in the transfer of title thereto" (Bartels, 1965: 56).

On the business concept of marketing, the economic process was divided into production and distribution. Marketing was focused on distribution. It was a technical process that dealt with "physical distribution and the economic and legal aspects of transaction" (Bartels, 1974: 73). In this process, the sale of products was often seen as the heart of marketing, even though it was not the whole of it. Such a view was congenial to those who viewed marketing as a science, and, as such, an activity quite distinct from ethics.

The problem with this view is that it is too narrow, in at least two different ways. First, it does not capture all the areas in which marketing now takes place. Beginning in the 1960s and 1970s a number of marketers argued that other organizations than business organizations used the various tools of the marketing mix (see Hunt, 1976: 18). Whether it be the police, museums, public schools, anti-cigarette groups, "all of these organizations are concerned about their 'product' in the eyes of certain 'consumers' and are seeking to find 'tools' for furthering their acceptance" (Kotler and Levy, 1969a: 11–12). In these ways, marketing expanded beyond the realm of business (as usually understood).

Second, though marketing, as so viewed, involves scientific aspects, this is only part of what constitutes marketing. For example, it is true that marketing involves consumer research, and this can (and should) be done scientifically. But it also involves decisions on which products to produce, how to go about promoting and advertising them, what kinds of data will be collected on consumers and how it will be used, as well as a host of other activities. Some of this involves scientific studies, for example analyses of consumer data. But also part of these activities are various decisions about whether information in ads is deceptive or not, whether consumers' privacy is violated when the data is collected, and what kinds of return policies stores should have. These decisions, whatever they are, are not simply matters of fact or science, but involve questions of what ought (both legally and morally) to be the case. Accordingly, marketing must be seen more broadly.

The generic concept of marketing

One prominent response to the above criticisms was the suggestion that marketing should be seen as "the application of marketing functions or techniques for both economic and social, business and nonbusiness processes" (Bartels, 1974: 73). In short, we should opt to define marketing not in terms of its subject matter (e.g. the economic distribution of goods), but in terms of the technology by which the subject is pursued (Bartels, 1974: 74). This revised view of marketing was intended to capture the greatly extended scope of marketing.

But what is it that brings these various techniques and tools under the "marketing" umbrella? Similar kinds of surveys, research on consumer behavior, focus groups, data-collection, use of incentives, and even advertising might be used by others in non-marketing ways. Hence, what is it that transforms the use of these techniques and tools into marketing ones?

The answer was that these tools are all being used in the service of exchanges or transactions, which are the real core of the marketing universe. Thus, marketing was even more broadly interpreted as involving exchanges or transactions, and the cause-and-effect phenomena associated with them (Bagozzi, 1975: 32). As Kotler claimed, "The core concept of marketing is the transaction. A transaction is the exchange of values between two parties. The things-of-value need not be limited to goods, services, and money" (Kotler, 1972a: 48). On this view the exchange is the real subject matter of marketing which was then seen as "the science of transactions" (Hunt, 1976: 25; Bagozzi, 1978: 536).

When one takes this approach, marketing is defined not by economic exchanges with an aim for profit, but by the transactions in which people engage in which various values are transferred from one party to another so as to satisfy the wants, goals, etc. of the individuals involved (Kotler, 1972a). Marketing is not even defined, on this view, in terms of the tools of marketing, though it is through these tools and techniques that the exchanges were to be fostered. Instead, "marketing is specifically concerned with how transactions are created, stimulated, facilitated, and valued. This is *the generic concept of marketing*" (Kotler, 1972a: 49; emphasis added).

As a consequence some in marketing have concluded that other areas involving exchanges of values are also forms of marketing: for example teaching, the military, and religion. In fact, any exchange appears open to being brought under the marketing umbrella. "What in marketing is 'selling' in the school is 'teaching,' in the church 'proselytizing,' in politics 'propagandizing,' in the military 'indoctrinating.' The marketer who adapts his product to the market is doing what the teacher does in organizing his class presentation, the preacher in sermonizing for the needs of his congregation, or the housewife in catering to the food tastes of her family" (Bartels, 1974: 75). This kind of approach apparently led Billy Graham to compare marketing efforts on behalf of religion and Christianity to those involved in selling soap (Fromm, 1955: 109).

This view of marketing was captured in 1985 when the AMA adopted a new definition of marketing that identified it as "the process of planning and executing the conception, pricing, promotion, and distribution of ideas, goods, and services to create exchanges that satisfy individual and organizational objectives."[5]

On this view, marketing becomes identified with a set of techniques and a mindset that seeks, efficiently and effectively, to attain various goals, and to manage those involved in attaining those objectives. The satisfaction of these goals is to be through exchanges that the marketer tries to create. As such, marketers seek to change behavior, though the specific ends remain open. In this sense, the *nature or concept of marketing*, as defined here, is indifferent with regard to its ends. Since the objectives referred to are individual and organizational, many have taken them to be simply self-interested ends. But nothing in this definition requires this.

In these discussions, we can see marketers grappling with just what is marketing. But if the business view of marketing noted above was too narrow, surely the generic view is too broad. There are several problems here.

An ancient philosopher, Anaximander, concluded that all that existed was water. He has been roundly criticized for such a view because if everything was water, then that term became useless to pick out that distinctive substance that fills streams, lakes, and oceans. Similarly, some marketers have also criticized the generic view of marketing. They have argued that so to expand the boundaries of marketing is to needlessly confuse what is marketing (Luck,

1974). Robin objected that Bagozzi's notion of a "generalized exchange" extends the boundaries of marketing beyond the realm of usefulness (Robin, 1979: 607).

The point is that when a term is so stretched to cover everything, it loses its meaningfulness; it becomes worthless to pick out some phenomena from others. Two people having sex are engaged in an exchange (of sorts), but that doesn't mean that all other exchanges are forms of sex. However, it is this kind of reasoning that has led some marketers to the above faulty conclusion that all these areas are forms of marketing. We should recall Hunt's sage advice that "A good definition of marketing must be both properly inclusive and exclusive" (Hunt, 1976: 19). If everything turns out to be marketing, we have failed in our attempt to capture what is special about marketing.

Second, some have thought that the underlying problem here is that marketing only holds for markets, not for non-market (hence, non-profit) activities. They ask rhetorically, "Why else do they call it 'marketing'?!" (see Luck, 1969, 1974; Robin, 1979). But, as the above comments on the business concept of marketing should indicate, this response is mistaken. The history of marketing for the past several decades reveals that marketing need not be tied to traditional markets (involving the buying and selling of goods and services). Marketing has clearly been extended to the political and social realms. Non-profit organizations also engage in marketing.

However, what is correct about this objection is its contention that it is important to distinguish between markets and other areas of life, whereas the generic view collapses them all into one form of life. Such a reductive view neglects (or denies) the different values, standards, assumptions, and expectations that compose different areas of life. To do so poses important conceptual and ethical problems.

Markets, families, religion, education, science, the courts, politics (to name a few) are all different areas of human life because of the different values, standards, etc. that compose them. This is not to say that the values and norms in these areas are utterly different from each other. In fact, they are instances or specifications of more general principles, norms, and values that apply to all these areas. Still, these overarching values and norms are instantiated differently in these various areas.

Accordingly, people operating in one area will tend to have a different mindset than those in some other area. Think of the differences, for example, among accountants, marketers, physicians, and musicians. They go about their tasks very differently, due (in part) to their different beliefs, values, practical principles, and assumptions. Various exchanges do take place in all the areas these individuals work in. But to claim that the exchanges in all these different areas are forms of marketing exchanges is to transform those areas by inserting values, norms, and assumptions from marketing. This is due to the fact that many of the values and assumptions of marketing (hence, its mindset) have arisen out of markets.

To appreciate this point, one might consider how marketing would operate if it were viewed as a form of religion (perhaps theologians made this claim), and the relations within marketing were governed by what we recognize as religious values and assumptions. In such a case, marketing relations would, supposedly, be governed by notions such as grace, forgiveness, holiness, prayer, sacredness, and salvation. Surely marketing would look quite different from how we ordinarily think about it! A similar transformation takes place when religious, family, and scientific relations are seen as instances of marketing exchanges or relations.

In effect, the generic account of marketing fails to attend to contextual features critical for marketing. By identifying exchanges (abstractly identified) as the heart of marketing this approach eliminates from those exchanges what makes them *marketing* exchanges. In doing this it has also, unwittingly (perhaps), excluded important value and normative assumptions crucial to marketing.

As I noted above, whereas one of the dangers of morality is the moralization of all of life, the corresponding danger of marketing is that of the "marketization" of all of life. This is what occurs with the generic concept of marketing. In fact, it offers a concept of generic exchange, not of marketing. Extensions of morality and marketing are both mistaken and dangerous.

We do not want an account of marketing that implies that all these areas are forms of marketing. However, we do want one that will permit us to recognize that marketing, in various ways, may take place in those areas – which we may then want to approve or disapprove. In short, there is an important difference between what marketing is and how (and where) it should be applied. Those areas to which it may be applied (whether desirably or not) do not thereby become forms of marketing. An account of marketing should leave open the possibility of discussing whether those applications of marketing are desirable or not.

IV Marketing as a Practical Activity

Accordingly, I propose that we consider marketing to be a set of coordinated activities that, in response to background interrelations between marketers and society members, are designed to create, communicate, and convey, through voluntary exchanges, something those targeted will value, and to do so in ways that fulfill the objectives of marketers and/or their organizations.

This is not, as such, a definition of marketing as much as an initial explication and promissory account of marketing that needs to be filled out in this section (and the rest of the book).[6]

What is clear from this statement is that marketing is a complex, cooperative human activity, involving networks of explicit and implicit understandings, agreements, and rules, through which various external goods (for marketers as well as those targeted by them) may be produced (see MacIntyre, 1984; Solomon, 1992). In addition, marketers may realize various internal goods through their activities, for example through "strategic imagination and competitive intensity" (MacIntyre, 1984: 188), and hence the use of their analytical and practical skills. Accordingly, marketers may both care for the excellent performance of their tasks and take pride in the resulting work. As such, marketing is an example of a social practice.

My aim in sketching out below the basic features of this view is to reveal various ethical dimensions that are integral to marketing. The result is that it becomes implausible to maintain that marketing is simply a science, or that it is an amoral activity. Once this point is secure, the door will be open to developing a moral framework that can provide guidance when issues of marketing ethics arise.

There are four basic features of this understanding of marketing:

(a)   goal-oriented action
(b)   capacity for responsible choice
(c)   instrumental relatedness
(d)   competition

Goal-oriented action

Marketing exchanges are directed or goal-oriented exchanges. They are not like other exchanges that may be open-ended and non-directed. People sitting around a campfire or at the dinner table, or even hanging out at a coffee shop, may engage in (conversational) exchanges of which no one knows (beforehand) the likely outcome. In contrast, in marketing exchanges marketers intentionally and actively seek to bring about an exchange which is designed to attain an end they seek.

These exchanges can be simply individual ones, though even then they occur within a social context of values, expectations, norms, and ideals that affect these exchanges. However, increasingly, marketers are interested in developing explicit, ongoing relationships with customers within which individual transactions may occur, and customers play a role in creating these exchanges.[7] Since these relationships involve more than a simple series of actions, there may be goals not only for the particular exchanges but for the relationships as well. The most recent AMA statement builds the management of customer relationships into its definition of marketing. However, this unduly narrows the view of marketing, since it would still be marketing even if a marketer focused only on individual exchanges, rather than longer-running relationships. Focusing on relationships may be a better way of doing marketing (at least in some instances). But even poor or unethical marketing remains marketing.

In approaching exchanges and relationships with this goal-directed mindset, marketers may not only modify their own behaviors to attain their objectives, they may also seek to modify (either in the short or long term) the behavior of those they target. As Kotler says, "marketing managers seek to influence the level, timing, and composition of demand to meet the organization's objectives" (Kotler, 2000: 5). As such, though marketers may be interested in informing customers about products and even satisfying their wants or needs, they are also intent on eliciting a certain behavioral response, viz., to buy a product, to vote for a candidate, to use a condom, etc. (see Kotler, 2000: 12; Andreasen, 2001). This characterization of marketing does not imply any particular ethical conclusion, though clearly questions of ethics must arise at this point regarding how this is done. In short, this is an ethical opening here that requires filling.

Marketing involves not only meeting the objectives (ends or purposes) of marketers but also supplying something of value to those they target. It is frequently assumed that in so doing marketers are (merely) seeking to satisfy their own ends and hence are selfish. However, neither marketers nor their customers need be viewed as wholly selfish, though clearly they are interested in their own well-being.

There is an important difference between being selfish and having self-interested ends. Something can be in a person's self-interest, but not be selfish, simply because the interests of others either are not involved or do not conflict with one's interests. Something is selfish only when it overrides the interests of others when those interests should be given precedence. Such selfishness is often attributed to Adam Smith and marketing's origins in market exchanges. However, even Smith spoke of the self-interest of shopkeepers, not their selfish interests. When people exchange goods in the market, the fact that each person looks to his or her own self-interest does not make those actions necessarily selfish.

A marketer's (or a customer's) own (ultimate) ends or purposes (in this context) might be his or her own interests, or those of the marketing firm (or its employer). These purposes might be for profit, for reputation, fame, or power. They could also be for other goals such as the satisfaction of consumer needs, or the fulfillment of various social values and norms. What those goals are, in fact, is an empirical matter and will depend upon the setting in which marketing is applied. Though the ultimate objectives (ends) are generally taken to be those of the marketers themselves, there is no need to define these simply in terms of profit or narrow self-interest. Hence, there is no necessity to the claim that marketing is based on self-interest and the law. This is particularly the case when marketers engage social issues in the form of social marketing. Then their concerns may be focused on the interests of those they seek to help, rather than on their own self-interests. Still, this is a form of marketing.

The fact that both marketers and customers voluntarily exchange certain things of value entitles both marketers and customers to make certain moral demands of each other. One such demand is that they exchange or transfer their "goods" only in certain ways, for example, not by stealing them from each other, or compelling the other to give them up. Some, but not all, of these rights will be captured in the law. Together they define (in part) a realm of freedom within which people may engage in marketing exchanges.

Finally, a marketer's proximate objectives (purposes or ends) are those that work to accomplish his or her own ultimate ends or purposes. In this context these proximate ends might be to focus on making production as efficient as possible, lowering its costs, mass-producing goods, or keeping the product stocked and the consumer informed about the product (a *production orientation*). Or marketers (businesses) might focus on aggressively selling and promoting the products they have (already) made (a *sales orientation*). Marketers then focus especially on persuading the customer to act in ways the marketer wishes. Perhaps this approach would best attain marketers' ultimate goals. Or they might focus on satisfying consumer wants. Some identify this as a *marketing orientation*, though it might be better to say *customer orientation* since the previous two stages are also forms of marketing. Then marketers seek out the wants and aims of customers and attempt to fulfill them, though this does not rule out also trying to influence customer behavior at the same time.

Sometimes these three different approaches to exchange relationships are portrayed as different stages in the development of marketing. This suggests that the last stage is the highest and most appropriate. Others maintain that these are three different ways of going about marketing (Levitt, 1986). The implication here is that marketers might, in different circumstances, adopt one or another of these approaches. Indeed, they might even mix them in various ways. With the development of modern economies and society, there does seem to be some tendency towards the last approach, but it is too strong, I believe, to say that therefore these are developmental stages in marketing such that the last stage is the highest (and best) stage.

In any case, the customer-orientation approach is also known as the *marketing concept* (see chapter 2). This should not be confused with the *concept of marketing* (which we are discussing here), even though this conflation frequently occurs. For example, Stanton et al. say that "the essence of marketing is a transaction or exchange. In this broad sense, marketing consists of activities designed to generate and facilitate exchanges intended to satisfy human needs or wants" (Stanton et al., 1994: 5). In this way, the marketing concept absorbs the concept of marketing. This is undesirable and fails to capture conceptually the changing practical nature of marketing. Once we move to focus on the exchanges at the heart of marketing and these are postulated to occur only when those involved satisfy their respective wants or desires, one can see how far along one is to the marketing concept, viz., that marketing correctly understood must focus on the satisfaction of customer wants and needs. Still, this would mistakenly identify one form of marketing with marketing itself. It is clear that exchange partners (individual or business) are crucial to marketing. But to say this is not to identify what that role is, since marketing can take, and has taken, different views of exchange.

Capacity for responsible choice

Marketing is a form of voluntary exchange. If the latter notion means anything, it refers to transactions that proceed from the unconstrained choice or will of the individuals (or organizations) involved. Accordingly, marketing presupposes some minimal level of capacity or competence to make choices and the related responsibility for the choices made. In short, it presupposes its participants are capable of a basic form of self-determination or autonomy. If one takes candy from a baby by offering some worthless object in return, even though this might be viewed as an "exchange" in some sense, this is not the sense in which marketing speaks of exchanges. For marketing exchanges, each party must have a minimal level of competence so that they know what they are doing and can be said to have voluntarily engaged in an exchange. Whether such capacities and competencies are simply innate, requiring only maturation, or also require various resources and enabling conditions is a matter of dispute. But their importance is not disputed. What counts as minimal levels of competence and knowledge is the subject of considerable debate in which different normative views clash. However, that there must be such minimal levels is simply part of the concept of marketing.

In fact, both marketing and morality assume that (mature) individuals are, in general, capable of making decisions for themselves and taking responsibility for those decisions. Such views lie behind the questions that are raised regarding marketing to children and the vulnerable. In this sense, we can understand the statement of the American Marketing Association, at the outset of its Statement of Ethics, that marketers are responsible for their choices and actions (see appendix I). Of course this assumption of responsible choice applies not simply to marketers but also to those whom marketers target. Later chapters will discuss the strength of one's capacity for choice and the extent of individual responsibility that different forms of marketing require. However, that people must have some (minimal) capacities for choice and responsibility arises out of the nature of marketing as well as morality.

Information

The fact that marketing presupposes that its audience is capable of making (voluntary) choices and decisions implies that they have (or may obtain) relevant information. It is not enough to have an engine if you don't have the fuel for the engine. Information is the fuel for capable choice. This requires that the parties must be able to communicate with each other (Stanton et al., 1994: 5; Takala and Uusitalo, 1996).

Indeed, the exchange relation not only rests upon, but also presupposes, an exchange of information as well as that of a product or service. The person with whom the marketer seeks to engage in an exchange must have certain information and beliefs about the nature and conditions of that exchange. Similarly, the marketer must have particular beliefs about the customers (or potential customers) with whom they seek to engage in exchange(s). In short, such information is a two-way street.

This information requirement is captured by talk of the right of consumers to be informed about the purchases they seek to make. President Kennedy enunciated, in the 1960s, such a right in his proclamation of a consumer bill of rights. Of course, consumers are not the only ones that have a right to know in this exchange relation. Marketers also have a right to know about relevant features of their customers. Further, these rights imply corresponding responsibilities of the exchange partners to provide relevant information. In short, as above, we have a complex moral relation of rights and responsibilities at the heart of marketing.

Finally, such communication presupposes that the participants are able, at least in some general sense, to distinguish false from truthful communication. If they could not, communication would not take place. Potential customers would not be informed, but distracted or perplexed. Each side to the exchange would have little or no idea about what the other side proposed. Marketing would break down. Accordingly, marketing carries assumptions regarding truthfulness. This doesn't mean, of course, that both marketers and customers do not engage in trying to deceive the other or simply telling the other lies. However, the ability to distinguish lies and deception from truth is crucial for the capacity for responsible choice. In the simplest exchanges the exercise of this capacity might merely require that a potential customer be able to inspect the product. However, in more sophisticated exchanges, other means will be required to make these discriminations, for example other companies that certify products, regulations on deception, trusting relationships with marketers. Thus another side of this aspect of marketing is that marketing involves some assumption that fraud or deceit cannot (as a matter of general fact) characterize marketing.

Freedom

Since marketing exchanges are voluntary ones, each party must be free (in some appropriate sense) to accept or reject the exchange offer (Kotler, 2000: 12). Otherwise the decisions and choices regarding an exchange would be a delusion. Armed robbery is not a form of marketing exchange, even though an exchange might be said to occur. Surely one has a "choice," viz., to be shot, but this is not a free or unconstrained choice. And though a person chooses to save his or her own life, it is a choice that, absent the robber's pistol, the person would not have made.

Accordingly, the voluntary exchanges marketing seeks to bring about must not only offer a choice, but one in which a person is not coerced or intimidated by the marketer into making a particular choice. Any pressures upon that individual must, at least, not go beyond some minimal level. This does not mean that to say that something is voluntary is to say that it is wholly unconstrained. Due to social conditioning or the expectations of a particular role – for example wife, student, employee, etc. – a person might voluntarily make a choice or act in a certain way that is, nevertheless, significantly constrained by his or her social and cultural circumstances.

Nevertheless, since the constraints within these roles are not imposed by marketing, they do not (ordinarily) prevent those within the roles from engaging in marketing activities. The point is that the person could have, to a greater or lesser extent, done something else, but the person's choice or will played an effective role in the particular situation. There were other "choices."[8] Such freedom underlies the legitimacy or justification of marketing. It is a plausible basis for talk about a consumer right to choose, such as Kennedy also included in his list of consumer rights. However, as identified here, it is not a right to a cornucopia of products from which to choose, but a more modest right that voluntary exchanges require uncoerced choices. How extensive the range of choice is will differ from time to time, and from country to country. Whatever that range may be, marketing can only exist within a broad spectrum of situations in which it does not seek to impose, coercively on others, various decisions or actions on a person.

The debate regarding marketing, then, is not whether freedom is required, but how much and what kind(s) of freedom. Any freedom within the market must be within certain bounds, regulations, and laws. The realm of marketing is not one of disorder or anarchy. In fact, some constraints are crucial to people being free (or autonomous) and responsible for their behavior.

Accordingly, questions are rightfully raised when, for example, some marketers seek to take advantage of pressures they can place on potential customers: for example, children nagging their parents for a product, people feeling pressured to buy beauty products, the role of fear in advertising and in sales, and the role of uncertainty (if you don't buy now, it may be gone). Part of the objection to such activities is that they run up against the issue of coercion or freedom. How this should be worked out we must consider below. The point here is that there is a base assumption of freedom and voluntariness in marketing to which all arguments on marketing may (and must) return.

Marketing makes few assumptions about what conditions are required for people to be free. However, two are worth noting. First, if people are not (physically) forced or constrained by some individual person or organization to act in a particular way, marketing assumes that, in general, they are free. That is, "externally" people are free if other people or institutions are not coercing or constraining them to act in various ways that a person could not reasonably or ordinarily resist. Freedom in this sense does not speak to various material conditions that people might have to enjoy, or to exercise, a freedom they have from coercion. Second, marketing freedom also has an internal dimension. "Internally" people are assumed to be free to make various choices (this is required for their autonomy and responsibility). Minimally this means that people may choose to act in self-interested ways, or in ways that accommodate or focus on the interests of others (even though these may – but need not – coincide with one's own interests). In short, people are not constrained to act simply in an egoistic fashion, always and only seeking simply their own interests. In fact, some social and political marketing appeals to people's concern for other people. Similarly, some ordinary marketing appeals to one's concern to protect one's children, spouse, parents, the environment, etc. Accordingly, though many marketers (and others) assume that human beings are simply self-interested, neither marketing nor other facts about human beings warrant adopting this as an assumption about human beings upon which to build a theory of marketing, let alone a theory of marketing ethics.

Instrumental relatedness

Marketing seeks to move those it targets to accept or buy something that the marketer is offering or proposing to them. People who disagree or are dissatisfied with a marketer's products or activities may decline or remove themselves from the offering, i.e., they may exit the proposal or relationship. In this, they may exercise considerable influence or power over marketers, especially when they do so in some coordinated fashion, such as boycotts. And though they may communicate their views to marketers regarding their products, they do not have a voice (in the sense of entitled participation or equal say) in the final determinations. Even though some current marketers argue for much greater interactivity with customers or stakeholders, marketing is not a democratic or egalitarian relationship.

This is not to say that marketers may not, or should not, also recognize various rights of customers to have input regarding what marketers are doing or how they are doing it. In this sense, customer rights to information, safety, etc. may act to shape the final decisions made by marketers.[9] However, those rights have typically not included the right to participate in the final decision-making authority of marketers. Of course, marketers might decide to recognize such a right. And some argue that they ought to recognize such a right. But nothing within the nature of marketing itself requires this.

The preceding suggests that the relation of marketers to those with whom they deal as customers is an instrumental relation. Of course, this does not mean that our marketing relations with others, since they are instrumental, cannot also include respect or dignity-observing aspects. Most of our relations are multi-layered, marketing exchanges and relations included. It is possible in an instrumental relation also to have regard and care for the dignity of and to respect those one deals with. Such respect is due to any moral agent. Still, in marketing, these relations are set within its goal-driven processes and must contend with larger individual and organizational objectives.

This instrumental relatedness is not, however, simply unidirectional. In marketing, each party must do something that fulfills an objective or desire of the other. There are two aspects to this feature of marketing.

To begin with, marketing exchanges are driven by the various wants or objectives of each party. Of course, prior to their encounter with marketers, some may not believe (or realize) that there are things for which they may have (or develop) certain wants (or needs). Due to the influence of marketers they may come to have these desires. Conversely, customers may seek to get marketers to sell products and services they would not otherwise have considered offering. So the heart of marketing is to be understood in terms of the efforts of some to get others to act in certain kinds of ways for ends that they themselves take as (or may be brought to see as) valuable. Kotler speaks of marketers as being responsible for demand management (Kotler, 2000: 5).[10]

In addition, each party must have something of value to contribute in the exchange, and each must believe that it will benefit (all things considered) from the exchange. Each party believes it is appropriate or desirable to deal with the other party (Kotler, 2000: 12). What one party wants may be that the other party buys something from him or her. Or it might be that they want the second party to stop doing something. In the case of social marketing, what the marketer wants might be that certain people stop taking drugs, stop using fire carelessly in national forests, or stop abusing their wives and daughters. In political marketing, it might be that marketers want a particular group to cast their ballots for a certain candidate. In any case, there is something that the marketer wants to get the targeted person or organization to do.

This means that those people in society who have nothing of value to contribute to a marketer (or to those who hire marketers) are out of luck. They cannot take part in any exchanges by which they might be able to obtain what they want or desire. Hence, a society structured to fulfill its ends and needs on this basis is a society in which those without anything that others want will be left out of the system, i.e., will not have their wants and needs attended to. The upshot is that the well-being of people in such a society is determined by their contribution to others, rather than the needs they have or their being viewed as equals.

Finally, to say that marketing is importantly an instrumental relation involving a coordinated set of activities also suggests, but does not imply, that these activities are undertaken in some rational fashion. It is possible to coordinate activities that have an instrumental nature in a variety of ways. Any of these would, on the present account, count as marketing. However, there is also great pressure among marketers to rationalize these activities to make them as efficient and as effective as possible in attaining their own objectives. In part, pressure for such a way of proceeding stems from the influence of competition.

Competition

If you assume, as marketing does, that marketers seek to fulfill their own objectives by getting those they target to do certain things, that the various objectives or wants at stake often overlap, that there are multiple marketers and potential customers, and that there is not an abundance of, but limited, goods or resources, then we can understand how competition has been closely linked with marketing. In fact, there is a range of levels of competition and conflict that are associated with marketing.

Marketing as war

At one end of this continuum, some claim that marketing is a form of war. This is, at best, a metaphor with regard to one extreme form of marketing.

The war metaphor is used to characterize the situation of those industries which are under conditions of particularly intense competition. However, this is a dangerous and inappropriate metaphor.

To begin with, though this metaphor need not characterize all forms of marketing, this is something that its advocates tend to forget. Marketing takes place in smaller towns and in small and medium-sized industries where competition may be much less intense. Further, the point of the war metaphor is to indicate that certain extreme measures that would not otherwise be justified are justified, for example espionage, deception, lying, theft, and even physical violence. In short, the war metaphor is used to justify suspending (or reinterpreting) certain common moral rules. However, even the war metaphor does not mean that anything goes. Not even the military believes that. We are all too familiar with the reality of war crimes. If one country threatens the very existence of another country, the second country may have morally justified reasons to use various means, including deception, to obtain private or secret information about the first country. It might even use physical force to protect its very existence. But businesses, even large businesses, are not countries. The conditions portrayed here do not exist in the case of competitive markets, since it is of the nature of participating in such markets that one grants that one may not be able to successfully compete against others. In short, fair competition with others may put one out of existence. And if one's competitors are using unfair competition, for example deception to acquire one's own private information, it does not follow that one is justified in using similar means to protect oneself. This may simply lead to the *rationalization* that "We were forced to do it, since everyone else is doing it."

Finally, the war metaphor cannot justify physical violence as one of the means to promote one's marketing. Theft, lying, and espionage are also not justified. They will be discussed in later chapters. Still, it is highly competitive forms of marketing that give rise to efforts to learn more about competitors and to strategize regarding these relations (see chapter 2). It is also such forms of competition that force marketers to identify what their competitive advantages are and to try to play to them.

Marketing as a game

Another metaphor that marketers use proposes that the competition that typifies marketing (and business more generally) should be viewed as a kind of game (such as poker). The suggestion here is that marketing has its own rules that permit various forms of deception and maneuvering in an attempt to best the other players (Carr, 1968; Levitt, 1970). Partly as a result, game theory and strategic theory are widely applied to marketing. This game metaphor can be useful to suggest a kind of practice, as noted above, that does differ from other areas of life, though people do talk about "war games," the "game of life," and even the "game of love." It also captures the competition that exists between marketers in attempting to win over customers.

However, the danger of this metaphor, like the war metaphor, is that it suggests that the rules of marketing are quite different from those of the rest of life. And though marketing is different from other spheres and practices of life, this does not mean that it is utterly separate, or that ordinary principles and values relating to truth, coercion, and justice simply have no grip there. Poker players who hide cards up their sleeves and don't pay their debts learn otherwise. Further, though not all games have referees or umpires, for example a game of poker or even a friendly game of tennis, for more competitive games, and those involving larger numbers of individuals (and organizations), competition and the activities of marketing are dependent upon there being some form of external regulatory agency that exercises control over the competitors. Hence, it is hypocritical to deny any role to regulatory bodies such as the Federal Trade Commission (FTC), the Food & Drug Administration (FDA), and the like. Not only do they help to control the competition, they make it possible. Finally, unlike ordinary games in which a person may decide whether or not to participate, and in which the results may be trivial, the broad scope and importance of marketing activities are such that individuals today cannot avoid involvement in them and having their lives significantly impacted by them. Hence, most marketing activities do not nicely fit the way we ordinarily think of the games in which we participate. Accordingly, we should also be wary of interpreting marketing as a kind of game.

Marketing as social practice
In fact, the game metaphor is best understood to suggest a broader view of the competition that typifies marketing. Such competition spans a wide variety of radically different situations, from that in which two marketers may go head to head in an intense form of zero-sum competition, on the one hand, to that of social marketers who must "compete" with the scarce resources (money, time, etc.) of potential "customers" that prevent them from responding to the social marketers' proposed exchanges. That is, in some cases "competition" may be not so much with other people and their desires, but with time pressures, or the lack of resources a person may suffer in trying to decide to do something a social marketer seeks (see Andreasen, 1994). Here the "competition" is not with other people, but with other determinants of the person's choices, for example their conflicting desires or needs. This is a different sense of "competition," which leads one to note that marketing is

bound up not only with traditional notions of competition, but also with conflicts within a person and between persons regarding marketing exchanges. In these situations, marketers may also cooperate with their exchange partners in fulfilling both their objectives.[11]

What marketers consistently face are situations in which they must overcome some obstacle or other to succeed in their efforts to create, communicate, and convey something that a targeted group may value (or may come to value). Such obstacles are defined within a social structure and set of understandings of social and individual behavior in which influences may flow back and forth between marketers and their (potential) customers.[12]

Within these social contexts, the competitive exchanges of marketing, not to say its more cooperative forms, require various social conditions, such as laws, trust, and morality. The social settings within which marketing operates are not simply unrestrained markets. Instead, they involve and require referees (from professional organizations and government) and the professional codes, regulations, and laws by which they constrain and channel marketing activities.[13] They require trust, though the levels of trust may vary. However, without some form of trust, free and voluntary exchanges would either not take place or would be severely restricted due to the need to protect oneself. Indeed, the more complicated the general type of exchange, the greater the trust that may be required. In short, the competition of marketing is tied to cooperation and to trust as well. The less trust there is, for example in various forms of cowboy capitalism, the greater the protection people will seek and the less ready they will be to engage in marketing exchanges.

Accordingly, marketing is characterized by competition that is spread over a *continuum* that stretches from intense, traditional forms of contention to forms of cooperation where the "competition" may occur only within the different parties to an exchange. In short, marketing involves competition and cooperation, as well as zero-sum and win-win situations. To view all marketing as a form of war is to present a one-sided view that is sometimes used to justify ethically questionable actions. On the other hand, to view marketing as a game may be helpful, so long as one does not exempt it from appropriate moral rules, recognizes the social contexts in which it is played, and takes notice of the forms of trust that inhabit it. In any case, it is this broad, rather than narrow, sense of competition that is linked with marketing. As such, competition permits, rather than excludes, cooperation between exchange partners as well as competitors. Some refer to such organized forms of activity as "social practices." This notion encompasses games and wars, but other forms of activity as well, and suggests the importance of socially recognized rules and background institutions.

Comparability and justice

Finally, when there is a marketing exchange, whether it be highly competitive or strongly cooperative, be it on a single occasion or within the context of an ongoing relation between marketers and those they target, the question will inevitably arise as to whether what one receives or does in response to a marketer's proposal is comparable in some rough fashion with what one must give up or do in order to receive it. Hence, questions of the fairness of such exchanges are inevitably a part of marketing. Consequently, after an exchange, those involved may be pleased, or feel angry, cheated, etc., not only with regard to what they receive but also with regard to the terms of their obtaining it.

Accordingly, questions regarding the *justice or fairness* of marketing exchanges and relationships are an inherent part of them. In effect, marketing is thereby essentially linked with some form of justice as exchange. Bagozzi claims that in "restricted exchanges" parties to this exchange seek to maintain equality; in short there is a "rule of equality." This is said to be "a central tenet of the marketing concept" (Bagozzi, 1975: 33). Following this rule means that participants in such "restricted [marketing] exchanges" do not attempt to take advantage of the other; this also works against deceiving the other (Bagozzi, 1975: 33). What this means, and the limits of such a view, remains to be worked out. What is important is that this form of justice must be considered in such marketing exchanges.

However, questions of fairness and justice extend to any version of marketing, not simply to the restricted forms of the marketing concept to which Bagozzi alludes (see chapter 2). The amount each agent receives in an exchange is not simply a neutral, non-moral issue, like the amount of water that falls in a spring rainstorm. The proportions received are the direct result of human intervention. They raise basic moral questions of the justice of exchange.

Accordingly, the form of justice that can be sufficient for marketing is a question that needs to be addressed. Since marketing defines itself through exchanges and relationships, which directly place us on an individual or micro level, one question that arises is whether this is sufficient for questions of justice at other levels (e.g. meso and macro). What is not in question, however, is that some form of justice is bound up with marketing.

Summary

The upshot of the preceding is that marketing is a practical activity infused with morally relevant values, norms, and assumptions. To view marketing simply as a scientific or neutral activity is to confuse a part with the whole. Though marketing uses various scientific tools and technologies, their use comes with values and assumptions that define that use as one of marketing. Marketing is the resultant complex form of practical activity. It is not simply the tools of surveys, focus groups, etc., or even exchange relationships, let alone advertising or distribution. It is at home in the commercial marketplace, but can also be extended outside that domain. It constitutes a social practice. This is why it may be so difficult to transfer a marketing approach to some societies and why, whatever society it is found in, it will take on its own special forms.

The morally relevant norms and values we have seen embedded in marketing have included autonomy, freedom, justice, trust, truth, and well-being, as well as related rights and responsibilities of both customers and marketers. Without these one does not have marketing. And with these one has some of the essential elements to construct a marketing ethics which will *not* have to be imposed on marketing, but will be part and parcel of marketing. Such a view is the basis for the integrated marketing ethics that marketers need.

We have also seen that, though marketing makes various assumptions about human motivation, it need not assume that humans are simply self-interested (and hence selfish), though it may (and does) assume that they seek to satisfy their own self-interests, among a number of other values and concerns they may have. Finally, one can imagine that those people and organizations that identify with and adopt this form of social practice may develop a mindset that tends to view things instrumentally as they seek to achieve various objectives through voluntary choices in a competitive context.

With this view of marketing we can talk about the various dimensions of this complex practice, while not extending the concept itself too far, and not necessarily approving (or disapproving) of all the forms it takes.

V Towards a Marketing Ethics Framework

The preceding sections have already suggested major parts of a marketing ethics framework. These include recognition of moral problems that marketing may encounter (section II) and some of the values, norms, and assumptions of marketing that would be relevant to resolving those moral problems (section IV). It should be clear that moral problems do not come stripped of any context or situation. They come embedded in the various situations and challenges that marketers daily face.

The previous section has sought to make clear that at the heart of marketing is a set of values, norms, and assumptions that place marketing squarely

within the bounds of morality. They are bound up with any marketing relation or any exchange which marketers seek to foster. It is important to be
clear what exactly this means. It does not mean that marketing or marketers
are always moral (in the sense of doing the right thing) in whatever they do.
This is to confuse the normative sense of "moral" with its meaning or conceptual sense, which has, so far, been at stake. In the conceptual sense, morality contrasts with what is non-moral, for example which shoe a person puts
on in the morning or the height of Mount Le Conte. Such examples don't
involve morality; they are non-moral (or amoral). But whether a customer
makes free or coerced choices, is given accurate or false information, or is
treated justly or unfairly in an exchange are all issues that fall within the
concept of morality. The answers themselves to these issues may be better or
worse, moral or immoral in a normative sense. But, conceptually, they are all
moral issues whichever way they are answered.

This is not an insubstantial point. It means that marketing involves activities which directly (and indirectly) relate to the basic interests and relationships of humans and human society. Its activities fall within the moral ballpark,
even if there are disagreements over which course of action is the correct one
(in a normative moral sense). It also means that marketers cannot escape
charges of immorality by declaring that marketing is really a science, or simply
a question of self-interest that cannot be morally evaluated. In short, a consideration of any (or all) of the above values and norms is inherently relevant
to marketing.

So the question of marketing ethics is *not*: How do we get morality into
marketing? Rather, the question *is*: How do we engage the various moral
values and norms necessarily involved in marketing? Further, how can we
adjudicate conflicts between them, as well as between them and other values
and interests which marketers, consumers, and society have? This will require
further specification of these general norms as they apply to particular instances
within the various areas of marketing. But how to do this, and what may
we expect?

These questions may be understood empirically or normatively. An empirical theory would tell us how marketers (and others) actually go about making
moral judgments. Several different empirical theories of marketing ethics have
been advanced by marketers (see Hunt and Vitel, 1993; Mayo and Marks,
1990; Ferrell and Gresham, 1985). What is striking about many of these theories is that they do not proceed from field or psychological studies of how
marketers actually make moral judgments. Instead, they draw on ethics or
moral philosophy to portray a process of decision-making – from perceived
ethical problems to the application of deontological norms and the evaluation
of consequences – that leads to an ethical judgment, intentions, and behavior

(see appendix II). From such models various testable propositions are then drawn.

The rationale for this empirical approach is to provide marketing managers with knowledge that would be useful in "controlling" ethical behavior in their organizations.[14] However, if this is the aim of such studies, then marketing managers would best look, not to theories about how marketers make ethical judgments, but to a host of other individual, organizational, and societal factors that play a role in people's moral behavior (see chapter 5). On the other hand, how one might manage ethical behavior raises normative questions (not simply empirical ones) regarding how this should be done. And this is a normative question. Finally, if it is important, as Hunt and Vitel suggest, that such an empirical theory should be "consistent with moral philosophy" (Hunt and Vitel, 1986: 15), then it is crucial to have a defensible normative moral philosophy that would tell us how ethical decisions should be made in marketing. It is, then, to a normative account of moral decision-making that I now turn.

A challenge that is frequently posed contends that because normative theories do not tell us what people actually do, they are (or must be) unrealistic. Now, an ethics must always seem somewhat unrealistic if to be "realistic" is equated with what people actually do or what in fact takes place. Instead, an ethics is supposed to supply standards, grounds for criticism and evaluation of what happens. It is to provide guidance to those inside (and outside) of marketing as to how they might change current practices. This presupposes two things: First, not everything is always what it should be, and, second, it is possible for things to be different. Here is where the "unrealistic" charge enters in a second way, since whether something could be different depends upon the nature of the situation and the possibility of changing it. Is it possible with little effort? With a lot of effort by a lot of people? Within a short period of time? Within a decade or perhaps even a century? Was criticism of slavery in the U.S. unrealistic at the beginning of the nineteenth century? It was possible to change it, we know, since it was changed; but it took the next seven decades to abolish slavery constitutionally, even though forms of servitude persisted for decades in various places in the U.S.

It is mistaken, then, to hold that an ethics is unrealistic if its prescriptions are not acted upon, or don't become "reality," as they are offered. Similarly, it is just as incorrect to say that an ethics is realistic, if its recommendations could only be adopted through a radical change of the underlying psychological nature of humans. It is between these extremes that a meaningful ethics may be found (or constructed) that offers "realistic" guidance to marketers even if that guidance may take effort and time to put into place. What ethical framework can we turn to, then, to resolve marketing's ethical challenges?

Folk guidelines

We might begin by noting what a marketing ethics will *not* do. It will not make a decision or judgment for a person. It will not "give" them an answer, so that they do not have to decide or make a judgment themselves. Thus, different people who use a marketing ethics may come up with different answers. This should not be surprising. People come up with different answers using the same economic theory. However, both ethical and economic theories attempt to supply procedures to reduce these disagreements or to help make them intelligible. Ethics is not, then, a cookbook of recipes such that if you simply follow them you will end up with the right answer.

Nor will the moral framework of a marketing ethics be composed of simple rules, or various folk guidelines, which some have offered to help resolve these issues (see Laczniak, 1983). Among these are the "Look in the Mirror" test, the "Morning Paper" test, the "Sleep Well" test, and even the "Golden Rule." These are often mentioned as guides to moral action in marketing (not to mention business and life more generally). Someone says that if you can imagine yourself sleeping well having done something, then it is morally permissible (or perhaps even obligatory) to do it. Or we are told that if a person would not flinch at seeing what he did yesterday in the morning paper, then (again) it is morally all right to do.

Surely there is some truth to these folk guidelines, just as there is some truth to most stereotypes. Still, there are major problems and inadequacies with them. For example, there are some murderers or thieves who might enjoy seeing their acts reported in the morning newspaper. This doesn't make those actions right. Further, there are things a person might do morally with another person that he or she would not want presented in the morning newspaper – not because they are unethical, but because they are private and should stay private. In addition, such guidelines do not tell us which one(s) to use or how to choose among them when they conflict. Moreover, their simplicity makes them too easy, even moralistic, to use. They can easily be invoked and just as easily, it seems, dismissed and not taken seriously. They are like the slips of paper in fortune cookies, quickly read and easily forgotten.

Finally, the Golden Rule, "Do unto others as you would have them do unto you," has an ancient lineage. But again it is too simple to use as such. There are any number of people who might want to share bribes, nepotistic favors, or even physical injury (think of sado-masochists) who would not be stopped by this rule. Some fanatics might even be willing to have themselves exterminated if they found out that they were among those they so vehemently oppose. Besides, this rule itself does not specify who "others" are. If members of certain races don't even count as "others," then again the Golden Rule will fall short.

So the folk guidelines are much too simple. They cannot constitute the backbone of a marketing ethics.

A single moral principle

Some ethicists have taken a very different approach. Instead of appealing to various "folk guidelines" or "rules of thumb" they have attempted to abstract from them and from the moral norms noted above a single basic moral principle that would cover all the preceding norms and moral situations marketers face. This has proceeded in one of two directions.

On the one hand, consequentialists, such as utilitarians, have argued that the preceding moral norms all take their moral significance from the consequences of the actions and rules involved. In particular, they urge that if we are morally serious we must look for those acts or rules that would produce "the greatest possible balance of good over evil . . . in the world as a whole" (Frankena, 1973: 34; italics deleted). Whether we are talking about instances of freedom, justice, or well-being in marketing, classical utilitarians contend that the morality of the issue rests upon producing the greatest good or happiness (for the greatest number).

On the other hand, deontologists have argued that the morality of actions is tied to certain inherent features of those actions, rather than their consequences. Some, such as Kant, have claimed that they can formulate a single moral principle that holds independently of the consequences. Kant urged us to ask whether the maxim (or subjective principle of our action) could be willed to be a universal law for everyone (the Categorical Imperative). For example, if a marketer is considering lying to a customer about the materials used to make a certain product, she should ask whether she could will that there be a universal law that required all people to lie when they were asked about the make-up of something concerning which they were considering an exchange. In such cases, Kant thought the answer would be "No," since if there were a universal law along these lines, no one would or could engage in such exchanges since they could not know what it was they were thinking of acquiring. Obviously, this principle has connections with the Golden Rule. Still, the Categorical Imperative is not the same and avoids some of the problems of this simpler folk guideline.

Debate regarding these two ethical positions has lasted for centuries, with little indication of agreement in sight. Utilitarian views tend to suffer from various problems including:

(a) How do you measure the consequences of your actions?
(b) How do you make interpersonal comparisons of the effects of different actions (and/or rules) on people?

(c)   What do you do if you cannot determine what the consequences will be?

(d)   How do you distribute the consequences of your actions or the rules society might adopt? (see Frankena, 1973; Shaw, 1991)

So too deontologists such as Kantians also struggle with various objections to their theories. They face the following problems:

(a)   What is the correct formulation of the most general, non-consequential-ist principle?

(b)   How is one to know when one has the correct application of such a general principle to particular situations?

(c)   Do the universal principles deontologists defend require us to treat loved ones and friends in the same manner that we treat strangers and enemies?

(d)   Since we repeatedly look to the consequences of our actions in other areas of practical life, why believe that such consequences are not rele-vant, even if not conclusive, in arriving at moral determinations?

Consequently, though there remain avid defenders of each approach, there are also equally ardent opponents of each approach. Given the significant issues each basic principle faces, and the fact that two centuries of argument have not produced a broad consensus for one or the other of these two approaches, it is unlikely that there is any single principle that we could adopt or meaningfully use. Is there any way to avoid this impasse?

A pluralistic view

There have been some who have advocated combining, in some manner or other, the basic consequentialist and deontological principles just described (see Frankena, 1973; Hunt and Vitel, 1986, 1993). This would be an excellent idea if it would overcome their shortcomings, rather than simply combine them. However, it seems dubious that doing so would overcome the difficul-ties they suffer as all-encompassing principles.

Instead, to develop a marketing ethics we should return to the several moral values and norms that were identified above as crucial to marketing. From this discussion, the following six principles or values emerged as central to marketing: Autonomy, Freedom, Justice, Trust, Truth, and Well-Being.[15]

Underlying these values is the view that people (and their organizations) are (or may be) responsible for their actions and the effects they have in the world about them. We are not simply the victims of some fate which toys with us. We may affect the world about us in ways that will change it. And, it makes sense to say that we are (or may be) responsible for (at least some of) the effects we are involved in bringing about. Obviously, we are not responsible for all the effects our actions bring about. Other people and organizations play contributory (or even preeminent) roles in what occurs. Still, we do have responsibilities for what we have a role in making (or allowing to) happen. The difficulties lie in determining the nature and extent of those responsibilities. The preceding values help to determine the configuration of those responsibilities.

These six values are not reducible to some single value or principle. Though they are sometimes characterized as middle-level principles (in contrast to the "basic" principles of utilitarianism or Kantianism), they are constitutive of a marketing ethics. Hence, such an ethics will be pluralistic. This is a moral position that a significant number of ethicists have turned to in the past few decades (see Hampshire, 1989; Wolf, 1992; Berlin, 1991). Thus we are faced with invoking a variety of relevant values and principles and then seeking to determine which combination of them is most weighty, or most significant, within the particular contexts that we face.

Though these values and norms may take forms particular to marketing, they are not unique to marketing, but are the same ones that we use to characterize other areas of life. When used in marketing they are part and parcel of decisions regarding product development, forms of market research, kinds of advertising, etc. which will impact customers, stockholders, marketers themselves, and the environment. As such, their role in marketing decisions and the impact of these decisions on the well-being (their self-interests and capacities) of people both inside and outside of marketing firms must be ascertained and evaluated.

In short, marketers do not face moral problems abstractly, but as they arise while trying to create, communicate, and convey something valued by designated people that will fulfill their own objectives. For marketers to use the values and norms embedded in the marketing context, we must proceed in two directions. First, we must make them more specific or particular and, as such, usefully relevant to each situation (*specifying*). Second, we must balance them off against each other, so that we can define a coherent course of action (*balancing*). This will require identifying some sort of process whereby marketing values and norms may be adjudicated.

Specifying marketing's values and norms
With regard to the first point, the following chapters examine the particular nature and roles these values and norms play in marketing, for example research, distribution, advertising, etc. Among some of the more general features of such norms and values the following deserve mention.

Each of these values and norms will have its own specific forms. Freedom looks to issues of coercion, voluntariness, physical and/or psychological pressures. Trust concerns matters of vulnerability, confidence, knowledge, and risk. And autonomy involves questions of choice, self-determination, knowledge, and lack of coercion. There is overlap here, but there is also difference. Each value or norm will have its own "metrics," as it were, by which marketers might seek to determine the extent of their fulfillment as well as the nature of the demands they place on marketing actions and policies.

The violation of some values and norms (or their more specific forms) will be more grave or troubling than the violation of others. Hence, identification of some minimal basic marketing moral standards which underlie the less basic moral standards is important (see Strawson, 1961; Walzer, 1994). This might be done by identifying a threshold level of capacities which must be guaranteed to everyone (see Nussbaum, 2000). Above that level there are other forms of these values and norms which reach more broadly, and to which adherence may be more voluntary. On this level, there might be several different, more complete forms of well-being or full capacity development (Nussbaum, 2000). In any case, the closer we get to these minimal, central standards the less willing we are to permit some people to violate them.

In short, it is important to distinguish, as many others have before, the minimal (and obligatory) aspects of morality from other broader (maximal or ideal) aspects of morality that are open to a wider range of choice. Together they constitute different forms of a good life. As such, we don't all have to be musicians or scientists as part of the good life for ourselves. However, we had better all avoid (all things being equal) violence against others, as well as exploitation and deception of them. We don't all have to buy brown bread and listen to Mozart. But we had better not be charged unfair high prices for whatever we buy, as well as not coerced into buying it. In short, marketing ethics must distinguish between those forms of its values and norms that are most crucial, and those which are more peripheral. The more essential elements of a marketing morality are the ones whose violation would be most disruptive of the role morality plays in addressing the human predicament or condition (see Warnock, 1971).

Still, some broader vision is crucial of how these narrower principles and values at the heart of marketing might fit together into a good or flourishing society and the lives of its citizens. Without such a view, criticisms regarding the materialism and commercialism that marketing is said to encourage would lack grounds for possible discussion. In addition, a basis for resolving disputes among the various values and norms would be missing. The development of this general vision of a flourishing way of life will arise, through a reciprocal process, out of the specification of these norms and values. It will also be the result of empirical knowledge we gain about ourselves and the choices we face. Such a society will involve, I maintain, significant concerns for equality, freedom, and opportunity, as well as protections from vulnerability and/or exploitation. It would also open up possibilities for the development of various human capacities for excellence, compatible with the like development of the capacities of others (see Nussbaum, 2000). Thus this model gives a touchstone for measuring marketing exchanges against what we know, from other sources, about human capacities and development. It also gives us a chance to give a proper place to self-interest within a larger moral framework. The result should be a stronger and more reasonable basis against which to measure marketing and the exchanges it involves. In this way, arriving at a marketing ethics is a constructivist task. In effect, the end we seek to create is the ultimate criterion of marketing success. It is a form, if you will, of well-being or happiness.

In defending this constructive pluralist view, I am not saying that these values or principles are reducible to their contribution to the good life, something independent of them. That would be to run contrary to the pluralism I defended above. Instead, the various forms they take are (partially) constitutive of a good life and must be viewed in this broader context, even though they are not thereby reducible to it.

Further, these values are not clear from the outset, ready to hand, as it were, only lacking application. They cannot simply be imposed from the top down. Instead, they must be built from the ground up. This is what the following chapters do. We don't start with a fully articulated normative vision and then apply this to various situations. Rather, in working through various situations we develop the more specific and useful forms of these norms and values, and do so in a manner that articulates more fully a view of a flourishing life in light of which marketers undertake the activities they do. One desirable aspect of this approach is its compatibility with the view that there is much we have yet to discover about humans and morality.

Ultimately such specification requires a discursive, deliberative dimension. Waters and Bird (1987) make a nice distinction between principles and values that are commonly held, as opposed to those that are held in common, meaning that they are held publicly and through joint discussion. It is this joint deliberation that is important for the specification of our values and norms and the justified determination of our moral views. The fact that, far too often, this does not take place in many (marketing) organizations is what contributes to higher levels of moral stress and difficulty resolving moral problems.

Balancing values and norms
The second prong of this pluralist view involves the balancing of marketing values and norms. This is required to combine their more specific application

into a mix that can be justified in light of the minimal and maximal aspects of morality noted above. Marketers should be comfortable with this, since they themselves developed the notion of a "marketing mix" (product, place, price, and promotion) which were linked with a certain end of the firm or its "success." What we face here is, in effect, an "ethics mix" (or the "marketing ethics mix") which is linked with success in a broader, ethical shape.

Too often marketing ethical models propose that the process is carried out by a single individual who is the sole agent of moral decision-making, and that this involves some reflective inner monologue by which each agent comes to a decision. It is little wonder that each person finds it extremely difficult to weigh or balance these various considerations off against each other, all by him- or herself. Such an individualist model lies behind the moral stress that some have characterized businesspeople (and others) as experiencing (see Waters and Bird, 1987).

Instead, this process must occur through mutual discussion, dialogue, and deliberation whereby we may arrive at the moral view about which we may be the most confident and which is most likely justified. The process is one that is theoretically viewed as ultimately arriving at agreement, even though this may not, in practice, happen in any particular case. This is not simply to argue for consensus, let alone convention, as the touchstone for making our specific moral judgments. Rather, these discussions must take place within a context in which various criteria are fulfilled.

First, people should have access to as full empirical knowledge as possible. Nevertheless, we recognize that people's knowledge is, in fact, bounded and this plays a significant role in marketing ethical decisions. Still, expansions (and corrections) of knowledge that pertain to the ethical issue at hand are always relevant. Thus, the preceding values and norms must also be placed within their social, legal, and historical context. An adequate portrayal of marketing and morality is that marketing may reflect as well as initiate moral changes in society. Our individual moral views occur only within a social context that may support or undermine them. Though an individual may give voice to a particular moral view, the practicality and ultimately justification of that view will depend on it possibly fitting into a larger social framework according to which others may also act in line with those moral views.

Second, such discussions require appropriate levels of sensitivity to the implications and consequences of alternative actions for others. The role a person fulfills may steel them to these dimensions of their actions. When that happens it may also deaden their ethical sensitivities permitting them to engage in callous, unethical actions. Of course, one's experiences of being in certain situations (not to mention being on the receiving end of mistreatment by others) may well add to one's appreciation of those situations. In any case, such sensitivity should extend not simply to different proposed actions, but also to how those actions might impact a society of flourishing individuals.

Given this approach one can easily understand the place of looking to others as role models (or exemplars) to see how they have interpreted these situations, what their responses to them and the actual consequences were, and what were the responses of others around them. This is, in effect, to look to the role of the virtues in marketing ethics. Hence, marketers may also ask: What kind of person do we wish to be? What kind of person are we in the midst of creating? Similarly, the role of moral imagination finds a natural place here in examining the nature of each ethical issue one faces and developing creative responses.

Finally, a marketing ethics must consider all those relevantly involved. Accordingly, this view has (in a broad manner) similarities to the notion of stakeholder theories. Since the roles people have and their relations to each other carry differing moral weight, marketers will have more stringent responsibilities towards some of those affected by their actions than others. In this way, this view will also focus more closely on some stakeholders rather than others. It won't simply be a matter of balancing like effects on all stakeholders, or of balancing their various interests, but of weighing the different effects and relations with stakeholders. In short, there are different kinds of stakes, some more direct than others, not simply some larger than others. Some will simply be observers of what is going on, with little or no stake in "the game." A marketing ethics must sort out these different relations.

In any case, through the process described here the aim is to arrive at an "overlapping consensus" of both those involved and those who stand outside the direct marketing actions. It is a consensus that would hold not simply for those in this or that society, but (ideally) across societies (see Nussbaum, 2000: 76; Rawls, 1989). Of course, there will be differences over the interpretations here. Some will be factual, others metaphysical, and yet others will be moral. Theoretical resolutions may not be possible for some of these conflicts. But this does not mean, given the preceding three conditions, that the ethics of marketing is simply subjective.

Some implications

The preceding gives us a clearer and more complete view of the complex activity that is marketing and how it relates to ethics. In this light, we can outline some implications.

Some have suggested that the concept of marketing needs to be expanded in light of various problems in society, for example environmental deterioration, resource shortages, explosive population growth, world hunger and poverty, and neglected social services (Kotler, 2000: 25). Accordingly, some speak of "humanistic marketing," "ecological marketing," or "societal marketing." Each of these views calls upon marketers "to build social and ethical considerations into their marketing practices. They must balance and juggle the often conflicting criteria of company profits, consumer want satisfaction, and public interest" (Kotler, 2000: 25). Ben & Jerry's and The Body Shop are frequently cited as examples of businesses that have adopted such a marketing view.

What I have argued is that marketing already involves ethical considerations. The real struggle is over the ways in which these ethical considerations should be balanced with other values, such as self-seeking and profit, not whether they should be taken into account at all. Hence, marketing ethics, as I have characterized it, includes considerations of social responsibility, i.e., how marketers should treat both those inside and those outside the marketing firm (e.g. individual customers, the local society, non-governmental organizations (NGOs), and governmental institutions).

Since the interpretations and assumptions regarding these values and norms may differ there is not one single, solid, undifferentiated "thing" called marketing. There are various forms marketing takes, including narrow, profit-oriented marketing, as well as social marketing, ecological marketing, and even radical marketing. Part of the task of an ethics of marketing is to sort out the ethical issues each of these faces and where they succeed or fail. Accordingly, an account of the nature of marketing does not answer the many ethical challenges above. However, it opens the door to answering them in that it places marketing within the moral arena and characterizes it as a practical activity involving various values, norms, and principles.

What marketing may become will be the result of thinking and arguing about its various (value and moral) dimensions within the social contexts in which they operate. However, other forces also operate on marketers and marketing that will affect its future. We must believe that the outcome is not simply "fated." We must assume that through human choice and individual and collective action we can alter that future.

This, then, gives my answer regarding how to determine what is ethical within the field of marketing.

First, we must correctly understand the nature of moral problems and issues, as well as recognize when they appear in a marketing context.

Second, we must identify the crucial values and norms such as autonomy, freedom, justice, trust, etc. as they define the broad activity of marketing. Those participating in marketing relationships are frequently unaware of these moral features of actions, exchanges, and relationships. However, this does not mean that they are not present.

Third, we must specify or particularize these values and norms in the contexts marketers face (something that I undertake in subsequent chapters). In doing so, we must consider their various interpretations and ways in which their content has been filled over the years, and we must do this in light of which interpretations will best work towards the end of moral marketing. The folk guidelines noted above only inadequately capture many of the underlying ethical beliefs that are embedded in this complex structure.

Fourth, the preceding process is not something that involves some inner monologue but communication and dialogue with others, who are willing to listen to facts, to discover new things about themselves and society, and to change their views accordingly. Both those affected and those not affected at all may provide helpful insights into the moral demands marketers face. Stakeholder theorists sometimes forget the importance of those not party to various moral disputes.

Finally, the preceding will involve a two-pronged attack – looking both at the particular interpretations of these middle-level values and, at the same time, balancing them against each other and their implications for the development of a good or flourishing life. It is clear, in any case, that ethical marketing requires that those involved take into account a wide variety of normative considerations.

Is this framework for a marketing ethics unrealistic? Over the past decades we have seen topics previously disparaged as "soft" or "subjective" brought within the realm of crucial components of marketing and management discussions. Some suggest that discussion of morality is now where discussion of safety was years ago (Waters and Bird, 1987: 22); slowly however, safety has been brought to the fore. Others suggest a similar comparison between the discussion of quality and the discussion of morality (Soule, 2005; Waddock, 2004). Both safety and quality are now essential parts of discussions of everyday marketing. So too discussion of morality is moving in this direction. The forms this discussion takes will differ from those taken by safety and quality, but like them, they will be present.

VI Conclusion

Marketers face a host of ethical problems. Satisfactory responses to these challenges will be possible only if we understand that marketing is itself a practical, value-laden activity, which falls within the moral arena. Just as there have been disputes over the nature and extent of morality, so too there have been similar disputes about the nature and extent of marketing. This chapter has portrayed some of these differences. It has developed three main points.

First, a satisfactory view of marketing is one that views it as a practical activity that is neither limited simply to a narrow range of distributive business activities nor so broad as to encompass all human interactions. As such, marketing involves a set of coordinated activities that, in response to background interrelations between marketers and society members, are designed to create, communicate, and convey, through voluntary exchanges, something targeted people will value and will do so in ways that fulfill the objectives of marketers and/or their organizations. This view of marketing is not limited simply to the sale of products, but may also take into account marketing activities dealing with social and political problems. At the same time, I have resisted suggestions that various realms of social problems and politics are thereby transformed into forms of marketing. In addition, I have suggested that these marketing exchanges are part of a broader set of active relations between marketers and customers which a complete view of marketing (ethics) would capture. A marketing ethics that views marketers as the active members, and customers simply as passive, would be one-sided. It would not capture the full ethical drama that marketing involves.

Second, I have presented this view as not constituted by some narrow economic form of self-interest, but as a kind of practical activity that encompasses broader value and normative bases of a social and moral nature. Some have spoken of such a view as "humanistic marketing," i.e., marketing that includes various social responsibilities. Unfortunately, this term is frequently used to refer to philanthropic or morally desirable activities, rather than activities that are morally required and obligatory. Further, this approach to marketing often treats the values and norms involved as "added on to" or "appended" to marketing. On the contrary, the moral values or norms I have elicited in discussing marketing are embedded within marketing, not simply something that must be imposed on it. They are central to the relations between marketers and customers that I have also contended are part of any complete view of marketing. In addition, a marketing ethics encompasses not only activities that are morally desirable, but also those that are morally required or obligatory. Once it is so viewed, such special phrases as "humanistic marketing" or "societal marketing" are no longer needed.

Third, I have also argued that it is possible to reason about the value and normative dimensions of marketing. A marketing ethics is not simply subjective or merely a matter of feelings. Ethical claims or appeals that are rationally justifiable require a kind of reflective equilibrium theory – appealing to full, concrete empirical knowledge and the due consideration of others (see Rawls, 1971). This involves a form of open dialogue (and hence transparency), within a framework aimed at the realization of the above values embedded in ongoing marketing relationships, in essence, a form of sustainability. In any case, a marketing ethics is not simply an individual matter, but a social or collective affair.

In this manner, this chapter has also laid out the initial outlines of a framework for an ethics of marketing. In each situation we must identify the relevant values and normative features. These will be related to more general values and norms that form a system of morality whereby human relations are organized so as to develop human capacities within good or flourishing societies.

This constructive pluralist view also implies the importance of humility, since it also allows that there is a great deal we may yet learn about morality and humans. Some of this learning may result in the replacement of old ways of doing things. At the same time such changes may be fought tooth and nail by those committed to past ways of marketing and living with which their identities are bound up. In the end, some people's views are not changed by argument so much as surpassed with the passage of time as more people adopt different and opposing views. This is more a psychological and sociological point, than an ethical one. Still, it is an important one.

What additional tools marketers can use to respond to moral challenges will come out in the following chapters and their discussion of the particular levels on which marketing operates. We turn in the next chapter to marketing's view of customers and ways in which it researches and segments its customer bases. This is one of the most crucial areas for marketing ethics.

Notes

1 <http://www.bartleby.com/73/1736.html>, accessed August 7, 2007.
2 There is a similar danger (I shall contend later in this chapter) when marketing is extended to all of life.
3 I say sentient life, rather than human life, since morality includes humans but also (at a minimum) the higher forms of non-human life, such as dogs, cats, horses, monkeys, etc. It can be immoral to treat them in certain ways as well. Those who believe this is true also of mosquitoes and salamanders have a much more difficult argument to make.
4 This definition was originally adopted in 1935 by the National Association of Marketing Teachers, the predecessor of the American Marketing Association.
5 AMA webpage; downloaded July 2, 2004.
6 This statement is similar to, but differs importantly from, the latest definition of marketing from the American Marketing Association. The latest definition, announced in 2004, is that "Marketing is an organizational function and a set of processes for creating, communicating and delivering value to customers and for managing customer relationships in ways that benefit the organization and its stakeholders."

7   A point emphasized to me by Craig Smith.

8   There are clearly great complexities here. Some will argue that women or people without capital may be subject to coercion within the roles they play as wives or employees. I do not deny that here. What I assert is that marketing operates within broader limits, and within these boundaries individuals can make different choices.

9   President John Kennedy identified four consumer rights: to safety, information, choice, and to be heard. However, these were rights primarily against the government to have their interests taken into account. To the extent that they applied to businesses, they were viewed not as rights to participate, but as rights to have their interests acknowledged and responded to.

10 Marketers frequently speak rather casually of wants, needs, interests, and demands. However, these are not necessarily the same, and, strictly considered, have different implications. I will use "wants" as the more general notion here. It is not obvious, in any traditional sense of "needs," that marketers are particularly concerned with the needs of customers, so much as their wants (or desires). By seeking a response from their audience based on their wants, etc., marketers are seeking to engender voluntary responses that will fulfill their own objectives.

11 A corollary of the preceding is that marketers must not assume an overly strong competitive view of human nature. There may be people who are content with their status quo and engage in little, if any, competition with others. There are others, however, who are strongly competitive. Marketing must allow for both types.

12 It is better to characterize marketing in this way than to begin with individual exchanges, abstracted from everything else, and try to build an account of marketing based simply on the model of zero-sum, intensely competitive acts.

13 De George (1993) refers to the importance of societal background conditions.

14 This point was emphasized by an anonymous reviewer of this book.

15 I don't claim that these are the only values and/or principles embedded in marketing, but they are important and basic ones.

Chapter Two

Marketers and their Markets

I Introduction

Marketing, as portrayed in chapter 1, is a norm- and value-laden set of activities that, in response to background interrelations between marketers and society members, seeks to create, communicate, and convey something of value to particular people through voluntary exchanges in order to fulfill marketers' objectives. In addition to identifying the multiple values and norms crucial to marketing, I have also sketched a general ethical framework within which marketing decisions should be made. This model offers the best way in which to approach the (ethical) questions marketers face. But this framework doesn't, by itself, answer how marketers should proceed in particular cases. For this, marketers need to make these values and norms more specific, as well as to identify additional strategies and guidelines to direct their marketing.

One of the most frequently cited marketing guidelines is that marketers should seek to satisfy their customers' wants and needs. Called *the marketing concept* (TMC), this focus on customers has, for the past half-century, been one of the most prominent interpretations of marketing and how marketers ought to go about their business.[1] In the 1990s, the development of relationship marketing extended the focus of the marketing concept to building strong relations with customers to satisfy their wants and needs (see Cravens, 1995: 235).

There is, however, some irony in this situation given the number of complaints from customers and consumer groups regarding the ethical practices of marketers. The examples at the beginning of chapter 1 are a reminder that the relation of marketers and customers raises more ethical issues than any other in business. Customers may receive wonderful goods and services, but may also experience serious problems and suffer considerable anger and frustration through this relation.

What further steps ought marketers and others to take to sort through the jungle of moral claims and counter-claims here? Are marketers ethically out of step with their customers? What about customers? After all, this is a relationship in which some customers give marketers good reason to be wary, distressed, and angry. Some return products they only wanted to use for a special occasion. Others switch price tags, steal products, and cheat on coupons. In fact, at times the marketer–customer relation seems to be a dysfunctional one, filled with anger and mistrust. Still, at other times, there is both gratitude and respect shown on both sides.

We need to do three things at this point. First, we must look more closely at the marketing concept and its implications regarding the relation of marketing to individual customers. What assumptions and implications are involved in this relationship and in the marketing concept? What guidance can the marketing concept provide? This relationship is not simply a personal relationship, but occurs within the context of marketing. It generally develops when the marketer is (or represents) a firm of some sort or other, which is in competition with other firms for that customer. So, too, customers seek out firms that can satisfy their wants. They too have limited resources (finances, time, etc.) with which to fulfill their wants. Hence, this complex relation cannot be understood outside of the various institutions and social structures within which it is embedded. In these circumstances, the marketing concept is an inadequate ethical guide. It leaves many difficult questions unanswered. However, a discussion of it will allow us to identify further basic assumptions of marketing, some of which need to be modified, for ethical marketing to be possible.

Second, we must examine various specific relations that marketers undertake with customers. In the present chapter, I will focus on marketing research, competitive intelligence, and segmentation. In later chapters questions regarding product development, pricing, advertising, and retail sales will be considered. In probing the topics of this chapter, we want to know how marketers should go about determining and identifying who their customers might be. What relationships should marketers try to establish with customers? Since they are, in these activities, in competition with other businesses, how should they relate to other marketers who are going after the same customers? In short, how are we to interpret the various roles that marketers play when they seek to satisfy the wants and needs of their customers? Answering these questions will help us determine what ought to be the nature of marketing and its relations with customers.

Finally, we must further develop ideas presented in the previous chapter regarding how marketers can resolve disputes involving ethical conflicts. How can this be done in the various relations that marketers have with customers?

As previously noted, there are no simple algorithms or rules to be used to make these determinations. Still, a number of moral tools important to moral reflection can be introduced. Further, some coherent strategy for invoking and coordinating the basic values and norms of marketing is needed. In the end, however, dogged consideration, discussion, and reflection on the values and norms that define the relations of individuals and the marketing organizations they face are what is necessary.

II Marketing and the Marketing Concept

The relation between marketers and customers is the central issue of marketing. However, within the broad nature of marketing, marketers may relate to individual customers in any one of a number of ways. What marketers require is something that would further specify how they should engage in marketing. In particular, marketers seek guidelines as to how they should go about marketing in ways that would enhance their chance of being successful.

For the past half-century, a "customer orientation," or "the marketing concept," has been the most prominent and influential view (both inside and outside the U.S.) regarding the general relation of marketer and customer. It is appealed to not only by commercial marketers but even by social and political marketers as the best answer as to what should guide a company's marketing efforts (see Kotler, 2000: 16; Houston, 1986: 86–7). As such, the marketing concept is offered as normative, rather than a descriptive statement. With the development of the internet it has been said that "it [the internet] is . . . forcing marketers to finally make good on those marketing-concept promises" (Donath, 1999: 10). Consequently, the marketing concept is at least part of the answer to marketers' need for strategies to apply the ethical values and principles that define marketing.

There are several questions here: What is the nature of the marketing concept? What guidance does it provide? And, how adequate is this answer to marketers' need for ethical guidance? The conclusion I reach below is that this concept delivers inadequate guidance to marketers, in part because it builds upon a view of marketing rejected in the previous chapter. Attempts to rescue it through modifications embodied in what is called "the societal concept of marketing" are also unsatisfactory. Marketers require a different approach, one that will be developed later in this section.

The marketing concept (TMC)

One of the earliest statements of the marketing concept was offered in the 1950s by Peter Drucker, who formulated it in terms of the satisfied customer being the "only one valid definition of business purpose" (cited in Webster, 1988: 31; see Drucker, 1954: 37). Companies whose purpose is customer satisfaction were said to be "customer-driven." Similarly, Levitt says that the marketing concept is "the idea that success is most assured by responding in every fiscally prudent way to what people actually want and value" (Levitt, 1986: 215).

Numerous businesses have adopted this view. L. L. Bean has displayed a poster in its offices which declares that "A Customer is the most important person ever in this office . . . in person or by mail" (Kotler, 2000: 49). Burger King has advertised "Have it your way." Marshall Field & Company has trained its employees according to the view that "The customer is always right if she thinks she is right" (Kotler, 1987: 281).

Of course, such statements are not intended to suggest that marketers are simply out to satisfy the wants and needs of customers. This is only one part of the marketing concept. A second part is that this customer orientation is the best way to ensure the profitability of a business. And a third part is that efforts to satisfy customers must be integrated throughout the firm (see Drucker, 1954; Bell and Emory, 1971). Still, it is the focus on satisfying customers that is the main distinctive feature of the marketing concept.

Now such statements regarding the marketing concept are oftentimes frustratingly unclear as to what exactly marketers believe they are to satisfy regarding the customer. Some claim that marketers ought to seek to serve the wants and desires of consumers. However, marketers also readily speak of satisfying customers' needs, interests, demands, values, or preferences.

Many marketers notoriously treat these terms as interchangeable, even though they are not. In contrast to wants and desires, needs are requirements without whose fulfillment a human being cannot continue to exist (or at least exist in some normal way). People might not be aware of some of their needs, whereas they are aware of their desires and wants. Simply because a person wants something, it does not follow that it is a need or that it should be fulfilled.

Similarly, desires and interests are also different. Interests (and needs) involve objective considerations that wants and desires do not. Hence, people may be mistaken with regard to their needs and interests in ways in which they cannot be with regard to their wants and desires. Preferences are like desires or wants, rather than needs or interests.

So when the marketing concept says that consumers are sovereign, and that marketers should seek to satisfy them, what is it that marketers should seek to satisfy: wants, desires, interests, needs, or preferences? The simplest and most plausible answer is that the marketing concept urges marketers to satisfy the wants and desires of customers. It is these that are directly expressed in the marketplace choices and purchases of customers. And it is these that marketers aim at. Accordingly, Kotler notes that under the marketing concept, the marketer would "make no judgments about the contribution of these consumer wants to consumer health or welfare. If consumers want cigarettes, alcohol, junk food, and so on, this is their business. Marketing is a responsive tool, not an educational tool" (Kotler, 1987: 285–6). This kind of statement strongly suggests the amoral perspective noted in chapter 1 that many marketers have identified with the marketing concept.

It is wildly implausible, of course, to charge marketers with satisfying (all) customer desires. Customers have too many desires, and marketers too few resources. Further, marketers have not interpreted the marketing concept as implying that they are to satisfy simply the presently expressed desires of customers. Instead, there are several criteria according to which marketers may choose among customer wants.

To begin with, marketers are to satisfy those wants that fall within the area of their competencies (or competencies they can develop, compatible with their overall strategy and moral requirements). The fact that some groups of customers want something does not mean that any particular marketer must seek to satisfy it. Marketers are neither philanthropists nor government agents. They are limited by their resources and competencies. These will be linked with their strategies and long-range planning. Hence, the customer wants that marketers tend to go after will be determined in this broad context. Since marketers are not obligated by the marketing concept to satisfy any or all wants that customers have, it follows that (on this view) customers don't have rights against marketers which would require them to provide what they want or, even, to develop additional competencies to meet those wants. This is a *practical condition* that places boundaries on the marketing concept.

In addition, marketers must consider the law. Simply because someone wants something a marketer doesn't have to seek to fulfill their demand. Some of those wants may be for illegal items, for example explosive devices, certain kinds of chemicals, or child pornography. Marketers are enjoined by the marketing concept to seek to satisfy customer wants, but they must make a determination whether the law permits that they fulfill those wants. Hence, marketers may, if they so choose, provide tobacco and alcohol to the average customer (of a certain age), but not certain deadly chemicals or enriched uranium.

Finally, marketers must consider the effects on their objectives (e.g. profitability) of using their competencies within the law and their own strategies to fulfill customer desires. In short, the marketing concept appears to assert that marketers will be able best to achieve profitability if they will focus on satisfying customer desires, within the above conditions. It is up to the customers to decide what to buy or not to buy. Marketers are not their parents or baby-sitters. Paternalism is undesirable, and the marketing concept captures this by calling the customer "king" or "sovereign." On such a view, then, satisfying customer wants is a means whereby to achieve profitability.

Accordingly, this standard account of the marketing concept embodies a view of marketing which is limited, supposedly, to self-interest and the law (see Gaski, 1984). It is this amoral view that gives rise to the skepticism regarding marketing ethics which was criticized in the last chapter. However, inasmuch as this view eschews paternalism, values (such as self-determination and freedom) are still implicit within it. In any case, the marketing concept (as so interpreted) is an example of a form of marketing rejected in chapter 1.

Problems with the marketing concept

There are several specific problems with the marketing concept as a guide to marketing.

First, on this view, commercial marketing efforts to satisfy customer wants are wholly instrumental undertakings in the service of profitability. Accordingly, customer satisfaction does not have, in the marketing concept, any intrinsic or ethical significance. It is merely a means to the end of profitability. An implication of this is that the marketing concept, though supposedly focused on customers, may undercut itself, since the appeal to profitability serves as its ultimate marketing criterion. This opens the possibility of businesses shifting their aim from customer satisfaction to developing advantages over competitors and to seeking market dominance (Webster, 1988: 33). Webster has argued that this view of the marketing concept has led, under various financial models, to businesspeople focusing increasingly on marketing opportunities "in terms of the market's growth rate and the firm's ability to dominate its chosen market segments" rather than customer satisfaction (Webster, 1988: 33). And this has led, he continues, to a move away from concerns with customer satisfaction even as found in the marketing concept (see Webster, 1988).

Second, since the satisfaction of a present or near-term want is of greater certainty than the satisfaction of future and remote wants, and if profitability and satisfaction are the primary guidelines, there will naturally be an emphasis on satisfying present or short-term wants (see Abratt and Sacks, 1989). But this emphasis on short-term want satisfaction has created many of the ethical and other problems that marketing and society face.

Third, when marketers determine which customer wants to satisfy, they must take into account not only their own self-interests, but also the law. However, this cannot be finally decisive since the law may be silent on some issues, vague on others, or (sometimes) arguably unjust and unethical (e.g.

discriminatory laws). Because marketers operate with resources that might be seized, it is understandable that they must be careful about violating the law. Though this is primarily a practical or prudential consideration, it is clear that it may also have legal and ethical dimensions regarding their fiduciary responsibilities. But beyond this, consider cases in which the law is arguably unethical. For example, the laws, in a given country, may require that people not criticize their government. Marketers who undertake marketing programs that support this law would run afoul of various ethical standards embodied in human rights. In short, there may be moral issues where a marketer may have to say that, even though marketing certain goods, or doing it in a certain way, is not prohibited by the law or their self-interest, still they should not (ethically) do it. Abercrombie & Fitch's Christmas catalogue of 2002 received considerable notoriety as its text and photos promoted group sex. Nike used a demented man with a chainsaw chasing a woman in the forest, as part of an ad campaign to which others raised ethical objections. In later chapters these issues will be more fully addressed. Suffice it to say that it is mistaken to go from the (correct) view that self-interest and profitability play an important role in marketing to the (unjustified) conclusion that, absent other considerations, these may be fulfilled even if others, society, or the environment are harmed. The latter is proscribed by marketing ethics.

Fourth, the marketing concept, as so understood, does not take into account the various values and norms that we have already seen are presumed by marketing. For example, marketers do not, in fact, simply accept customers' views of what they want. Marketers may recognize that consumers may be under- or misinformed. This is *a cognitive condition*. "The customer does not always know what is 'needed'" (Houston, 1986: 86; see Kaldor, 1971). Consumers may not have a broad or informed view about what is technologically possible, what the impact of various products might be on society or the environment, or what their situation will be in the years to come. Real customers, as opposed to the ideal constructs in economics, don't have the full facts or may not correctly understand what is (or might be) available. Thus, marketers do not have to take their lead from the *expressed* needs and wants of customers (Houston, 1986: 85) since these may be mistaken or incomplete (Houston, 1986: 86). Consumers need to be informed and educated about the goods and services available to them. Clearly this holds for commercial, social, and political marketers. But with this come questions of the honesty, openness, and truthfulness of marketers in providing information to customers. Hence, it is a cognition condition with moral implications.

Finally, marketers may also view consumers as under-motivated (or "mismotivated"). Thus, they play an active role in seeking to attract customers and to influence what consumers want rather than simply waiting for consumers to make their wants known. Bell and Emory comment regarding the importance of gaining "knowledge of the consumer" that this "does not exclude the possibility that these needs may be 'stimulated' by business or that aggressive selling may be needed to persuade consumers to buy goods and services which have been created for them" (Bell and Emory, 1971: 39). Levitt speaks of the importance of "creating customers." He also speaks of marketers doing those things that will *make* people want to do business with you (Levitt, 1986: 19; emphasis altered). Commercial, social, and political marketers agree on this point as well. As such they do not passively view customer wants. They see *a motivational dimension* to this relation.

This motivational aspect of the marketing concept does not mean that customers are simply putty in the hands of marketers. Far from it. Still, the marketing concept leaves us hanging here as well. For example, when do attempts to motivate consumers amount to coercion or manipulation of consumers? Which wants are to be stimulated in consumers – those that are simply individual desires, or wants that have a more societal dimension, i.e., that take into account the interests of others and the environment? Accordingly, if the marketing concept realistically includes a motivational dimension, then it will also necessarily raise questions of freedom and self-determination.

In short, if one acts on the marketing concept one does not, and cannot, have a guide to moral marketing since it omits reference to the values and norms that are needed to answer the above questions. The marketing concept is not aimed, primarily (or even secondarily) at helping marketers face the ethical questions it raises and for which marketers need answers. In fact, it is silent on ethical questions. Inasmuch as its primary focus is self-interest (profitability) and the law, it places any ethical values outside of itself. It tells marketers to go to the ethicist for answers to questions about the ethics of what they do. Ethics is detached from marketing.

On the contrary, the relation of marketers and customers is much more complex (as I argued in chapter 1) than the marketing concept portrays. Marketers require better guidance regarding how to be successful in a manner that recognizes the reality of the market (and non-market) applications of marketing, while avoiding the preceding problems.

The societal marketing concept (SMC)

The conclusion that some have drawn from this is that the marketing concept needs to be conjoined with various values. This has been tagged the *societal marketing concept.*

Accordingly some contend that the goals of the TMC must be broadened to include the societal needs of those who are directly affected by one's products (Stanton et al., 1994: 11–12). Kotler claims that "the societal marketing concept holds that the organization's task is to determine the needs, wants, and interests of target markets and to deliver the desired satisfactions more effectively and efficiently than competitors in a way that preserves or enhances the consumer's and the society's well-being" (Kotler, 2000: 25). Years earlier, Schwartz noted that the societal concept is viewed as requiring marketers "to add consumer and societal welfare, as factors influencing marketing planning and performance, to the usual profit considerations" (Schwartz, 1971: 32).

In short, to fix the marketing concept, we need to add to it considerations such as community (and customer) well-being, fairness, and lack of harm. These value considerations, when conjoined with marketing profitability, will produce effective and ethical marketing. Thus, though the SMC acknowledges ethical values, it merely adds them on to what is already marketing. It tells marketers also to take into account the social circumstances and impacts of their marketing. The values and norms involved are external to marketing.

The societal marketing concept is a clear improvement over the marketing concept to the extent that it recognizes that marketers must consider not simply customer satisfaction and profits, but also the broader consequences and (moral) implications of their actions on other people and society. Can a marketing ethics be built on the back of this concept?

To begin with, both the name and interpretations of this concept suggest that its emphasis is on society, for example social welfare, philanthropy. In short, societal marketing is focused on what marketers do to society, something outside the marketing firm, or marketing itself. As such the societal marketing concept does not obviously apply to the research that marketers do, or to their relationships with other marketers. In this sense the societal marketing concept is too narrow for the purposes of a marketing ethics. It is also too narrow if it is formulated so that marketers must only address the effects on their target markets. Sometimes marketing campaigns have unintended consequences for customers who are not targeted. In addition, marketing activities in research, distribution, and packaging (for example) affect others who are not customers. Marketers need to be attentive to all these areas of impact as well.

Second, if the ethical values part of the societal marketing concept are simply appended to the marketing concept, their relation to profitability is a matter of crucial concern. Quite commonly one hears that such values and norms are subordinated to profitability. For example, we are told that "the societal marketing concept at no stage denies that the basic goal of a business enterprise is to ensure its long-term survival and profitability" (Abratt and

Sacks, 1989: 27). Now the survival of ethically upstanding firms is surely desirable, and this requires profitability. But, this denies the pluralism of values and norms by which marketing takes place and the difficult, but ethically unavoidable, judgments that marketers must make that sometimes require limitations on opportunities that might be profitable. The upshot is that the social marketing concept is not a significant advance over the traditional marketing concept. As Crane and Desmond contend, "societal marketing . . . may be less a moral transformation of marketing and more a minor adjustment or extension to the existing technicist 'scientific' marketing paradigm" (Crane and Desmond, 2002: 564).

Third, some marketers resist the societal marketing concept by claiming that for marketers to make any decisions regarding societal and customer welfare (other than those they make on the basis of profitability within the market) is to usurp the democratic process. These determinations, they contend, should be left to society to impose through its elected representatives. But any appeal in such an argument derives from accepting a simplistic dichotomy between society and marketing. And it is just such a dichotomy that the SMC fosters by treating the value considerations it identifies as imposed on marketing from outside. They are external to marketing. But then the obverse is correct too, for marketing to speak to these value concerns is for it to operate outside its own area. On the contrary, as I argued in chapter 1, such value considerations are embedded within marketing. Further, we do not have society making its decisions on the one hand and marketers executing them on the other. Marketers and business have significant input into what society decides. In addition, as we have seen, there may be a considerable time lag between the point at which society decides to act and the damage that some marketing practices may occasion. Accordingly, although the SMC has good intentions, it ends up fostering a view of ethical marketing which opens it to important objections.

Finally, defenders of the societal marketing concept rarely sort through the different normative considerations attached to it. Customer and societal welfare considerations are different from circumstances of fairness and ethical decision making. Instead of exploring how these various norms and values are to be woven together to create ethical marketing, SMC advocates often simply list a number of them and urge other marketers to make use of them. As a result, mention of these additional considerations does not provide the same direct guidance that the appeal to self-interest and following the law provides for defenders of the traditional marketing concept. Their reference to these normative notions is, in effect, an appeal for further guidance. What is a consumer's or society's well-being? How do we know? What is fairness in these circumstances and how does it relate to a customer's well-being? Hence, even if the societal marketing concept is an improvement over the marketing concept, it is more of a promise of an answer as how to engage in marketing, than an answer. Something more (or different) than this is needed.

The integrated marketing concept (IMC)

To respond to the previous difficulties, we need what I will call the *integrated marketing concept*. This concept recognizes the practical and ethical aspects of marketing, described in chapter 1, as constitutive of marketing. At the same time, it provides a framework within which particular forms of marketing may take these values into account.

Central to this framework is the view, developed in the preceding chapter, that marketing is a complex set of connected activities, values, and norms (both moral and non-moral) that form a practice, with internal and external goods and rewards for those who participate in it. It is, as I have said, the creation, communication, and conveyance of something of value to designated groups through voluntary exchanges in ways that also fulfill marketers' objectives. The integrated marketing concept enjoins marketers to integrate the various aspects of marketing in a strategic manner that provides the greatest value to those they target while making allowance for the background conditions within which they operate. In so proceeding, they define a manner of acting that constitutes the excellence or superior performance of marketing.

The question the IMC asks, then, is not what will best satisfy customers, but what constitutes superior performance on the part of marketers in participating in this kind of practice and undertaking these kinds of activities. How can they best design a set of activities that recognizes their competencies, resources, and resource needs, respects relevant values and norms, while providing the greatest value to customers (see McDonough and Braungart, 2002: 9)? The IMC is the integration of those considerations at their highest level. This integration affects all aspects of marketing.

There are several parts to this compressed statement of the IMC that require elaboration. To begin with, the IMC directs marketers to look to their own resources, competencies, and values in determining the nature of the superior performance at which they should aim. It is mistaken to think that marketers can simply develop any set of excellences. Just as some people have the capacities and competencies to be champion bicyclists, while others do not, so too different marketers and marketing firms have different competencies and capacities. Accordingly, part of IMC is that marketers must look to their own competencies and capacities (and those they can develop) that are compatible with the values and norms embedded in marketing.[2]

So too, marketers must look to their resource constraints and the economic drivers within which they operate. Depending upon these, they can develop or maintain these competencies while meeting the values and norms that define marketing. Resources sometimes expand and sometimes shrink; but they condition the specific forms of excellence marketers may achieve. In short, to be excellent, one must also know the economic (and other) drivers of one's practices. The limits of one's resources and those of customers must be taken into account, in both the short and long term here.

Second, marketers must look to the values that drive them, both those they can choose and those that operate as boundary markers and internal structures that shape and define how they operationalize other values as well as their competencies. For example, marketers are enjoined, as the American Marketing Association notes, to refrain from harming their customers and members of society.[3] This is a boundary marker – a minimal condition. However, what kinds of products they produce for customers is a matter of choice by marketers, though they must still ask whether those products make their customers better off afterwards. Excellence in marketing is not compatible with making people or nature, all things considered, worse off. It requires making them better off not only in the short run (i.e., in this particular exchange), but also in the long run (which applies not simply to this customer but also, as relevant, to future customers and generations) (see McDonough and Braungart, 2002: 185).

Third, the preceding competencies, resources, and values might be fitted together in different ways by different marketers and the results all be morally acceptable. In short, there is no one way in which all these parts must be put together. How this might happen will depend on the two other parts of the IMC noted above. One of these parts is the strategy that marketers adopt to service their customers. Here again, marketers may, morally, adopt different strategies, in playing to different competencies, and drawing on different resources and values. Ethics does not prescribe that only one kind of product be produced and marketed in one kind of way. There are multiple moral pathways.

Porter has suggested that different strategies might emerge when a company focuses on some subset of choices its customers make, the needs of its customers, or on the access that its customers might have to their products and services (Porter, 1996: 66–7). He mentions the Vanguard Group as a business that has focused on a subset of the choices its customers make. Bessemer Trust Company is said to target the particular needs of certain groups. And Carmike Cinemas is said to focus on the access to their product that people in smaller cities and towns have (Porter, 1996). Regardless of the final validity of this account of the sources of different strategies, the point is well made that businesses may validly opt for different strategies based on different ways in which they target their customers. Marketers must make these choices in light of their own competencies, resources, and values. Thus, given the values embedded in marketing, the strategy they might select – in light of their competencies and resources – that will best enable them to provide the greatest value to customers will constitute the superior set of activities that they can seek to fulfill as part of their own excellence.

Fourth, the IMC's remaining leg is that of the background conditions in which the marketing takes place. These conditions include the different laws, enforcement regimes, cultures, levels of trust, and conditions regarding social stability that define each society. The practice of marketing requires, as do other practices, certain background conditions for ethical values and norms to be acted upon.[4] In short, if you place people (and organizations) in impossible situations and then demand that they act ethically, you will be disappointed by all except the heroes and saints amongst us. Beyond this, the excellence that marketers can achieve is also conditioned by the background conditions of the societies in which they operate. A marketer who attempts to introduce certain products or services into a society whose culture is opposed to such products, or which finds other marketing practices offensive, is one who will not be long in business. Similarly, any system requires a certain basic level of trust to operate in any efficient manner. To the extent that marketing actions are rendered difficult because of a lack of trust between marketers or between marketers and customers, the practice of marketing can hardly achieve the superior performance of which it is capable. Marketing firms must consider these conditions in deciding whether to do business in various developing countries.

Among these background conditions is the assumption that marketing is the means that a society may best adopt to address the problems of how its citizens obtain the goods and services they require for their lives. These means are (explicitly or implicitly) viewed as part of how that society structures some of the crucial opportunities for people to live a good life. Those who engage in marketing are engaged in activities that presuppose the view that, through the voluntary exchanges of items that those involved value (though they may value different things), a better material (and social) life can be built that promotes the good life for people.

Accordingly, as participants in such a system, marketers also have responsibilities for the manner in which their activities fulfill (or fail to fulfill) these most general ends of marketing. At this level, the purpose of marketing is expressed in terms such as "What kind of society do we want to live in?" or "What is the role of marketing in fostering the good life?" The most general relevant standard here regards the flourishing life, understood in terms of fulfillment of the human capabilities marketing may affect. Questions of commercialism, materialism, and the commodification of life naturally arise on this level. Marketers must be able to address these issues. In doing so, marketing cannot itself bring about the flourishing life, but it can and must play a supporting role by providing people with the necessary goods and services for that life. Obviously answers to these questions are difficult to come by. These kinds of issues will be raised with particular attention in chapter 5.

Consequently, the aim of individual marketers is to produce and sustain a creative response (in light of their capacities, relevant values and norms, possible strategies, and background conditions) to the values people seek that require goods and services. This will involve considering not simply the present wants or needs of customers (and hence their current satisfactions), but the situations, problems, and challenges in which they value those wants or needs. People do not necessarily need gas-burning automobiles, they need transportation; they do not need wrist watches, they need ways to know the time (e.g. for some people cellphones seem to be replacing wrist watches for this purpose). Marketers must consider how they can provide value to designated groups in ways that address these general situations. People's specific wants and desires come and go. The things of underlying value to them are ongoing.

This is a more plausible approach than that of the (traditional) marketing concept, which urges marketers to focus on the satisfaction of customers, rather than on the provision of goods and services valued by customers. The reason is that marketers can't simply satisfy customers. They don't have electrodes embedded in the heads of customers that they can energize and create "satisfying experiences." Indeed, some people and customers will never be satisfied, no matter what a person or marketer does for them.

Instead, marketers have to offer something to customers such that customers value what they receive (and thereby may be satisfied that their aims are met). The danger in focusing on satisfaction – since "satisfaction" is something that occurs here and now – is that the temptation may arise to focus on the marginal or superficial aspects of the product to achieve that satisfaction. That is, as soon as one focuses on the satisfaction, rather than the valued means to that satisfaction, one may be tempted to alter the means in questionable ways. This happens in education when instructors dumb down courses to make their students "happy." It happens in medicine when physicians prescribe what their patients want so that they leave their office satisfied. And, it happens in marketing when researchers give their clients what they want (rather than an account of what is the case); when advertisers seek to satisfy their clients or even targeted customers without regard for the larger implications of what they offer; and when retailers are willing to tell customers whatever will satisfy them, rather than what will provide value to them. In each of these cases the results may well not be desirable, in a larger, ethical sense. In each case, the desires marketers satisfy might be uninformed, or ill developed. Instead, it is also important for marketers, educators, and physicians to act on the basis of a longer-range view which is, in part, captured by reference to the value of the services or products they offer to those with whom they deal.

Similarly, the integration at the heart of the IMC does not occur solely through aiming at profitability, even in the long run. Profitability is one important criterion. Without it a business cannot be sustainable. However, the desire for a simple (even simplistic) criterion of who has won and lost has led too many to fasten mistakenly on this single criterion. Indeed, insistence on profit maximization as the final marketing determinant is both the denial of the independent importance of moral values and norms and the effort to avoid having to make hard choices and tradeoffs.

In fact, there is no single, common value among the above considerations which marketers could seek to maximize. Instead, the values, norms, and other considerations must be balanced so as to create their highest level of joint fulfillment. This will involve appropriate tradeoffs. Justice may require some limits on freedom. Autonomy may impinge on the well-being of others and therefore have to be restricted. Self-interests are themselves shaped by the other values and norms one holds. Clearly we must yield on certain values or norms to realize others more fully (see Porter, 1996: 68–70). The excellence (superior performance) of the firm is to offer the highest value to those targeted compatible with the values and norms that define the practice of marketing. And this means that these tradeoffs must not violate certain minimal moral, legal, and economic conditions.

Accordingly, the IMC is compatible with the importance of profitability, though only within the pluralistic context already suggested. This view accords with the comments of prominent marketers and businesspeople. For example, David Packard commented, years ago, that "I think many people assume, wrongly, that a company exists simply to make money. While this is an important result of a company's existence, we have to go deeper and find the real reasons for our being" (Collins and Porras, 1994: 224). And though the view developed here differs from that of Levitt in many other ways, he too argues that "profit is a requisite, not a purpose of business" (Levitt, 1986: 6). To say, he contends, that "the purpose [of business] is to make money . . . [is] as vacuous as saying that the purpose of life is to eat" (1986: 6).

Instead, marketers must ask how these values can best fit together to meet marketing objectives (which are themselves subject to moral and non-moral evaluation) while creating, communicating, and conveying something of value to designated people through voluntary exchanges. Integrating these aspects of marketing at their highest and most consistent level of excellence will require imagination, care, attention, and perseverance on the part of marketers. The specific form that marketing activities take will differ depending on the conditions already noted (see Porter, 1996: 70–4). Since marketers are familiar with the marketing mix which involves balancing different items, the integrated marketing concept should not be alien to them.

The upshot is that different marketers will give different answers as to what constitutes the excellence of their marketing because they engage in marketing with different backgrounds, competencies, resources, etc. Still, they all remain subject to relevant ethical values and norms. Nevertheless, for all of them marketing excellence lies in the consistent, sustainable, realization of the value complex involved. Such excellence involves not simply the values related in the preceding discussion, but also other internal values. Some of these may be intrinsic values, for example pride in one's work, that are also thereby satisfied; others are extrinsic in the fulfillment of certain self-interested desires. In any case, the aim is to offer the best product or service within these complex circumstances. As such, the IMC is a full-value marketing concept, including moral and non-moral values as relevant. For marketing activities to achieve this form of excellence they must, quite clearly, be incorporated throughout a firm, such that there is consistency of action and a unified approach.

How will marketers know when they have achieved the excellence or superior performance at which they should be aiming? There are a number of indicators.

To the extent that marketing involves various internal goods related to the fulfillment of marketers' own capabilities, their need for intellectual challenges, etc. they will know quite directly based upon their own sense of accomplishment in having provided quality goods and services in a competitive manner. Some rewards will consist of the simple gratification of having done so, while others will have to do with financial returns and recognition by one's colleagues. These are indicators, or feedback mechanisms, as it were, as to how such marketing is going. It shouldn't be surprising that when marketers are doing well in some of these categories, but not well in others, they feel conflicted. Some of these considerations are ethical ones. Others are not. This is wholly fitting with the IMC.

Beyond this, they can look at the extent to which their marketing activities achieve recognition not only from peer marketing organizations, but also from other non-marketing organizations in society, for example NGOs, citizen groups, focus groups, community leaders. The breadth of positive response by various different kinds of organizations to one's marketing activities may serve as an indicator of the excellence those activities are achieving.

Surveys of customers regarding the social responsibilities of marketers suggest that they have become increasingly troubled, over the past decades, with marketing programs that do not integrate ethical values and norms into their activities. Hence, surveys of members of society may also give an indication as to how well one is doing. Likewise, if such individuals are pleased with the values they receive from marketers, they will be more likely to seek out the products of those marketing programs and to tell others about a marketer's products.

In addition, legislatures have increasingly passed laws and regulations that require marketers to give greater attention to the effects of their products and marketing programs on their customers and society. Marketing activities that fulfill appropriate laws and regulations will have fewer fines and suits brought against them. Fewer restrictive laws and regulations will be passed.

Finally, marketers can look to whether the integration of values and norms (moral and non-moral) of marketers and customers tends to coalesce at the micro, meso, and macro levels. The more this occurs – the fewer conflicts and battles that take place at (and among) these levels – the greater one's certainty of the excellence of one's activities and that one is proceeding in an ethically successful direction.

The process by which marketers achieve such excellence is an iterative process, going back and forth between the objectives of marketers, the background conditions under which they operate, the competencies they have, their economic resources, the moral values and norms they are subject to, etc., etc. Just as marketers do not assume that the particular forms that customers' values take may not be changed, so too they should not assume that their own objectives and procedures are not subject to evaluation and change. Part of engaging in this process is proceeding through discussions such as those in the following sections and chapters.

Summary

The aim, in all of this, for the individual marketer, is to achieve the most complete integration of these values and norms within a sustainable marketing organization. When this is not possible, depending on the nature of the case, it might be that certain marketing programs (and even organizations) do not have the moral justification to continue.

On an immediate level the aim of each marketer should be, assuming that all else is equal, simply to act according to the most clearly justified interpretation of the values and norms that are relevant in that situation. This will be subject to factual disputes, claims regarding personal bias, as well as the neglect of morally relevant features of the situation. More globally, the aim is to act on these standards in a manner that achieves their greatest integration with the aim of marketing.

The task of filling in this framework requires developing additional moral guidance for marketers by looking to the particular areas of marketing, and building, moral brick by moral brick, a structure on which marketers can rely when they undertake their various marketing activities. The general values and norms noted in chapter 1 provide an area within which to operate. The IMC presents a general framework through which to operate. But only by looking to these various practical areas can we fill in the details of the integrated marketing concept and its surrounding notions. The result will be more particular rules and guidelines.

An obvious place to begin is with the knowledge that marketers must have not only of their customers but also of their competitors. For this, a marketing information system is crucial. This is what we turn to in the next two sections.

III Marketing Research

Marketers require knowledge of their customers, their competitors, and the general circumstances within which they operate. They need to know what their customers value, what they will buy, what are their wants, attitudes, interests, and their reactions to company marketing strategies. Regarding their competitors, they must understand what they can and cannot do, as well as what they are likely to do. Finally, marketers must also understand the social, political, and other environments in which they carry on their marketing.

By "marketing research" I include not only research that is directed at specific marketing situations, but also research aimed at more general marketing problems and aims. The ultimate point of any such research is to assist management "in decision making related to the identification and solution of problems and opportunities in marketing" (Malhotra, 1992: 379). This means that marketing research within a company should be informed by that firm's strategy, and involved throughout the process that leads from the design of products to their sale. Since marketers believe that (potential) customers may be misinformed or poorly motivated, marketing research cannot be limited simply to identifying what customers (presently) want. And because values and norms are part and parcel of marketing, marketing research must be concerned, at least in part, with customers' future wants, their capabilities, interests, values, and even well-being (see Kotler, 1987). It is in terms of this broader, integrated view of what marketing aims to accomplish that marketing research programs and information systems must be designed. In short, the integrated marketing concept has a transformative role on marketing research.

The importance of marketing research and the information it seeks is obvious. If marketers don't know their customers and competitors, as determined by their strategy, they cannot fulfill the integrated marketing concept. Their chances of succeeding in their aims as marketers are extremely remote. When new products can cost millions of dollars to develop and bring to market, a huge waste of resources occurs if they do not provide customers with what they value. This fact is reflected in the billions of dollars spent on market research, as well as the millions of people on whom research is done to gain valuable information.

Marketing research is also ethically important since marketers can hardly know how they ought ethically to treat customers and competitors if they don't know what their circumstances are – for example their attitudes, perceptions, values, and rights. This is particularly the case in light of a concept of marketing that includes not only commercial but also social and political marketing. These latter forms of marketing involve marketers delving into ethically sensitive areas such as education, drugs, sexual practices, diseases, and government activities (Tybout and Zaltman, 1974: 357). Marketing research can help inform marketers about obstacles and opportunities if it is also alert to the ethical dimensions of potential marketing programs.

There are two main aspects of marketing research that raise ethical questions. First, what information is to be gathered? Second, how is it to be gathered? There is a third question – what use is to be made of that information after it has been gathered? – however, the answer to this issue is part and parcel of the rest of this book. The answers to these two questions are not simple. Further, they have been made more complex by increasingly sophisticated technology (e.g. computer databases, scanning machines, implanted chips, database mining) enabling researchers to acquire, intercept, and receive information on individuals and competitors. The result is that vast amounts of information can be gleaned in any number of ways and used for purposes that may (or may not) be ethically desirable. Consequently, the ethics of marketing research is of particular significance.

What information may be gathered?[5]

Marketing researchers might be tempted to think that any information that will be useful to promote the exchange relationships their firms seek would be desirable information to obtain. This would, however, be a dangerous temptation. There are two reasons for this.

First, to respect people's freedom is not to encroach upon them either physically or mentally in areas entitled to protection. We believe those areas are protected by various rights. Hence, crucial to one's freedom are rights of property, privacy, and personal security. If marketing researchers simply gather any information useful to them, some of that information may encroach upon their subjects' right not to be treated in certain ways. For example, in political marketing there is information about candidates, their spouses, and children, to which marketers have no right. To try to obtain such information by any means, including wire taps or long-range listening devices, is to violate their rightful privacy. It would diminish their freedom. Similarly, some products might be improved by learning about people's use of them in their bathrooms or bedrooms. However, to obtain such information through imaging devices without the knowledge or consent of those observed would understandably raise strong objections regarding the violation of people's right to privacy.

Second, marketing researchers should not simply seek any information that would further a particular marketing project since their aim is not (or should not be) to promote this or that project. They are not cheerleaders for a manager's pet projects. Instead, their aim should be to determine whether conditions would permit or undermine a particular project. As such, the aim of the marketing researcher must be to be as objective as possible. If they do not speak the truth, they undercut the very point of marketing research. Marketing researchers are reality checks, not project boosters. Of course, it is obvious that there may be many pressures on marketing researchers against saying what is true. Conflicts of interest may arise when the role they occupy requires that they provide honest, objective information, while their superiors may threaten them with the loss of bonuses, promotions, or even their jobs if they do not come up with the information that supports a special pet project of their supervisor. Dishonesty is a special vice in the case of researchers. But their own autonomy requires that they not yield to pressures or incentives that would distract them from their responsibilities. It is in such situations that the integrity of marketing researchers is tested.

So what information may marketing researchers seek from their subjects? A better answer, it has been contended, is that the nature of the information sought is that which a subject is willing to tell the researcher. Thus, some say that "the right to privacy involves the right of respondents to decide for themselves how much they will share with others their thoughts, feelings, and the facts of their personal lives" (Laczniak and Murphy, 1993: 59).

However, this is also too simple since an impressionable and suggestive subject might be willing to give information which is deeply personal and not appropriate for marketers to know. Similarly, children have been known to give private information regarding their families in answer to internet surveys on web pages they visit.

So, instead, the subjects who are willing to provide information to researchers must be morally mature agents, or adults. Their mental and emotional faculties must be sufficiently mature or in "good repair" that they can consent in an informed manner. In short, some form of (freely given) *informed consent* is required, rather than simply the willingness of a subject. Since we do not believe that children are capable of giving informed consent, their assent to providing certain information does not justify collecting it. With capable adults, their consent can be valid only if it is informed. For example, the consumer must have relevant information, and be able to understand the kinds of questions that are asked and their implications. In addition, they must not be coerced into giving that consent.

It appears, then, that there this is no piece of information which will always be private. Whether something is private will depend on the individuals and situations involved. Accordingly, the answer to our first question about what information may be gathered is naturally transformed into the second question about how the information is to be gained. On this view, a marketing researcher might (theoretically) ask for (or seek out) any piece of information, i.e. seeking such information would be morally permissible, so long as the subject gave his or her (informed and uncoerced) consent to marketing researchers acquiring that information.

Though this answer is correct, it is also too simple. Problems arise when a research project requires that the respondent *not* know the direct purpose of the research, since to have that knowledge would prejudice or bias the views from their respondents. Does marketing ethics here clash with marketing research reality?

Not necessarily, since there are alternatives to telling the whole truth, on the one hand, and lying or deception, on the other. One possible path is for marketing researchers to explain what they believe they can tell respondents and indicate to them that they cannot tell everything for the reasons just outlined. If respondents agree, research projects which do not fully reveal their purpose at the outset might proceed. But, clearly, in these cases subjects are indicating an important level of trust in the researcher not taking them down a path that will harm them, or which they will later regret. This places added burdens of responsibility on any reputable marketing researcher.

Under these circumstances, marketers have the responsibility to ensure that the questioning is directly related to their products and marketing, will not harm the subjects, and will not violate their trust. Further, they also have the responsibility to explain at the end of the research what the project's purpose was. This is particularly the case when a research project may generate strong emotional responses from the subject.

In short, marketers (and marketing researchers) are not entitled to all the information that would support their efforts to market some product. Their subjects (and potential customers) have rights that certain personal information not be sought or not be sought in certain ways. These rights are based on the principles of freedom and justice that are inherent in marketing. Further, marketing researchers need to be aware of potential conflicts of interest that may arise in their preparing relevant information for their (or other) marketing firms. Their role responsibility is to deliver that information which is truthful regarding the potential product, customers, and their circumstances, so long as it is obtained in an ethical manner. How, then, may such information be gathered?

How should information be gathered?

As we have seen, informed consent is crucial in pursuing marketing research, but this has to be tailored to situations requiring that informants not know the purpose of the research or some details of the research. However, since marketing research includes the two broad categories of covert and overt research, marketers must look for additional ethical guidelines.

In each of these categories, marketers should consider the *entry*, *examination*, and *exit* conditions of how the research project is carried on. There are ethical issues here regarding how marketing researchers approach people or arrange for them to be the subjects of their research, how they treat them while they are being researched, and how these research subjects depart from the study. In each of these cases, the relation of subject or respondent to marketing researcher is different than the relation of a customer to a marketer. This has important ethical implications.

Covert research

In covert research people become subjects of research without making any agreement with the researcher. Even though they may be meeting face to face with the researcher or one of his or her assistants, they are not aware that they are being studied. Consequently, from the standpoint of the subjects, there is little or no formal entry into research programs. They are selected, for reasons the marketer believes are good, to be relevant subjects. As such, the covert subjects of marketing research have not provided their informed consent to be studied. What justifies this mode of marketing research? The answer depends upon the specific forms involved.

Covert research might be done in a variety of ways. I will limit myself to two main approaches: distance public observation and engaged public observation. Whichever approach is taken, covert observation is often advocated as a way of finding out what people really think or do, when to ask them directly, or to observe them openly, might result in some less "authentic" or less accurate answer.

Distance public observation might be done in some disengaged manner, through observation of customer behaviors, at malls, bars, restaurants, etc. This form of covert research raises the fewest ethical questions, because when people are in public places they are aware that their behavior can be seen by others. Hirschman says, for example, that in cases in which "the researcher merely stands and observes from an unobtrusive vantage point, such as a car or street corner . . . [f]ew ethical problems are encountered because, like any citizen, the researcher has the right to observe others in public places" (Hirschman, 1986: 247).

This is, of course, true. But it does not speak to the issue of the records or reports made regarding such observations. Ethical issues may arise because the assumption even in public places (at least in free societies) is that our behavior is not being recorded by someone we don't see or who is unacknowledged, and who then reports this behavior back to others. It is true, of course, that with video cameras in stores and even on streets the strength of this assumption has been reduced. Our justified expectations of "privacy" in public places have been reduced. Covert research pushes this yet another step. Still, there is an important difference. The justification of video cameras in stores and on the streets is crime prevention, something that has a public purpose. Further, reports are not made of who appears in the videos, unless some crime has occurred. The justification of covert research is the private ends of marketers (and reports are created on the behaviors of those who are observed). This is a much weaker justification which disappears when the research documents the behaviors in which a person engages and is used to identify particular people who might be targeted for specific marketing campaigns. In such cases, privacy and the public interest should trump the private ends that may be satisfied through such research. To maintain the contrary is to defend a position that would reduce people's confidence that their public activities would not be used against them.

Accordingly, when researchers study people covertly in public locations, any documentation of their behavior must not be person-specific, or done in a manner that the particular individuals can be identified. Marketing research should not record the fact that Simon LaGrand bought a particular video, drug medication, or pair of women's briefs at a particular store on a specific date. When people go into the public realm, they understand that others will see them. They can hardly have any privacy objections along these lines. However, they do not expect, for justified privacy reasons, that their behavior will be recorded, transcribed, and made available to others.[6] In fact, it has happened that particular researchers have seen people they know while engaged in their observations. Some of these people may be buying things they don't want others to know about; or they might be together with others whom they don't want their spouses or employers to know about. In these cases, researchers must be prepared to deal with this unexpected information by respecting the privacy of people in public places. Such individual-specific information has no place in their research, nor in their reporting of it to their supervisors, the clients sponsoring the research, or even to other people (e.g. the bosses or spouses of the persons observed) who might use such information to the detriment of those observed, or the benefit of the researcher.

Engaged public observation might be done when a researcher actually talks with people to learn about their views, attitudes, etc. but without revealing who he or she is. For example, a researcher might send an agent out onto the street, or into a bar or retail store, to speak with people about their views, preferences, and/or attitudes. In each of these cases the researcher presents him or herself as just another person. In so doing, marketing research agents engage people ostensibly for one purpose, but really for other (research) purposes.

This form of covert research raises more significant ethical questions. In this form of covert research some people not only observe other people (something we know happens every day), but also engage those people by directing their contact along certain paths, recording their observations, and then reporting this back to others who might use it better to target similar individuals when it comes to selling them various products. They may claim that they implicitly gain the person's permission to speak with them, since the subjects of this research do not turn away but continue to converse. Still, this is hardly an informed consent, since their subjects, *ex hypothesi*, never know with whom they are actually talking or what is the real purpose of the conversation.

It is a presumption we make in our social lives that the people whom we meet are not engaging us for other purposes than we might normally attribute to them. Of course this includes making connections, finding out what we know, trying to strike up a romantic relation, attempting to make a good impression, as well as just enjoying our company or some discussion we are involved in. Our moral response to these various encounters will depend upon how we are approached. Sometimes we are caught off our guard. Still, if someone is simply trying to use us to find out what we know or to make connections simply for his or her own benefit, and doing this surreptitiously, we respond negatively. So, too, with the covert marketing researcher. They are deceiving us (in the covert nature of their observation) so as to use us for their own purposes. It is striking that one of the reasons for covert research is that permission to obtain such information might not otherwise be given. This should tell marketing researchers something about the moral nature of their actions.

Some respond that, for both engaged and distance public observation, since the researchers are not seeking to *harm* those observed, they do not require their informed consent (Bulmer, 1982). This is a form of moral thinking that considers actions or policies only in terms of their consequences. Such reasoning misses the point that the very observation which is not agreed to may cause harm. Suppose that a peeping Tom has no other intention than peeping. Still, his peeping violates the privacy right of those observed, even if they are unaware of the Tom's peeping and do not feel harmed by it (due to their lack of knowledge). In the case of the researcher, at the least, his or her behavior involves deception. Lacking that deception, the targeted individuals might turn the researcher away as intrusive.

Others claim that, without covert observation, some truthful information could not be acquired (Jorgensen, 1989). This is, of course, true. But it is significant only if we also believe that observers have a right to learn or acquire all truthful information. Some researchers seem to come close to holding this. For example, Denzin and Erikson claim that "any method that moves us toward advancement of knowledge in science without unnecessary harm to subjects is justifiable" (Denzin and Erikson, 1982: 143).[7]

This view is not only false, but also dangerous. Simply because our knowledge of consumer behavior might be advanced without deliberately seeking to damage a person's credibility or reputation, it does not follow that some researcher ought to probe for information about that person. Surely if such procedures would indirectly, but avoidably, harm a person they should not simply proceed without further ado. At the least, they require some additional justification for creating avoidable harm.

A more plausible effort to specify conditions under which this under-cover intrusion into people's lives could be permitted was made in the 1992 version of the Code of Conduct of the Market Research Society. This says that "covert participant observation should only take place without participants' permission when they are in a situation where they might reasonably expect to be seen or heard."[8] But consider the agency employee who becomes friends with people at a bar so as to learn about their beer consumption. Surely these local bar patrons are in a situation "where they might reasonably expect to be seen or heard." But they might also feel, were they to learn of the presence of the marketing researcher, that they had a "spy" in their midst.

To avoid problems of privacy violation, marketing researchers must consider the nature and conditions under which information may be covertly obtained in an engaged manner from subjects. The burden of proof here is on marketers as to why this information is so valuable that it justifies deceiving unwitting individuals in public settings. An alternative course of action that would test the moral stance of marketers is that, where they seek information which requires them to deceive their informants, those individuals must be informed of the deception at the end of the research; if marketing researchers are not prepared to do this, the research should not go forward. In any case, there should be no "reasonable likelihood that comparably accurate and reliable information could be obtained as efficiently through conventional investigative techniques" (Hodges, 1988: 31; Stafford and Stafford, 1993: 68). Finally, the proposed deception should not result in recorded observations that are person-specific.

There are cases, of course, when those people observed hold positions in a company such that their behavior may be justifiably monitored by their supervisors. Salespeople in a retail store would be in such a position. They might, accordingly, be visited by "mystery shoppers," sponsored by their own firm. In short, covert observation might be used in such instances as part of management's evaluation of the performance of salespeople. However, if marketing managers are to retain the trust and good will of their employees, those employees should know that this form of evaluation will be used.

Accordingly, the use of covert observation requires strong justification in order to be pursued on any specific occasion. The moral burden of proof is on those who wish to use this form of marketing research.

Overt research

Marketing research can take place through a wide variety of surveys, focus groups, experiments, interviews, etc. in which researchers identify themselves. There are at least four salient values here: freedom, autonomy, honesty, and privacy.

The first salient point about overt research is that no one must be, or is required to be, a subject. To force people to become research subjects is to encroach on their freedom, and to deny them a choice that is rightfully theirs. This right to choose is basic to humans and to marketing, and is bound up with our views of the freedom and autonomy of individuals. Still the forms this right will take will vary in different societies. Who marketing researchers can approach and how they do so must be sensitive to these different cultural forms. At bottom, however, those who approach other people (potential subjects) for their own purposes are not entitled or permitted to use coercion or manipulation so that they become subjects or respondents. People's freedom and autonomy ought not to be impinged upon in these ways.

For this right to be meaningful, potential subjects must have knowledge regarding the situation they face – so one might choose whether to take part in this research. Hence, one has a right to know what they are getting into. Here questions of honesty and truthfulness arise.

There are two general situations at issue. Suppose some information is not material to the research project, for example how much the researcher is being paid to conduct the research, or whether the researcher is happy working for the marketing firm. In these kinds of cases, the potential subject does not have a right to this information. Indeed, researchers may decline to provide such information not simply because of its immateriality to the project but for their own privacy reasons.

However, suppose a respondent wants to know such things as the name of the products being researched, the purpose of the research, the identity of the sponsor, the length of time it will take, whether they will experience pain or be subject to stressful situations, what kinds of things will be asked of them, etc. In these cases, the potential subject has a right to this information, unless there is good reason to believe that informing the subject may color or bias that subject's responses. For example, if a researcher wants to solicit people's views in a taste test of two colas, it would be silly to tell the subjects which cola was which. Respondents themselves should understand this. Further, deception is not needed here, but an explanation of the nature of the research. Other similar pieces of information that would compromise the research may also be withheld.

This does not give researchers permission to lie or to deceive subjects about the research in other matters. Instead, they may say, truthfully, that they cannot reveal certain information. Still, aspects of the research that would subject participants to pain or stress must be revealed. It is not a good reason to withhold information because a potential subject might not then take part in the research. Deceptions cannot be justified by claiming that the researcher has a more basic or overriding right to know the information. When people are going to give up their time, and possibly experience stressful situations, they have a right to know what they are getting into. This right is weightier than any right that the marketing researcher would have to the information the potential subject possesses.

Once again, the underlying principle here is that of informed and unco-erced consent. The freedom and autonomy of informants stand behind this principle. People have a right to know in what kinds of situations they are voluntarily placing themselves. The ethical issues that this principle covers cannot be solved, as some appear to think, by invoking the greatest benefit for the greatest number (utilitarianism).

For example, some marketing researchers suggest that the principle of informed consent can be violated and subjects deceived regarding a research program, since doing so will bring various advantages to the research project: the problem of subject reactivity is reduced; researchers can elicit more spontaneous behavior; they have greater control over the research situation; knowledge can be gained that would otherwise be compromised; and there is greater ease in determining the validity of some marketing theory (see Kimmel and Smith, 2001: 664). Some even point to increased sales. But all this proves little.

Marketing researchers in such situations can have little idea of what the full complement of benefits, let alone costs (including possible harm, physical or psychological, to a subject) will be. It is extremely difficult to measure these consequences not only across different human beings but also over the time the deception carries an impact. In addition, the mistrust and suspicion that people may subsequently bring to business and marketing researchers is something that should also be considered.

Accordingly, marketers should respect a subject's right to informed consent. How much a subject must be told about the research will depend upon the extensiveness of that person's involvement. A survey may require providing a subject with rather limited information. An experiment in which a subject is placed in stressful situations will require much more information, including the nature of the experiment, the stress involved, and the possibility of withdrawing from the experiment as it proceeds. The upshot, Kimmel and Smith plausibly suggest, is that "one should never knowingly deceive another without an overriding reason," which (reason) cannot simply be a personal or self-interested one, but a moral one that gives equal consideration to all involved (Kimmel and Smith, 2001: 678).[9]

A second point regarding overt research is that it should not be used for purposes other than research. As previously noted, researchers and subjects have a different relation than do marketers and customers. They are not, as such, in competition with each other. In effect, in overt research there is a trusting relationship between researcher and subject. This means that the researcher has certain responsibilities, like it or not, with regard to not violating that trust or potential vulnerability of the respondent.

It is for these reasons that it is ethically inappropriate for marketing researchers (or marketers themselves) to attempt to sell products under the guise of engaging in marketing research. To do this is to misrepresent one's actions and intentions. It raises ethical issues of honesty as well as trust. It undercuts one important foundation stone on which marketing rests.

Consequently, one must look with raised ethical eyebrows at the letters people receive that solicit their responses in a questionnaire regarding the environment, parenthood, guns, or whatever and then conclude with an appeal for funds. The questionnaire is simply a door-opener to the appeal to obtain funds for the causes or organizations sending out those letters. These instances are mildly deceptive, in that they try to draw us in on a survey basis, but then seek a contribution. We can walk away from it. There are worse examples of this ethical problem. Still, these surveys present themselves in a manner that belies their real intention. They foster moral cynicism regarding marketing research.

Third, researchers often seek to engage their subjects by promising confidentiality. In such cases, the respondent should be able to rely on this moral undertaking of the researcher. Unfortunately, there are many instances in which this is not the case. Some researchers send out questionnaires which are to be returned unsigned, but may still identify the respondent by the placement of "codes in the stapling, binding area, or under the stamp, or by [the] systematic misspelling of return addresses" (Tybout and Zaltman, 1974: 361). What is unethical about these practices is not necessarily that undesirable consequences result. For example, Tybout and Zaltman claim that "over time, promises of anonymity may be regarded suspiciously by subjects. As a result they may refuse to respond to personal or controversial questions or, more drastically, refuse to participate in research" (Tybout and Zaltman, 1974: 361). This is true, but then again this might not happen. Would such broken promises then be ethical if respondents did not become suspicious? Surely they would remain unethical since the rightful expectations of the respondents to confidentiality have been violated. Researchers have broken a promise which they have, supposedly, freely offered to the respondent. The breaking of such promises or the violation of these rights is simply wrong in itself. To engage in this behavior may also tend to create a tendency on the part of the researcher to engage in similar behavior in the future in circumstances in which the results are less benign. In short, individual moral failures must also be seen in a larger context of their implications for one's character and future behavior.

Of course researchers may rationalize this situation by arguing that they need to identify the respondents so as to be able to send follow-up letters or in order to analyze the results more closely. But in such cases the offer of anonymity ought not to be given. The danger which researchers face is that the demands of the research project and of the client for information from the project acquire a significance that overrides all other considerations. Then the researcher may easily fall into moral difficulties. By virtue of the researcher's promise of anonymity to respondents, they acquire a moral right against the researcher. There is, however, no moral right that the researcher retains to break this anonymity. The aim of more objective or more complete research is a desirable goal. It may even be supported by utilitarian considerations. However, the fulfillment of this goal sometimes comes at the cost of the corruption of the very relationships which allow its attainment. Thus, the advantage the researcher may gain appears to undermine the kind of end he or she seeks to attain. This is a form of inconsistency which deontologists such as Kant have claimed to be immoral.

Summary

The marketing research relation to subjects is not a competitive or a market relation, though exchanges (of sorts) take place in this relation. Though those engaging in the relation may be subject to constrained resources (time etc.), this doesn't make this a competitive relationship – even though other activities may be "competing" for that person's time. This is a good example of an instance in which the definition of marketing (in chapter 1) doesn't really apply to marketing research itself. This is not, however, surprising since there is no reason to believe that everything in a discipline partakes of the special nature of that discipline. Some physicians also engage in (medical) research, but that doesn't mean that such research shares all the features of the treatment of patients by physicians.

Marketing researchers are governed by various moral principles, but those of honesty, privacy, freedom, autonomy, and justice hold special prominence. They are also governed by principles of loyalty (fidelity or obedience) to their firm, employer, or client. Some of the problems of marketing research ethics arise when these different principles tug at researchers in opposing directions. Then conflicts of interest may develop against which researchers must guard.

In addressing the ethical issues that arise during marketing research, it is apparent that the resolution of particular issues requires an understanding of the specific contexts, as well as a view of relevant values and norms, knowledge of how they have been used in the past, and assumptions about human beings and a good society. For example, part of the reason that trust between researchers and respondents is so important is that we also want a society that encourages trust between its various members. Such trust encourages greater knowledge, requires fewer defensive mechanisms, and permits more efficient interactions.

In each of the particular cases marketers face, it is not merely a question of applying a simple rule and getting a quick answer. The difficult ethical issues in marketing research do not lie so much in identifying various rights that need to be respected as in balancing rights that pull in different directions, or balancing rights that pull in one direction against obligations and important interests that pull in other directions. It is only by discussing these principles in the context of the integrated marketing concept that we get a better sense of the nature and limits of these principles, as well as the actions and policies marketers should undertake.

IV Competitive Intelligence

In the current highly competitive environment in which new competitors may emerge, or present competitors develop new products or new marketing strategies, competitive intelligence is essential in order to be well informed about these threats, as well as the capabilities, vulnerabilities, and intentions of one's competitors. Having this knowledge may prevent one from being surprised or caught unawares by new product developments, new promotion strategies, expansion plans, or new price announcements from competitors. It may also help one to determine the moral, political, and economic circumstances within which one competes. Are one's competitors offering bribes to suppliers or special deals to retailers? Are they seeking special regulatory relief? Are new laws being suggested that would impact one's marketing strategies?

Marketers have self-interested reasons to know their competition and the competitive environment within which they operate. But they also have fiduciary responsibilities to their stockholders to be well informed about their competition. And given that their own marketing actions in competitive situations will affect their employees, suppliers, people in the community, etc., they even have a (derivative) moral responsibility to do so. The upshot is that knowledge about the competition is crucial for developing one's own overall moral marketing strategy.

But what information may marketers morally seek to obtain about their competitors, and how may they go about obtaining it? Here too there are ethical considerations that should structure one's competitive intelligence-gathering.

At the outset, it is important to note that there is a vast amount of information that marketers may legitimately acquire about their competitors. They can follow reports in the newspapers, on television, and in trade magazines. They can send out salespeople to openly monitor the public actions of their competitors. They can simply train salespeople to report salient information. They may visit trade shows and collect information given out there. They can monitor competitors' websites, the websites of trade associations, attend trade conferences, monitor patents, watch changes in pricing, follow advertisements for jobs, etc. They can even check out recent building permit requests at City Hall to see whether competitors are planning new building projects.

These sources of information are numerous and all morally legitimate because they involve information that is already public, either because it has been made known by the firm or because it concerns activities for which the firm could not reasonably claim a right to privacy. Through the identification, combination, and analysis of these pieces of information, some of them seemingly unrelated though otherwise publicly available, marketing research can develop a coherent and insightful statement about one's competitors.

However, there are much more dubious means of acquiring information about one's competitors. These include:

(a)　covert intelligence whereby one obtains information that is not public, through means of which competitors could not be aware and to which they would not consent;
(b)　deception and/or misrepresentation of one's agents who approach the competitor to gather information;
(c)　special forms of influence (e.g. economic incentives, blackmail) that place pressures upon individuals associated with a competitor firm in an effort to obtain desired information from them.

These are only some of the different ways in which a firm might acquire useful information about a competitor. The following will consider only the first two.

Covert intelligence

Covert intelligence involves cases in which marketers undertake surveillance to which consent has not been given. Examples include going through the trash of a competitor, using long-range listening devices (that can monitor conversations in other buildings at some distance), infrared monitoring devices, satellite photography, long-range photography, etc. In all these cases, by some means, whether hi-tech or low-tech ("dumpster diving") one firm seeks to gather information on the intentions, capabilities, vulnerabilities, and resources of another firm. This is information that the competitor firm does not want revealed, but it does not realize that covert means are being used to obtain it.

As in the case of marketing research regarding individuals, the ethics of these cases is not determined simply by what a competitor firm does not want. It might not want, for example, that any information about it becomes known by its competitors. However, that does not determine what is moral in such a case. What we want and what is moral are two different things.

Consider the example of dumpster diving. The trash of a competitor is sometimes viewed as a rich source of information. Sorting through a competitor's trash may reveal a host of valuable information that can give an advantage to another firm. Sam Walton trumpeted the fact, in his autobiography, that he would go through the trash of some of his competitors to find valuable information on them. Now, dumpster diving can be done either while the trash is on the competitor's property, or after it has left that property and been placed in some public place. To do it while it is on a competitor's private property raises the issue of trespassing. But, in the U.S., once one's trash is in a public location, it is no longer legally one's own. Courts have ruled that it is not illegal to go through it. But what about the ethics of doing so?

Procter & Gamble was involved in a notorious case in which information on Unilever was taken from its trash bins. In published reports, there is a difference over whether the trash bins were located on Unilever's property such that for anyone other than an employee of Unilever to go through them would constitute trespass and be illegal. Unilever claimed that this was the case (Mortished, 2001: 1–2). However, others, including P&G, contend that no laws were broken (see Prescott, 2001: 1). What is clear is that this operation involved hiring the Phoenix Consulting Group, whose founders had taken part in the Vietnam War's Phoenix program, an intelligence-gathering CIA effort against suspected Vietcong supporters (see Mortished, 2001: 1). Agents of the Phoenix Group went through Unilever's trash and obtained extremely valuable information regarding Unilever's marketing plans regarding present and new products.

When John Pepper, CEO of P&G, learned of this case, he called the CEO of Unilever, Niall FitzGerald, to admit what had happened and to offer to settle the matter. In this case, Pepper, a strong supporter of competitive intelligence, concluded that P&G's agents had gone too far. He not only admitted it, but also took direct action to correct the situation.

Had P&G done anything ethically wrong? Pepper seemed to think so. But if you have thrown something away, haven't you relinquished your property rights to it and, if so, how could there be an objection if someone else picked it up for themselves? This is the line of reasoning that U.S. courts have taken. Of course, if this trash is still on your property, you might object to a person's trespassing to pick this object up, but there could hardly be any objection to collecting the trash itself.

Further, some argue that, if one business acquires private or confidential information on another business through documents it has discarded, but not shredded or rendered unusable, the first business is not to be faulted. In the

U.S., the Economic Espionage Act of 1996 is couched in terms that require marketers to make some reasonable attempt to protect themselves. If they haven't and information is acquired by others, they may not complain (legally). However, ethically some believe they would have a complaint. For example, the Society of Competitive Intelligence Professionals (SCIP) maintains that such activities are not proper. What is the nature of the ethical complaint?

Consider the simpler situation of going through someone else's trash to obtain confidential or private information. Inasmuch as they have thrown it away, they are giving up their property rights to this material. Still, they are doing so with the intention that it not become public; they intend that it no longer exist – that no one else have it. They acted in this way with this under-standing of the moral norms of this society and industry. It is not simply that they no longer wanted this information, but didn't care if others collected it. Rather, they believed that operating in this way was in accord with a tacit moral understanding that this was the morally appropriate way of wholly eliminating such material. This was part of the background conditions on which they were relying. It would not have been morally appropriate to leave it on a park bench or to throw it out of the fiftieth-floor window of headquar-ters. Instead, one way we protect the privacy of information and things we no longer want is to put them in the trash.

In fact, we have various ways of ensuring privacy in our society, for example, pulling the shades down, shutting a door, speaking quietly, writing in our diary, as well as putting things in our trash. These will vary from society to society. This is why it is important to know the context of one's moral decisions.

Still, one's own privacy in any society always requires some sort of restraint on the part of others. Otherwise there will be little left of privacy. Sometimes it is as simple as an averted gaze, or refusal to listen to what is being said. With businesses it is more complicated. When some businesses operate on the basis simply of the current legal situation, then every business must take added precautions to protect what, morally, should otherwise be private. The moral concern here is that if my privacy is only what I can protect from others who are using any and all technological devices they have to discover what I am thinking, writing, or saying, then I have virtually no privacy left. So too the privacy of a firm (and its competitors) relies on the self-restraint of other firms. When this is bounded only by the laws, the realm of privacy has been effectively reduced.

Another form of covert intelligence is that of obtaining aerial photographs of a competitor's plant that is being constructed. Photos of a construction site may reveal important information about manufacturing processes, plant capacity, etc. Far from a fanciful case, this is a real one that was judged to be illegal (Kotler, 2000). But is it unethical too? And what about buying satellite photos of that site? John Prescott, the editor of a journal on competitive intelligence, contends that "covert collection methods such as aerial photography of a competitor's new manufacturing plant are [ethically] inappropriate" (Prescott, 2001: 2).

However, in such cases and given the preceding discussion, it might be argued that the plant owner should be well aware of these possibilities and take appropriate actions to protect important information, since some people will try to take advantage of such situations. Still, this leaves the ethical dimension without response. The response is similar to the one above. Such behavior contributes to a decline in trust between competitors and people in a society. It raises the costs of doing business for everyone, simply because some are inclined to take advantage of "opportunities" of this nature. It is not behavior that could be acted upon openly and by everyone. It requires some form of stealth. It focuses the area of competition not on the excellence of one's own products and services, but on gaining advantages by knowing the ways in which competitors produce or bring their products and services to market. And when such information is used to improve one's products, the information is not new information a firm has itself generated that adds to our body of knowledge; rather, it is the redistribution of knowledge that has, instead, been stolen from its competitors.

In the end, these forms of covert intelligence are a way of imposing potentially significant costs on a competitor, while seeking to reap potentially significant benefits for oneself. Nevertheless, a firm engaging in this activity will also have to undertake these defensive measures itself. In addition, these costs also restrict the ways in which people can communicate within a business, the trust they may have of others, the physical openness with which they do their business, etc. In short, these measures have the potential effect of transforming business into something that must be done under extensive cover, in bunkers, and behind specially constructed walls or blinds. It transforms a form of business life into something much less desirable. Though the rationale for businesses engaging in such covert intelligence is that they may gain some information that would give their products a competitive edge, the result, instead, may simply be a pyrrhic victory for all involved.

Deceit and misrepresentation

Competitive intelligence may involve deceit and misrepresentation in a number of different ways. Consider the following case. Suppose that a firm advertises a job and solicits employees of a competitor to apply for the job. At the interview, they are pumped for information regarding their own work and firm. But no job is ever offered. In this way, a business might use phony job interviews to milk information out of a competitor's employees. Clearly there is deception in such a case. Not only that, but this process wastes the time of the employees, and may compromise their present position (assuming that they are still working for the competitor). Hence, it may also place them in a vulnerable position. It may seem like a clever way to gain information, but it is not ethical. It violates our principles regarding truthfulness and honesty. The fact that one may gain something for oneself (or one's company) is not the kind of excusing condition that justifies such deceitfulness.

But what if a job were offered? Then there would not be deception, at least if it was a real job. Those competing for the position were only taking part in an effort to obtain that job. In this sense, any time wasted on their behalf was part of this competition. Nevertheless, if the aim of the exercise was to gain trade secrets from the other firm, then this would still raise other ethical questions, since the person (and the firm) might face ethical and legal challenges regarding theft of the property of one business by those at another business.

The preceding tactic can be used in reverse. Widget Inc. might send an employee to interview at a competitor, but without telling those interviewing him at the other company that he is still an employee of Widget. In fact, he might make up a story that he has recently been let go – or perhaps unjustly fired – and could supply some useful information if he were hired. Of course, he seeks the information his company wants and then returns to his existing job. In fact, the chairman of Staples sent his wife to apply for a job with Office Depot. Though she stopped this charade before the interview, she supposedly learned some of their training methods (Crock, 1996: 176). Other variations include sending an employee to go on a plant tour of a competitor's facility (Fitzpatrick, 2003: 6), or having an agent of a firm pose as a potential supplier of another firm so as to gather important information on that firm (see Fitzpatrick, 2003: 8).

Another form of deceit or misrepresentation is to have an employee pose as a student in order to obtain information that he or she could not otherwise obtain. Samantha calls up a competitor firm, posing as a student doing research on that firm and its business. For a report she is doing she solicits information that the firm would not otherwise give out. Sometimes this involves actual students posing as ordinary customers in order to obtain information, which is then reported back to a competitor of the firms interviewed. In one real case, students were required, as part of a class project, to do research for a business firm on one of its competitors. The students were encouraged to obtain information on the targeted firm by presenting themselves, as they were in fact, students in a class trying to understand that firm. They even used university stationery to communicate with the firm

(Ansberry, 1988: 37). Students in the class were told not to lie, but they didn't say that they worked for the other firm, because the targeted firm did not ask them! In this case, the targeted firm let its guard down. The students' class provided a cover or a disguise for them.

In all these cases, some form of deceit or misrepresentation is used to try to obtain information that could not otherwise be procured. One way in which some seek to justify such behavior is to argue that it is part of the "game" of business that permits such deception, as one competitor vies with another. In fact, many in marketing do believe that such deceit is frequently engaged in and as a consequence is acceptable (Paine, 1991: 426). The rationale here is not simply that it is widely done ("everyone is doing it"), but also that since they are competing in this manner, one must protect oneself by doing the same. In short, they adopt a tit-for-tat strategy, arguing that the use of similar means (i.e. deceit etc.) to protect oneself is justified. This leads to the *rationalization* that "We were forced to do it, since everyone else is doing it."

To begin with, we should be skeptical that "everyone" is in fact engaged in unethical forms of competitive intelligence behavior. Studies of moral decisions make it clear that most people have a bias against believing that other people are as moral as they themselves are (see Messick et al., 1985). We tend to believe that we are fairer, more honest, and more moral than our competitors (see Messick et al., 1985; Paine, 1991: 426). People tend to believe that others are more prepared to take advantage of them and deceive them, than they themselves would be. For example, 45.9 percent of the respondents to a questionnaire administered to 451 participants in seminars on intelligence-gathering approved of getting information by posing as a graduate student working on a thesis. A striking 85.6 percent of the respondents believe their competitors would use this method of intelligence-gathering (Paine, 1991: 426). Similar figures have been found on many other occasions. These results should remind us of our tendency, documented in various studies, to believe that the moral level of others' behavior is usually lower than our own. People tend to be somewhat mistrusting and suspicious of others. They then often use this as a rationalization and defense of their own morally unjustified actions. Of course this fulfills the expectations of their opponents. A kind of self-fulfilling prophecy takes place.

Second, even if it is true that many in business use deceptive forms of competitive intelligence, this does not, in itself, justify this kind of behavior. It is also true that people, in their ordinary lives, cheat, lie, steal from, and deceive each other. But this fact does not justify other people adopting these kinds of behavior. If a business had a right to information about another firm which that firm would not give it, then using deception to obtain it might be justified. But that is not the present situation. This information, we are assuming, is rightfully private. The only justification that is offered is that obtaining such information may help the firm using the deceit to out-compete other firms, to produce better products or services, or, at least, to be more profitable. However, these are not moral reasons, but self-interested ones.

Third, the real appeal in such cases is that unless one also does something morally wrong (e.g. deceive someone), some other, more important value, for example the well-being of the firm and those part of it, will suffer (unfairly). This may be true, but what it justifies is using sufficient defensive tactics so that one is not exposed to espionage. All members of the firm need to be trained in the ways in which competitive intelligence may be acceptably gathered, as well as the ways in which they may unwittingly give up crucial, private information. Of course it will never be possible to identify each and every technique of competitive intelligence. People are inventive. Hence, general values, examples, and guidelines are required. An ethical culture must be fostered which will help answer such questions. The upshot would be that if some use unethical practices, then, even if they thereby obtain helpful information, they should not be rewarded, but punished. Similarly those who give up private information need to be retrained, if not punished.

Finally, it may be argued, in some of these cases, that those people who, when misled or deceived, provide private information to competitors are rather gullible, overly trusting, or perhaps simply stupid. They believed what they were told. In these times, they should be more guarded, less naive. This is some truth to these charges. They do need better training. Still, this is a case of blaming the victim. Its implication is that the person who does not trust other people, and is always on his or her guard, comes out the winner. The further implication, however, is that cynicism, skepticism, and defensiveness come to characterize larger and larger parts of society. Trust is replaced with distrust; a willingness to help gives way to guardedness against requests for help. Society (and business) ends up the loser. In any case, this kind of rationale regarding being more guarded does not justify the deception, though it does suggest that firms do have a responsibility to train their employees to be more wary of those who would take advantage of them.

Accordingly, there appears to be little ethical rationale for such deceit. As noted above, it is unlikely that a company has a right to such information about its competitors that would justify employees using deceit to obtain it. Hence, an overriding right cannot be invoked to justify their deceit. Nor can the greater competitive edge of the company be the justifying basis. Absent some further rationale, there is no obvious reason why the welfare of the company that is willing to employ deceit should take precedence over that of the company whose information is being obtained by that deceit. This ethical stance is captured in the code of ethics of the SCIP, which enjoins against such deceit, while directing its members to reveal who they are in all interviews (see appendix III). In short, marketers cannot avoid these issues by claiming that simply "everyone does it," when it comes to these questionable methods.

V Segmentation and Target Marketing

Marketing research and competitive intelligence inform marketers about important characteristics of potential customers as well as their competitors. Given this knowledge, which people should marketers approach as customers? Everyone? Only certain people? Based on the information they have developed regarding potential customers and their competitors, marketers must make a strategic determination as to which customers to target. However, strategic decisions regarding which customers to focus on require not only such information, but also consideration of company objectives, competencies, resources, and marketing ethics. What ethical issues must marketers must be attuned to here?

One form of marketing is simply to refuse to pick out any particular group, but market to anyone who is interested and has the means to acquire one's products. Such mass marketing was the prominent form of marketing during much of the twentieth century. However, during the latter half of the twentieth century this changed dramatically. Though some products such as salt, sugar, nails, twine, and rope are still mass-marketed, the number of mass-marketed products has dramatically declined over recent decades. In itself, mass-marketing would not appear to raise any special ethical issues over and above those that arise simply with marketing. Since mass-marketing does not distinguish between this and that group, it does not raise the ethical issues such distinctions might occasion.

In contrast, market segmentation and the targeting of particular groups of customers raise a number of special ethical problems. Segmentation begins with the simple notion that it is impossible, or at least unlikely in most situations, for a marketer to please everyone with a particular product. Therefore marketers divide up the total market into a number of smaller groups which have a similar set of characteristics with regard to the products they might buy or acquire. They then focus their efforts on those customers in the segment that might be most interested in their products given the product's qualities, its price, the way it is promoted, and where it is offered. This is widely said to be one of the most crucial aspects of contemporary marketing. Levitt has gone so far to say that "If you're not thinking segments, you're not thinking" (Levitt, 1986: 128).

The scope of a market segment will be more or less extensive depending upon the number of individuals who fall within its defining characteristics, for example selling to families with infants or to high-end buyers of luxury automobiles. Hence, if mass-marketing is at one end of a spectrum, individual marketing is at the other end. In between are various degrees of segmentation. Kotler refers to these as:

(a)   segment marketing
(b)   niche marketing
(c)   local marketing, and
(d)   individual marketing (Kotler, 2000: 256–9)

In each one of them an increasingly restricted group of customers, who have similar desires, economic resources, buying attitudes and habits, as well as geographical location, are chosen to be targeted by marketers. Niches are much smaller segments and local markets smaller yet. Individual marketing is becoming increasingly possible due to advances in technology that allow customers to specify, in advance, the particular qualities they want in the products they purchase. Levi Strauss, Andersen Windows, Harrah Entertainment, and others have explored various forms of marketing in this direction.

Identifying segments

How are such groups or segments to be identified? It is possible, of course, to divide people up in an endless variety of ways. Further, there is nothing ethically questionable, as such, about any way in which you divide up a population, whether by age, gender, income, psychological features, or geographical region. Sociologists, psychologists, and demographers might use a variety of different criteria. But they are not marketers and what they do is not segmentation.

Instead, segmentation is the selection of various characteristics that "hang together" with regard to a marketing mix (including the product, price, place of distribution, and promotional efforts) that might be offered to members of that group. In short, marketers segment populations for the purpose of developing different marketing mixes that uniformly and efficiently target particular groups (this includes being able to out-compete others). As such, whatever segments they develop must be substantial enough to target, capable of being reached, distinctive, and actionable (see Kotler, 2000: 274).

The ethical issues that arise with regard to identifying various segments to target turn on the special features used to select (or to exclude) certain groups and the implications of so doing. We might distinguish exclusionary segmentation and heroic segmentation.

Exclusionary segmentation takes place when certain groups are excluded as potential marketing segments because they have features which, for morally questionable reasons, marketers choose not to identify as potential target markets. This might occur if a company defined the segments it was prepared to target by leaving out various groups because of other social prejudices against that group, even though members of that group would like to purchase the company's product. Of course, it might be that, if the company sold to that group, other groups might avoid or boycott its products. Still, if this occurred when these groups were identified by their color, ethnicity, caste, or sexual orientation, this would be a morally objectionable form of segmentation.

For example, in the past General Motors would not sell its Cadillacs to black people, since they thought that this would diminish the aura or prestige they wanted to surround their cars. Similarly, there are other cases of companies not picking certain segments due to discrimination, rather than for competitive reasons. A similar situation arises with red-lining, in which there are certain sections of a city (usually occupied by minority racial groups) to which banks or lending institutions will not lend money to buy houses. Accordingly, the ethical guideline here requires that market segmentations not exclude (or include) various groups based upon morally unjustified considerations such as racial bias, homophobia, gender bias, etc.

The upshot is that segmentation, if it is to be done ethically, must not be done on the basis of discrimination against people for morally unjustified reasons. Of course, whenever one segments a market, some people are included in that segment, and others are excluded. Those that are excluded should not have a moral ground to complain, such as racial or gender discrimination. It might occur, however, that excluded segments not targeted may complain about lack of attention by the marketer. Perhaps some segment of white straight males complains that they are not targeted, but gay males are. In such cases, unless the excluded group can demonstrate that it would be morally wrong to exclude them, their complaint will not be justified.

Heroic segmentation involves cases when marketers go beyond what is normally required for moral segmentation by a company. An example of this occurred when Merck realized that a drug (Mectizan) it had developed for animals could also be used on humans to prevent the devastating disease of river blindness. People suffering from river blindness is a special market segment – a group of people who have a pressing need. In the vast majority of cases, however, they do not have the resources to purchase this drug. In fact, the countries where they live were not able to purchase the drug, nor were there the channels of distribution in place to distribute it. Nevertheless, Merck proceeded to develop those channels of distribution and distribute the drug free to these people.

In short, segments ought not to be identified for targeting which would exclude people for unethical reasons such as occurs in exclusionary segmentation. On the other hand, marketers who identify segments that require special treatment, as in the case of river blindness, go above and beyond the call of duty. Morality does not, in general, require such behavior. Still, without such special efforts the moral life would be poorer.

Targeting segments

Since markets are segmented, not for some purely intellectual purpose, but in order to target potential customers, an important part of the consideration of segmentation is how marketers do in fact market to various segments that have otherwise passed moral muster. This raises a host of ethical questions, some of which will be dealt with in later chapters, for example, on promotions and advertising. Nevertheless, apart from the particulars of those issues, certain segments may be targeted in ways that raise additional ethical questions.

Beneficial targeting occurs when, because marketers have focused on particular groups of individuals, they can provide them with superior services and products. Because marketers may better be able to track niches of consumers or even individual consumers, they may inform them regarding products or services of which they would not otherwise be aware. This can occur on their home computers or even on their cellphones. So long as the customers wish to be so informed, this is clearly a benefit to them. Hence, the ethical issue here regards matters of intrusiveness that may arise in informing people about products and services. If such messages are unwelcome, then marketers are hurting their own cause as well as intruding on the privacy of their customers. In addition, there are issues of privacy regarding the use of the particularized knowledge that marketers can now accumulate regarding a person's buying choices and habits. In the case of cellphones there may also be issues of fostering behavior in some people that absorbs them in receiving and sending such messages to the exclusion of more immediate and direct forms of human experience of others and the world about them.

Defensive targeting occurs when a segment is defined by certain features that make it a desirable marketing target, but whose members will tend to misuse the products marketed to them to harm themselves or others, unless certain special, defensive marketing precautions are taken. For example, suppose a marketer identified a market segment of people inclined to drive much faster than the speed limit and who were more frequently arrested for doing so. This group would be happy to buy some device, for example a radar detector, that would allow them to speed and not worry about arrest. Ethical questions arise to the extent that people think that breaking this law is unethical and that the marketer is helping these drivers break the law, as well as risking their own lives (and those of others). The less this is believed, the less this is a problem.

But then consider a case in which marketers identified the market segment of those individuals who have been arrested for drunk driving. By searching court records it is possible to identify these people and to target them for a device that will measure their breath to see how much alcohol content it registers (Stanton et al., 1994: 145). Does this raise any ethical questions? It might not, if the result was that those drivers did not drive with elevated levels of alcohol in their blood. But suppose it was determined that marketing to this group gave such individuals a sense that they could drink and drive, by simply keeping their blood alcohol content below a certain number. This might give such individuals a false sense of capability to drive after having consumed alcohol. Second, it should be recognized that such devices might not be absolutely accurate on any particular occasion – false readings do occur. Or they might not be properly used by the person employing them (perhaps their vision has even become blurred!) and they believe that they can drive. In these cases marketers who target this segment would be acting carelessly in an ethical sense.

An ethical guideline here would be that segments which may foreseeably be expected to misuse a product to the physical harm of themselves or others ought not to be targeted by a marketer, unless special, defensive steps are taken to prevent such misuse. Of course, there are important questions here about whose responsibility is the misuse of a product. But if such misuse may be expected, then marketers have some form of contributory responsibility if they segment their markets to target such groups. Another guideline would be that segments ought not to be identified and targeted that would use the product to engage in acts that break the laws or moral norms that are widely viewed as being of significant importance in a given country. Defensive targeting would avoid such segments. If, however, they were targeted, an ethical marketing program would seek to reduce or eliminate these illegal and/or unethical consequences.

Vulnerability targeting occurs when a segment is identified that has a certain weakness, or vulnerability, which may lead those in it to being harmed if a product is marketed to them. It should be emphasized that even though a marketer identifies a segment that has special vulnerabilities and markets a product or service to it that relates to that vulnerability, there may be nothing morally unjustified in doing so. Indeed, it might be that such a segment deserves special targeting. The point, rather, regards how that is done. Is it done in a manner that seeks to remedy, or, at the least, does not take advantage of that vulnerability? Or does it exploit that vulnerability for the self-interested ends of the marketer?

The fact that a marketer seeks to profit from marketing to those with vulnerabilities does not mean that marketers are thereby exploiting, or taking unfair advantage of, that segment. Marketing of any sort to such segments takes place within a market system, such that the wants and needs of those vulnerable people may, in general, be met only to the extent that they have the resources to do so, and marketers may derive some reasonable profit.

Still, the fact that marketers are profiting from these transactions may well raise questions of whether they benefit from the troubles of those they target. Accordingly, whenever, marketers target a group that is vulnerable and does so with regard to that vulnerability, they must exercise special sensitivity to and awareness of what they are doing, how they are doing it, and what the results are. What they must not do is benefit from these people's vulnerabilities in a way that does not constructively address them. Hence, if they seek to sell a product to people with certain vulnerabilities, but the product does not redress the problems they have, but makes them worse off, then they are benefiting from the problems of others in a manner that is exploitative. On the other hand a product may directly address a group's vulnerabilities, but it might be priced at such a level that only those with access to exceptional resources can obtain it. Questions of exploitation also arise in this context, as the pharmaceutical companies have learned with their drugs for HIV/AIDS.

Vulnerability targeting usually pertains to those segments which have various weaknesses that stem from abilities, resources, or the like that they lack. Hence, it occurs when minority groups that lack power, social standing, or resources are marketed to in ways that do not address these problems, but take advantage of them. This particularly raises questions when the product marketed is itself potentially harmful. For example, G. Heileman Brewing Company was faulted for marketing a high-alcohol-content malt liquor called PowerMaster to inner-city black populations. Part of this criticism was due to the especially high alcohol content (5.9 percent) of this product and the harm it might pose. However, it was denounced even more because the billboards and advertisements for PowerMaster played on the theme of power, which it linked with a product that was marketed to populations who lacked power, not in the form of alcohol, but in the form of real social and political power. Similarly, there is a host of other segments, for example children of certain ages, the aged, the senile, the bereaved, etc., that, though plausibly target markets, raise significant questions regarding how they are targeted, for example the kinds of commercials or advertisements, the types of promotions, the instructions on the packages, etc., that should be used. When marketing campaigns are directed at the weaknesses of these groups, and in ways that do not correct those weaknesses but exploit them for the marketers' own ends, such marketing campaigns are justly criticized as unethical. These issues are considered in more detail in subsequent chapters.

Finally, a form of vulnerability targeting may also arise when, due to the special attention marketers give to individuals and niches of individuals, those customers become inordinately attached to the goods and services of the marketer. For example, if the special attention that Harrah's Entertainment gives to gamblers leads some to spend more and more of their money at Harrah's to their own great detriment, then marketers such as Harrah's need to be alert to these harmful affects of this form of target marketing (see Salkever, 2004).

In any case, the general ethical guideline here must be that though people may be segmented on grounds that relate to their vulnerabilities (e.g. sickness, senility, cognitive immaturity), the targeting of these groups ought not to be done in ways that harm the customer or take advantage of those vulnerabilities solely for the self-interests of the marketer, rather than to lessen or remove those vulnerabilities. This issue will be discussed further in chapter 4 below.

VI Conclusion

The relation of marketer and customer is complex and filled with many ethically challenging issues. At the outset, I discussed the marketing concept which has been widely touted as the prime directive for marketers in their relations with customers. Various problems with the marketing concept, and the societal marketing concept, led to the formation of an integrated marketing concept, which better captures the practically moral nature of marketing.

The remainder of this chapter has discussed additional moral features of marketing as they relate to marketing research, competitive intelligence, segmentation, and target marketing. To address important ethical issues in these areas, we must consider various relevant values and norms within the situations that marketers actually face. The values and norms of marketing, the background conditions, and the strategies marketers adopt all must come together to address these questions.

Some suggest that developing an ethical marketing approach requires that we engage in descriptive studies to determine what is generally done, or what the public thinks about various marketing practices. While this is an interesting and important suggestion, these studies do not necessarily help advance our understanding of what marketers ought to do (see Schneider and Holm, 1982: 90; Robin and Reidenbach, 1993).

Instead, just as we did in the previous chapter, we must follow the arguments and reasons which people offer for various courses of action. And to do this, I have sought to identify the relevant moral values, principles, and rights involved in the above areas of marketing, discussed the contexts within which those values and principles apply, and drawn together the relevant moral factors so as to make what seemed the best judgment. There is, as such, an interpretative aspect to marketing ethics. Marketing can be viewed as a text that must be interpreted within its historical, ethical, economic, and political contexts. The moral thinking it requires involves moral seeing, imagination, and judgment. It is not simply a case of mechanically imposing principles on situations, or calculating costs and benefits.

In the following chapters, I apply this approach, centered within the integrated marketing concept, to other crucial areas of marketing. It is true that, as long as certain current competitive relations significantly define the circumstances of marketers, there are limits as to what they can do individually. Still, there is a great deal they can collectively do and that society as a whole should urge them to undertake to promote ethical marketing. It is this discussion that I continue in the next chapter on product development, pricing, and distribution.

Notes

1   It should be understood when I do not specify the context of various claims I make that they are made with respect to the United States. This is not to say that they do not apply to other situations and countries. However, it may also be that they do not.
2   This point has been previously made in chapter 1. Still, the compatibility of these competencies with moral values and norms is important, and hasn't been directly made before.
3   The AMA lists "to do no harm" as its first general norm (see appendix I).
4   Lacking appropriate background conditions, various "system responsibilities" of marketers may come into play (contingent upon their abilities, knowledge, and proximity) to bring these conditions about. The point here is also true of other institutions and moral behavior in general.
5   In the present section I will address marketing research with regard to individual subjects. In the next main section I will consider marketers gathering information on their competitors.

6   Hence, the video recorders in stores etc. do raise ethical issues. The store owners have a right to protect their property, but they risk violating the privacy right of customers. Announcements that behavior in a store is being recorded are essential here. Also those videos ought not to be used to reveal the behavior of specific individuals. Nor should they be used for the entertainment of store employees or owners.

7   By such "unnecessary harm" Denzin and Erikson apparently mean that "the method employed [does] not in any deliberate fashion damage the credibility or reputation of the subject" (Denzin and Erikson, 1982: 143). But this test would be met if one unintentionally did so, even though it might not make the victim of such damage feel much better!

8   Rule A14; cited in Stafford and Stafford, 1993: 68. In the most recent (2005) version of this code, this rule has been removed.

9   Kimmel and Smith, 2001 suggest only the bare outlines of the rule mentioned here. Their formulation lacks the further elaboration given to it here.

Chapter Three

From Product Development to Distribution

I Introduction

The development of products, their packaging and pricing, as well as their distribution, may not strike most people as very glamorous activities. Nor do they receive the attention that advertising and promotion garner. But they are basic to marketing. Marketing research and segmentation may be the architectural plans, but the topics discussed in this chapter are the resulting structure. As before, ethical issues pervade the decisions marketers make here. Three areas of ethical concern are of particular importance.

First, decisions regarding which products to produce involve ethical issues related to product quality, planned obsolescence, and the effects of those products on consumers and the environment. We are tempted to see products as neutral material things. They are not. They are bundles of responsibilities, promises, and consequences to which marketers must be attuned.

Second, how are those products to be packaged, labeled, and priced? The packaging and labeling of a product may provide necessary and important information to customers, or may obscure and inhibit their knowledge of just what they are purchasing. Packaging decisions may contribute to deceptiveness regarding the package's contents, the safety of products, as well as the environmental impact of the packaging. The pricing decision is terribly important for more than the simple reason that it is what a customer has to pay in order to acquire the product. It sends various signals to producers and consumers about the product. At the same time it may also raise questions of fairness, discrimination, and exploitation.

A final major ethical topic relates to the distribution of products. Once products have been produced and packaged, and their price determined, they enter into the channel of distribution whereby they make their way to wholesalers, retailers, customers, and eventually the ultimate consumers. Marketers often form relationships with others who cooperate with them to accomplish their own ends in these distribution channels. What forms and uses of power are justified in these relationships? For instance, does justice set limits to the amount of power that the channel leader may exercise in a channel of distribution? What is the role of cooperation and trust within these channels? More broadly, what responsibilities do marketers have within the channels of distribution they use?

This chapter can address only a few of the ethical issues in this complex mixture of topics. To do so, I will draw on relevant moral values and principles I have already identified. My aim is to develop their applications to these different contexts in a way that will both deepen our understanding of them and expand our understanding of their roles in a marketing ethics. Finally, my intention is also to develop further the kind of moral reflection exemplified in the preceding chapters. In this way we can continue to fill in the ethical framework initially sketched in previous chapters, and to lend guidance to marketers seeking to address these issues in a responsible manner.

II Product Development

Businesses are under considerable pressure to develop products that will be favored by customers over those of their competitors. Part of the pressure to develop new products derives from the declining profits associated with products that have been around for some time. It is remarkable that a large percentage of the many products that businesses sell today did not exist a decade or two ago. This illustrates the importance of innovation. On the other hand, there is a high rate of failure of new products. How, within the framework laid out in the preceding chapters, are marketers to think about this crucial aspect of marketing?

In the following I will concentrate on consumer products, rather than business products. By a "product" I simply mean anything that has certain attributes or characteristics (be they tangible or intangible) a producer or manufacturer might offer in an exchange with customers, who believe (or can be brought to believe) they are of value to them. Accordingly, "products" include physical things, services, places, experiences, events, ideas, and information.

It is striking how little is explicitly said about the ethical issues that marketers ought to consider in product development. For example, with regard to the criteria for developing a product for the market, we are often told to consider whether an adequate market demand may be expected, what financial criteria need to be satisfied, and whether the product fits within the company's overall marketing structure and objectives. However, in addition, marketers must also consider a number of substantive ethical considerations, including the following: How safe is the product? Might the product be offensive to some groups? Will the product cause harm (in the near or distant future) to the environment? Will the product maintain its value over time? Does it embody substantive advances, or do claims regarding "new and improved" versions simply refer to superficial "bells and whistles" that have been added? Will the product not only satisfy customers in the short term but also solve various problems that customers have? To what extent do these products help to address society's problems?

These questions (and many more) are relevant, depending on the circumstances, to particular product offerings, as well as to entire product lines. They do not, to be sure, constitute a comprehensive list of ethical issues that face product development. However, their identification requires openness to ethical issues, and hence to questions of the impact and implications of products on those who buy and consume them. To the extent that marketers are wholly absorbed in their own competitive races and financial details, it may be difficult, at times, to take these issues into account. Recognition of ethical issues often requires taking some distance from the fray.

Ethical issues in product development

The first step for marketers to respond to the multiple ethical challenges that accompany their products is simply to recognize them. Endless ethical problems arise because the potential ethical issues they involve were not noticed. Marketers may be so involved in solving other problems that they don't see the ethical issues before them. They also get into ethical problems because they often detach any responsibility from themselves and place it on to others, for example the customer, the government, or society. They refuse to take responsibility for their own actions, since they believe that they are protected by a market which veils their own participation in these ethical issues and neutralizes any responsibilities. Both paths are exercises in denial. I will briefly consider three important areas of ethical issues in product development: value durability, safety, and environmental impact.

Value durability

By the "value durability" of a product I refer to the likelihood that a product will continue to maintain its value over time. This may not occur for a variety of reasons. Some products are designed with current fashions in mind, and may consequently lose their value (as they go out of fashion) quite quickly. Others are made "cheaply" so that they break down more quickly than others. Some lose their value because they are replaced by new technological developments. And some products might be built such that they do not incorporate, but seek to block the use of, technological developments that could make more durable and valuable products. As the reasons for loss of value differ, so too do marketers' responsibilities.

It would be an implausible ethical view, of course, to argue that marketers have a responsibility to produce products whose value will not decline in any of the ways noted above. This is implausible since technological advances do occur, and people's taste in clothing, cars, etc. may change. If "ought" implies "can," we cannot say that marketers ought to produce products with value that does not alter.

In fact, some products may hold value for some people simply because they are "new," which implies that older products are no longer valued as they were before. This reminds us that the products marketers produce are intimately tied up with what people may be willing to buy, given the range of values, desires, and knowledge people have, as well as the promotion and advertising campaigns on behalf of those products.

Similarly, the development of products that incorporate new technological innovations that will improve the performance of current products on the market would also seem to be an ethical "no brainer," at least where there are legitimate and distinguishable technological differences. But what about holding back such technology because it is less profitable than older technology, even though the newer technology would be more beneficial to the customer? Perhaps with different technology the lifetime of the product, for example a battery, would be longer, but customers would buy fewer batteries. Or perhaps the product would function more efficiently, for example a car's carburetor, and hence burn less gas. Would withholding such technologies raise moral issues?

There is no moral requirement, in most cases, that marketers provide the very latest technology to customers. Excellence in marketing does not require each and every piece of the latest technology; however, if one marketer does not do this others may, so there may be competitive pressure. But is there also moral pressure? Surely marketers have responsibilities to their own firms and stockholders. However, this may pressure marketers in different directions, depending on the effects and costs of incorporating new technologies. An ethical concern would arise here if marketers colluded so that none of them would offer the more sophisticated technology so as to continue to sell current products. This would not be a matter of violating a direct duty to particular customers, but it would be an anti-competitive action and hence a failure to fulfill the macro-level features of a good society. It also raises potential ethical issues of manipulating customers and thereby exploiting them. Marketers would not be fulfilling the integrated marketing concept.

However, suppose that marketers consider developing products that add features which do not significantly improve their present product. A few more bells and whistles can be used to draw in new, or even repeat, customers. In this way, some customers can be moved to buy newer versions sooner than they otherwise would have done. New technologies which would render the present product obsolete can be put off to the next year. There are at least two ethical issues here.

First, are marketers honest with regard to the minor and superficial changes to the product? If they are, there is no problem. If not, how is this product promoted and advertised to customers? If it is offered as a "new and improved" version of the present product and this is done in ways that suggest that the improvements are substantial, then customers may be deceived, and possibly manipulated, into buying this product. This would violate important principles part of the integrated marketing concept.

Second, the firm's marketers might instead pitch this product development as a matter of fashion more than technology. Suppose this is done in order to move customers to buy newer versions sooner than they would have as these features were introduced over time. Now certainly fashion applies to at least some technological products, just as it does to clothes, food, and entertainment. So we need to ask whether creating a fashion aura about a product (even a technological one) raises ethical issues. Doing so is surely tied in to the desires of people to be seen, to be admired for how they dress, what they carry, or what they use. In short, people want to be "with it."

Here the distinction between a moral minimum and the good life is helpful. It is not clear that marketers who produce products with changes in styles (and do so without deception) violate some moral minimum of behavior that relates to not doing harm to other people. However, it might be argued that doing so does run afoul of important views of the good life as one focused on important matters, rather than simply questions of appearance and style. The problem with this answer is that since there are many different views of the good life, this is less pressing as an issue than are other issues that violate some moral minimum. Some might choose to lead an aesthetic life, a life focused on styles, fashions, etc. Such a life, others charge, is superficial; it results in the waste of discarded items, and is an inadequate way of expressing one's personality. Still, the charge against those who live like this is not that they are acting immorally, but rather that they are living a life less good than it might be.

Accordingly, marketing decisions to produce such products raise questions of a diminished contribution to people's good life. They also raise ethical issues regarding the manipulation of people to acquire such products. This charge may be brought on the level of the individual product as well as the more general level of the atmosphere or cultural climate that fosters the desire for such products. To the extent that people understand the seasonal and yearly fluctuation of styles, and approve of such, they cannot be terribly aggrieved by fashion marketing. Still, this requires that they understand the nature of such marketing and how it is that they have come to have desires for such products. From the side of marketers, they ought not to undercut other important values regarding the desirability of products of continuing value etc. when they do so.

In short, it is not the responsibility of marketers to expunge from humans the desire to be fashionable or to stand out through wearing special clothes, driving fancy cars, or even using gadgets that have special features. However, to the extent that such desires are more superficial than other desires, marketers raise ethical questions when they promote the fulfillment of these desires over more important desires and values. And they specially do so when they promote such lifestyles on the basis of envy, or even fear of the disapproval of peers, in their advertising campaigns. To the extent that such products can only be developed if they will be promoted or advertised in ways that encourage these forms of life, then ethical questions also arise regarding such products.

Safety

Products may pose safety risks in a wide variety of ways. Think about tobacco, heavily sugared cereals, fatty foods, lawn mowers and other machinery that can injure a person, as well as pesticides, poisons, firearms, and explosives. The Dalkon Shield, the Suzuki ATV, super-absorbent tampons, some vaporizers, baby bathtub seats, Dell laptop batteries, Ford Explorer/Firestone tires, football helmets, and the Ford Pinto are actual products charged with having caused real harm to many people.[1] And this is but a small list of the many products that carry various dangers. Indeed, almost any product may pose dangers and become hazardous under certain conditions. Those safety risks may arise from the materials of the product, its design, production, use, how the product was advertised, or some combination of the preceding. Rarely is it only one of these. In developing products marketers must have a sharp eye out for the possible harm that proposed products may cause.

A traditional guideline has been that a marketer's responsibility is to produce the products which people will buy, but that it is the customer's or user's responsibility to ascertain whether, and to what extent, such a product may cause them harm. Of course marketers are not to conceal features of a product that may be harmful, but it is up to the customer to acquire relevant information regarding the product and to act accordingly. In short, *caveat emptor* (let the buyer beware) guides both customers and marketers. Inasmuch as customers must be wary of the exchanges marketers offer them – they must look out for themselves – a lack of trust underlies this view.

This may be a useful guideline in some situations where buyers and sellers have approximately equal knowledge, or where the costs involved in acquiring that information are minor (e.g. flea markets). But for most customers today, products are of such complexity that it is difficult, if not impossible, to know what features they have that may result in their own harm, or the harm of others or even the environment. The assumption of roughly comparable knowledge, or at least the ability to gain that knowledge if one is attentive, that is made by the *caveat emptor* doctrine simply does not hold in the case of the cars, computers, cellphones, or medicines we buy. Customers are at a significant disadvantage. Some other ethical guideline is needed that will help level the ethical playing field.

A more plausible ethical guideline for marketers would be that they must exercise due care in their production and marketing of a product. On this view, marketers must take all reasonable measures to ensure that their products do not have features that will cause harm to customers. This does not mean that people might not be harmed by a product. Someone who buys a pocket knife and simply cuts his finger does not have a reason to complain to the manufacturer or marketer. Instead, for a customer to have a justified complaint the product must have been defective in some manner. The marketer must have failed to exercise due care in designing or producing such a defective product, i.e. he must have been negligent in some sense.

Hence, marketers must make special efforts not to be negligent when it comes to designing and producing products. What is the standard of negligence that is to be applied here? This is a large question, widely discussed both in ethics and in the law. First, there are no absolutes here. The particular answers will differ from society to society. Second, among the factors that would seem appropriate to consider are those of the probability of the harm occurring, as well as its likely severity, and the costs involved in protecting against it. It will also involve studying possible misuses of a product, how the product might respond in out-of-the-ordinary contexts, and the effect of wear and tear on a product. If certain dangers cannot reasonably be prevented, suitable warnings or safety features should be on the product.

In short, on this view, marketers cannot simply place a product on the market and expect consumers to protect themselves from possible harm from that product. They are in a position to know, far better than customers, what the real and potential dangers of the product are. Hence they must seek to protect the customer against them. Doing this requires that they look to various situations that might be anticipated which could cause harm to the customer and then devise ways to prevent them from happening. The due care standard places these ethical (and legal) responsibilities squarely on the shoulders of the marketer.

The most demanding standard marketers face in determining which products to place on the market is the strict liability standard. This focuses on defects in the design or manufacturing process and on the resulting harm, but does not require producer negligence. In short, this assigns the responsibility to manufacturers and marketers when a person is injured by a product and the product has a defect (or is defectively designed). There need not be negligence on the part of the manufacturer or retailer. The product must simply be subject to a defect which has led to the harm of someone.

The issue of what is a design or manufacturing defect is crucial here. The mere fact that a product leads to some harm is not sufficient to prove that it is defective. On the other hand, the fact that marketers did the best they could in designing and producing a product does not establish that the product isn't defective. Defectiveness relates to the product being unsuitable for use in the ways for which it was designed, as well as for various other misuses of the product that could be reasonably foreseen.

This view places heavy legal (and ethical) responsibilities on marketers. Part of the rationale for this view is based on the belief that marketers are in a far stronger position to pay for the injuries a person sustains in using one of their products than is the ordinary customer. It is assumed that marketers have deeper resources from which they can compensate those people harmed by their products than do those individuals who are harmed. This argument assumes, quite clearly, a private system of production and a private system of health insurance, instead of a public insurance system that would take care of the harm people experienced, regardless of whose fault it was. Similarly, it assumes that if marketers are held responsible, in this way, for the safety of their products, far greater progress will be made in reducing harm to customers than if either of the other two standards were invoked. This is a form of consequential moral thinking.

A different defense of this view argues that marketers participate in a private system of production in which there are various rules which are required for the system to function fairly. One of these rules is that when the products of those who market them harm others due to defects in the product they should pay, even if they are not negligent in the production of those defects. The rationale is that since marketers have the knowledge and capability to eliminate defects, and since it is a defect in the product they produced that is the source of the harm, it is a matter of fairness that they are held responsible. This is a form of non-consequential thinking that looks to the moral relations involved, rather than the effects of people's actions.

These guidelines have direct implications for products such as guns, tobacco, and fast foods. None of these guidelines imposes absolute responsibility for the harm that people suffer from these products. Still, it is clear from the last two guidelines that marketers have legal and moral responsibilities that extend far beyond *caveat emptor*. Moral marketers of these products must not negligently produce a product which, because of some defect, harms its user. What will count as a defect is the difficult issue, both legally and morally. The recent record suggests that such a definition will involve standards of increasing rigor. In the case of guns, one of the major current issues is that of guns being unintentionally fired or used by children. Gun locks may make guns as safe as possible for intended uses. However, in the case of tobacco it is not obvious that this product can ever be made in a manner that will not harm its user as well as those in the surrounding area.[2]

There is also considerable discussion these days regarding fast foods – foods with high levels of fat (McDonald's, KFC), sugar (breakfast cereals, soft drinks), salt (chips, crackers), etc. – and the current epidemic of obesity in a number of countries (e.g. the U.S. or U.K.). Of course, obesity is also linked with lack of exercise, a demand for convenience, and parents no longer cooking at home.

What responsibilities (if any) does a marketer have to develop a product for the market that takes into account the health effects of its contents, for example high levels of fat, sugar, and salt? These are natural ingredients. They are not themselves harmful in the way that the chemicals in tobacco are. But in the amounts that many people eat – in terms of the size of portions and the frequency with which they are eaten – they are indeed harmful. Though eating one triple burger, fries, and shake isn't going to harm most people, the fast food business depends on repeat business, not one-time customers. Since marketers must address current situations, not some idealized world in which every customer exercises daily, they must make clear to the customer the nutritional features of these products, offer sizes that are in line with a balanced diet, as well as alternatives that are not harmful when consumed frequently. Hence, either the foods themselves need to be redesigned, or (perhaps and) the promotion and advertising of such foods needs to be changed. "Supersizing" may be good for profits, but it is harmful to customers.

There are several principles that are relevant here. The first is that marketers create a product that through the anticipated marketing will not harm individuals who consume it. In light of current products, both marketers and consumers should seek to reduce their harmful levels of fat, sugar, etc. The next best standard would be to inform the consumer as to the nature and potential harmful effects of particular products through adequate labeling and advertisement. A corollary would be that marketers should not deceive or mislead customers about these facts. Third, marketers should not advertise or promote those products in ways that lead customers not to pay attention to these facts. In short, they should not engage in promotions that create the harmful effects in question. Fourth, they should offer their customers choices for products that have lower levels of ingredients that are (potentially) harmful. And, finally, they should not try to entice young children into the consumption of these foods, through capturing the food courts at schools, or by offering children promotions such as those involving comic book characters, which focus their attention on matters irrelevant to the quality of the product they will consume. Recent agreements by marketers to limit the number of sodas sold in schools are a small step in the right direction (see Mayer, 2006).

Environmental impact
Finally, the environment is neither a customer nor does it have its own voice. And yet the impact on the environment of the products that marketers choose to produce can be quite significant. To address these issues, marketers can, of course, simply wait for guidelines from the government. This reactive response is not morally plausible. The government may not be aware of the nature of the products that marketers are thinking of producing. In addition, this assumes that marketers do not seek to influence any governmental guidelines in ways that are individually advantageous, but collectively destructive.

If marketers view themselves under the framework discussed in chapters 1 and 2, then they must also be thinking of ways in which they can not only reduce the negative impacts of their products on the environment, but produce products that have a benign effect (see McDonough and Braungart, 2002). Since the impact of current products may last generations, through pollution and the consumption of resources, to the extent that marketers are the source of those effects they also bear responsibility for them. They cannot simply disavow any responsibility since it is their customers who have bought and used their products. Assuming responsibility may involve altering production processes, as well as the materials used to make the product. Both changes can make them less directly environmentally harmful and more suitable for recycling.

Some environmental questions are bound up with the issue of the durability of products, due to their reliability and ease of repair. A great many of the products we presently use are designed and constructed in such a way that either they cannot be repaired, or their repair requires an expense that approximates to, if it isn't greater than, the price of a new product. So we get the bizarre situation that it is cheaper to throw away a radio, telephone, clock, or television rather than to get it fixed.

However the product that is thrown away must be carried to a dump and discarded. Often these products are made with scarce materials that are toxic and may leach into the groundwater or give off toxic fumes that may reach where people live. Marketers would wisely consider the argument that such products need to be made in a manner such that they can either be serviced or recycled. Various European manufacturers are starting to develop new best practices along the lines of recycling that others need to adopt.

What are the background standards marketers ought to adopt here? One suggestion has been the appeal to the precautionary principle. This principle comes in stronger and weaker versions. The stronger version would require that marketers not produce any products unless they can be shown not to have a negative effect on the environment. The weaker version requires that the products they produce have effects on the environment that, all things considered, are more desirable than the harm they cause (see Soule, 2003).

I suggest that both versions are important, though in different ways. The second version sets a moral minimum standard according to which marketers avoid unnecessary harm. To meet this standard is to meet their moral responsibilities. On this view, marketers ought to market products that have a minimal impact on the environment and can meet foreseeable sustainability standards. Some marketers have moved in this direction with "green" products. Unfortunately, too often the "green" in these products has been designed more for a public relations or advertising impact than an environmental one.

The first version (of the precautionary principle) offers an ideal to which marketers ought also to aspire. This is a goal or an ideal that embodies the excellence towards which marketers should be working, though they cannot be said to have failed some current moral obligation if they do not achieve it in the products they presently produce.

Accordingly, when marketers face problems relating to energy consumption, use of scarce materials, availability of important products to those who are poor, etc., the point is not to say that if a product does not solve one of these issues it is morally defective and the marketer ethically wanting. Successfully responding to such challenges, in any specific case, is not a matter of a strict duty or obligation marketers have. Nevertheless, there is, I suggest, an imperfect duty that marketers have to attempt to address these issues when designing and deciding upon the products they will market. It would be part of the excellence of a marketer to do so.

This standpoint is similar to those that marketers (and others) have regarding philanthropy. As in the case of philanthropy, it is noted that we may not be called to make donations to this or that specific individual or cause. However, a person who never made contributions to such worthy causes, assuming his or her ability to do so, would be viewed as less morally upstanding than one who did. So too marketers need to challenge themselves in their product development. At least part of the basis of this imperfect duty stems from the integrated marketing concept and its call for attention to the capabilities of people and how they are affected by the actions of marketers. To the extent that marketers seek to implement the integrated marketing concept they are challenged to go beyond their strict duties and obligations. Doing so may provide them not only with a comparative competitive advantage but an ethical advantage as well.

Customer responsibilities

Customers have their own responsibilities when it comes to products which may affect them and others negatively. They can plausibly argue that the days of *caveat emptor* are, by and large, long past. Still, they cannot argue that someone else is wholly responsible whenever a product harms or offends them, or when the fashion changes. If a person undertakes to use a product without inquiring how it should best be used, that person shares some responsibility for any harm encountered. When fashions change a person need not follow the next fashion design. When something offensive appears, the solution may be as simple as changing the television station. The world is pluralist in nature, not uniform. Society is the better for it. Similarly, customers also have responsibilities when it comes to the foods they and their children eat. They ought not simply to give their children whatever it is that the children ask for.

Finally, with the internet and product labeling there is a wealth of information that customers can draw on to determine some of the safety and environmental impacts of the products on the market. If they make no effort to act in accordance with what they can learn about such products, then they are complicit in the problems that marketers face.

So too, marketers must consider the above issues at the outset, rather than after the product has been designed, produced, and advertised. As Michael Mocwa suggests, "every product is an expression of an organization's ethical consciousness and ethical character" (Mocwa, 1987: 398). Products that, through their design or production, harm customers or the environment may be an indication of an ethical defectiveness within the organization that produced them.

III Packaging and Labeling

Most of the products we buy come with some kind of packaging which is labeled. Both packaging and labeling serve multiple purposes and raise other moral issues.

Packaging comes in an endless variety of forms and may serve to protect the product, help in its distribution (from manufacturer to wholesaler, retailer, and customer), make its theft much more difficult, or attract customers, as well as making the dispensing of the product itself much more convenient. In addition, it also has symbolic, aesthetic, and emotional aspects. Packaging can make a product look "special," highlight its best features, and make the customer feel good upon opening it. Some have argued that people seek out such packaging in order to give more pleasure and meaning to their lives (Levitt, 1970). Otherwise, Levitt maintains, their lives would be much more boring.

The use of labels on packages has grown tremendously over recent years. They may identify a product, but also describe the product, provide important information about it (contents, place of origin, how it should be cleaned), grade it, and seek to promote it. As with packaging, labels do not have simply an informational purpose. For example, labels on clothing don't just inform us who made the product, but may have emotional and psychological purposes as well. The Nike swoosh or the Lacoste alligator on a shirt doesn't simply tell people that the shirt was made by Nike or Lacoste, but that this is the kind of person who wears these clothes: "I have enough money to buy these clothes." "I am part of the lifestyle and the set of attitudes that this brand captures."

In both these areas marketers face ethical challenges to do with the information that customers need to have – or should have – regarding the product. Hence, deception and adequacy of information are important issues, while honesty and truth are relevant norms. Still, as already noted, these values and norms will be tested by other values of efficiency, attractiveness, and cost.

Packaging

Among the many ethical tangles marketers need to address when it comes to packaging, the following three are among the most important: the use of packaging to reveal or to cloak the nature of the product being offered for sale; the safety the packaging provides; and the environmental impact of packaging.

Communication of contents

Any marketer will, understandably, seek to place a product in a package that presents it in its best light, while making the item look appealing and desirable to the customer. As such, packaging can reveal – though it can also hide – what it encloses. An ethical issue arises, however, when this effort amounts to a form of deception, in that it hides undesirable aspects of the product for which the customer would otherwise reject it, for example when fruit or vegetable dealers place the rotten fruit or vegetables at the bottom of the package they are selling. Another familiar example is when a small amount of cereal is placed in a much larger box, to make it look as if the customer is making a large purchase. In this way, packaging may make it appear that the contents of a package are greater than they really are. This is the issue of "slack packaging." Some marketers respond that the contents have settled and that this explains the volume of empty space in the package. If this response is true, it would deflect this criticism. However, many believe the response is disingenuous since it is difficult to believe that the box was filled to the brim when it left the producer, and only settled to a level of about two-thirds on the way to the grocers' shelves. Ethical marketers must distinguish between rationalizations (or purported justifications) and real justifications.

Other marketers respond that many people seek to "package" themselves and their surroundings in ways that beneficially alter their appearance. They therefore claim that marketers are doing nothing different from what other people do every day. There are, however, important moral differences. If a man combs his hair and wears a nice suit, or a woman wears makeup and a sexy dress, this doesn't raise an issue of deception. Of course other current practices might: for example breast implantation or the augmentation of lips, calves, or biceps might well be regarded as deceptive, if, in a personal relationship, these facts didn't come out. In any case, we are not buying and selling individuals in the way in which we may buy and sell products. We don't have similar rights against other individuals to know what they "really" are, as we may with the products we seek to buy. Such arguments on behalf of packaging that cloaks the real nature of the product should not be accepted.

Safety
The responsibility of marketers to ensure the safety of the products they sell through packaging is a relatively new issue for them. There are two main concerns here. First, this issue (as it falls under packaging) requires that the product the customer receives is the one the marketer intended them to receive, i.e. not something that has been altered in ways that might compromise the consumer's safety. After the poisoning of consumers of Tylenol through cyanide being placed in some capsules, all marketers have had to seek ways to ensure that their products are not harmfully adulterated. In some products, of course, for example, fresh fruit, this is hardly possible. With drugs and other foods it is. Hence, marketers now enclose products in several levels of safety packaging.

This is both a practical and an ethical issue. The risks of legal suits, bad publicity, and customer disaffection may well move marketers to ensure that their packaging does not permit criminals to place deadly chemicals in their products. But there are also moral reasons and principles that lie behind such behavior. Among them is the underlying principle that marketers are ethically responsible for insuring that the product customers buy is not only the one they believe they are buying, but also one that has not been altered in ways that will harm them.

The second issue concerns children who might be able to get hold of a product, such as drugs or poisons, and do harm to themselves through ingesting or using it. Again this is both a practical and an ethical problem. The ethical issue concerns the responsibility to ensure that individuals who are cognitively and motivationally immature and lack the understanding of what might harm them are not able to gain access to these products. The practical issue in this, and the preceding example, is that of ensuring that sufficient safety is built into the packaging so that the product's integrity and use will be protected without rendering the product impossible to open.

Decisions in these cases will depend, in part, on the level of threats that exist. Responsible marketers cannot foresee all threats, but must make reasonable attempts to do so. However, once such a threat has become known, their responsibility is to respond swiftly and effectively to the new threat that has been identified. The account widely given of Johnson & Johnson's response in the Tylenol crisis illustrates the kind of response that responsible marketers would make in other cases.

Environmental impact

Though packaging serves many purposes, its instrumental nature is manifest once a customer has the product and the packaging is thrown away. This raises additional ethical questions of wastefulness and harmful environmental impact. What responsibilities do marketers have with regard to these two aspects of packaging?

Oddly enough, sometimes marketers do not realize that they may save significant amounts of money by paying more attention to these issues. In one prominent case, the Environmental Defense Fund worked with McDonald's to reduce the amount of packaging its operations consumed. This was good for the environment and for McDonald's.

Ethically, it would seem that the minimal amount of packaging should be used to accomplish the purposes listed above. Oftentimes marketers fail to consider whether there are simpler, more effective, less wasteful ways of providing a product to the customer, or they fail to consider the after-usage of the packaging. For example, people frequently do not properly dispose of the packaging that comes with the products they purchase. This is true in the U.S. as well as in other countries.

For example, soda cans and wrappers line the roadsides of many rural roads in the U.S. In Portugal, plastic containers are scattered about the sides of roads. In India, plastic cups that have replaced the former, biodegradable clay cups now litter the railways. The U.S. Environmental Protection Agency reports that in 2005 containers and packaging account for approximately 31 percent of the total municipal solid waste (by weight).[3] Obviously this creates a major environmental problem for cities and states. To the extent that the containers and packaging derive from the marketing process, private businesses are imposing these costs on the city and the state. By and large, marketers have been given a free ride when it comes to the disposal of their packaging. The costs have been borne by society and the environment. Nevertheless, marketers bear responsibilities for (pre-purchase) packaging, for the ease or difficulty of opening the packaging, as well as for the after-purchase use of the packaging.

However, since marketing involves a relationship between marketers and customers, we must consider both sides when it comes to environmental aspects of packaging.[4] What responsibilities do customers have with regard to environmental issues? If customers resist using their own shopping bags, oppose returning disposable bottles to a store, and prefer those forms of packaging that are less environmentally friendly (white cups over brown cups), then don't they share some of the responsibility for the results of current marketing practices when it comes to packaging? This is highlighted in instances, for example in the U.S., when there has been strong resistance by customers (as well as marketers) to small redemption fees for bottles and cans that might help to address these problems. On the other hand, customers may respond that their efforts along these lines seem to be of such insignificant consequence that it is not worth their effort. Clearly there is an important moral coordination problem here. Of course, individual marketers might say the same!

Still, the underlying ethical principle here is that marketers use the minimal amount of packaging materials possible, and those they use should be recyclable, recoverable, or reusable. An important part of the responsibility for fulfilling this principle lies with marketers who, though they have greater knowledge and abilities, do not use them to help set the stage for more reasonable packaging activities. Such responsibilities are not simply individual responsibilities of this or that marketer, but also collective responsibilities of all marketers. It makes sense that individual marketers can take some steps only if others will take comparable steps. This requires the kind of coordination that suggests a positive role for the government. At present, marketers charged with packaging are placing the responsibility for proper disposal on the customers, and in reality on the cities and communities, to clean up the results of contemporary packaging. In effect, they are externalizing part of the costs of the product's delivery and shifting the trouble of dealing with this aspect of the product on to the customer and the community.

Labeling

The label is virtually the last point of contact between marketers and consumers – a last opportunity to convey some information or warning to the customer. As such, whatever form labels may take (text, pictures, or other visual representations), they may provide extremely valuable information for customers and consumers. They can tell customers, for example, what is in a package they cannot otherwise inspect, when the product might be expected to perish, whether it contains a substance that might harm a customer, out of what substances the product is made, where it was produced, how it should be used, cleaned, or discarded, etc. And just as labels may be helpful, they are also the source of many ethical disputes as well. Of course, labeling will vary according to the type of product: physical, foodstuffs, financial packages (services), drugs, etc. I will focus on physical products here, rather than services.

There are two central ethical issues regarding labeling. The first has to do with the nature and amount of information that marketers are obligated to place on a label. Correspondingly, what information is a customer entitled to regarding the product? The second has to do with the potential deceptiveness of a label. Labels might be deceptive, but they might also be used to make up for potentially deceptive packaging.

Information

What information, if any, must labels include? If customers have a right to know what they are buying, then what does that right include? Can customers or society claim a right that particular labels must contain certain information? Clearly there are no simple or single answers here. It will depend on the product, the information involved, as well as those people who are potential customers. Marketers also need to consider that some of those who purchase and/or use their product, including some in the U.S., are illiterate. Those individuals need to have different labels than literate adults. In any case, it is important to distinguish between what right a customer has with regard to these topics and what would be nice or desirable from the customer's standpoint. Further, we shouldn't assume that the information to which they have a right must appear on a label; perhaps it may appear, equally well, in other places.

Finally, it is mistaken to think that the more information the better. Customers can be so overwhelmed with information (significant and insignificant) that their understanding of what they are buying is not improved but reduced. For example, warnings on labels can be so pervasive that customers discount the real threats they signal. In fact, labeling may become wasteful if it takes an important amount of resources to place on the package, but no one reads it or alters their behavior because of it.

Now, some information is simply practically desirable from both the standpoint of the marketer and that of the customer, for example the size of a garment, that the package contains chicken soup rather than black beans, etc. Since the interests of customers and marketers largely coincide in these instances, few moral problems arise.

However, when we look further at what information is supplied regarding the specific nature of a product or contents of a package, problems start to arise. Do marketers have a responsibility to inform customers about the particular ingredients of a product? As we have seen, this is the other side of the issue of whether customers have a right to know the answers to these questions and whether those answers should appear on the product's labels. Which principle(s) might provide guidance here?

It is clear that the mere fact that a person will buy some product does not entitle that person to know everything about the material contents of that product, since some of the ingredients of a product may be secret. The formula for Coke is secret and its customers do not have a right to know its ingredients. Hence, the right of customers to know what they are purchasing does not extend to features of the product (ingredients, software code, etc.) that are rightfully secret. Still, even in this case when the ingredients are secret, an implicit assumption is that there are no ingredients that might harm people who have particular sensitivities and allergies to them.

Accordingly, one likely inference is that marketers must reveal to customers and potential users ingredients that might harm them. This seemingly simple principle is actually very complex. Must the harm involved be some actual harm, or only something that is believed to be harmful by potential customers? For example, what about products that have been created through certain special processes such as, perhaps, being irradiated to kill bacteria, or made from genetically modified organisms (GMOs)? Further, must the harm be some physical harm, or might it include spiritual or moral harm, for example, if a product isn't kosher, Orthodox Jews will not want to eat it. Vegans would not want to use products containing animal ingredients.

The answers here will differ depending on context. In societies with low percentages of vegans and Jews, it may be morally acceptable that those marketers who target these groups specially identify and label their packages, whereas others do not. The fact that the package is not labeled, as it were, tells the customer that they should be wary of it. The absence of certain labels or information can itself be informative.

The case of physical harm is different. If a product may expose a person to immediate harm (poisons, peanuts, a particular way of using a product, etc.), even when that harm is not widely recognized by customers, then that information (or warning) should be placed on the label since such products may be dangerous to their users, regardless of their beliefs. The warnings may be in words, symbols, pictures, etc., or some combination of these. In countries in which the users may be illiterate, multiple means of ensuring that possible users are warned are especially important. An important problem here is the intelligibility of the warning. Information on some labels may be of such a technical nature that only an engineer will understand it. These labels fail the test of intelligibility.

However, some information about products may protect customers from more indirect, long-range harm. For example, information regarding various constituents (e.g. fats, sugars) can help customers to protect themselves from harmful effects they might incur years later. Here the moral point is that the greater the connection between the potential harm and one's own physical health, even if long-term, the stronger is the responsibility of a marketer to make that potential danger known on the label.

There are a large number of other issues various customers are genuinely concerned about: for example organically grown products, conflict diamonds, products that have involved the use of genetically modified organisms, irradiation, or child labor. Some of these involve potential harm to the consumer and the environment, while others regard harm to other individuals. Regarding the former there are significant scientific, political, and ethical disputes, for example over GMOs. What standards of proof are appropriate is one issue here. Regarding each of these areas of potential harm, various ethical and political disputes regarding the extensiveness of marketer responsibilities arise. Until there is greater clarity on these issues, it is difficult to know what the correct moral stance should be. The case of GMOs is an excellent example of how moral disputes may rest on factual, empirical, and scientific differences. As a result, marketers face a moral quandary from which there is no easy escape.

Some respond that if there is significant demand for such information (regardless of the answer to the scientific question) then some marketers will include that information on their labels and hence capture that market, whereas those who do not will forgo those customers. Though this market-oriented response might provide some guidance, this is not, as such, moral guidance. For this, marketers must ascertain the level of real and believed harm, the nature of the harm, its immediateness, its lasting effects, and their own responsibilities for informing and/or warning about such dangers. This is not to say, in the case of more remote, less significant harms, that customers should not be able to find out whether the products they wish to buy were produced in ways they consider harmful. It is to say that such information need not appear, at this point, on labels.

Consequently, labels may play an important ethical role as the last point of information and warning from the marketer to the customer. Added to the above ethical, political, and scientific disputes behind labeling must also be the cost of providing this information. Of course, it may also be costly *not* to include appropriate information, for example when people are harmed. But in cases when the information is merely useful or desirable, the costs may be balanced against the benefits customers receive, who those customers are, and the ethical level the marketer seeks to achieve.

Deception

A second problem area of labeling regards deception. When marketers use special terms, omit certain details, or make it difficult to find the relevant information on a label, customers may end up believing what is false. For example, a product that advertises itself as "light" or "lite" might reasonably be thought to have fewer calories or less fat. However, some marketers use these words to refer not to those meanings but instead to the color or the texture of the product. Customer suspicion and cynicism with regard to marketing is surely well grounded when they learn such details about these labels. Marketers have played fast and loose with customers. The war mentality that too many marketers possess undercuts claims to professionalism by these marketers and casts clouds of doubt and suspicion over their adherence to ethical marketing. Of course, in the U.S., the Food and Drug Administration can take action to control health claims with regard to "light," "high fiber," and "low fat." However, this is a law- or compliance-based approach rather than an ethical one.

Many other examples do not involve health claims but cases in which customers are misled regarding what they are buying. Suppose a marketer trumpets the syrup he sells as "maple syrup," but it has only 2 percent real maple syrup in it; surely many people will be misled. And Lowenbrau beer in the U.S. is not the same as in Germany, even though the label is the same. The U.S. distributors bought the label, but use different ingredients and a different brewing process. It is understandable that U.S. customers could be misled by such labeling strategies. Again, the terms "natural" or "recycled" can be given different, unexpected meanings by some marketers. And a product listed as free from one ingredient that is damaging to the environment, may contain others that also damage the environment (Menezes, 1993: 287).

Information on a package might also be deceptive through the way it is presented and the size in which it is presented. If people are in a hurry and don't read the small print on the labels that indicate that the product is actually somewhat different than they might otherwise think, they may be deceived into believing something is better or different than it really is. Similarly, marketers have tried to hoodwink customers through misleading labels on level of salt, sugar, fats, etc. The only thing that is surprising about all this is that marketers are then surprised when customers express their lack of confidence in and mistrust of marketers!

It is troubling that the AMA Statement of Ethics says very little directly about these issues (see appendix I). The most it says is that, in the area of product development and management, marketers must disclose all substantial risks associated with product or service usage. This is a good beginning, but falls far short of the ethical challenges marketers face. In addition there is a host of federal laws and agencies in the U.S. that pertain to labeling. Among them are the Food and Drug Act (1906), the Federal Trade Commission Act (1914), the Food, Drug and Cosmetic Act (1938), the Fair Packaging and Labeling Act (1967), and the Nutrition Labeling and Education Act (1990), all of which set various mandatory labeling requirements, and encourage voluntary industry packaging standards. The upshot is that various federal agencies set packaging and labeling regulations for different industries. However, beyond the many legal and regulatory requirements are the significant ethical issues that are raised above.

The underlying normative issue here is similar to other cases of deception. Marketers do not pass ethical muster if they simply meet the demands of the law (which, in some instances, they have helped to formulate to meet their own narrow interests). Instead, they must ask themselves two questions. First, what conclusions and inferences might the average customer take from their labels? The average customer is not so well informed as the "reasonable customer," who is relatively well informed. Nor is this customer an ill-informed or ignorant customer. However, within normal conditions, what expectations and beliefs might a customer acquire from the labels marketers place on their products? If these are at odds with the real nature of the product, then they are being misled and deceived. The labels need to be changed. Second, marketers should ask what labels they would use in a relationship that seeks to provide the best value at the best price to customers. The integrated marketing concept urges marketers also to make labeling decisions in light of this ongoing relationship in which they try to do what is best for the customer within their means and the constraints they face.

IV Pricing

Marketing discussions of pricing frequently portray it as a technical, objective undertaking wholly answerable through marginal analyses, cost-plus pricing, return on investment studies, and the like. Such discussions often take place at a very high level of abstraction. More practically we are told that among the items marketers are to consider are: the price customers (or perhaps retailers) expect; whether the product is a new or established one; the cost of the product; the nature of distribution channels; possible competitive reactions; the compatibility of this price with the firm's objectives, the level of demand; and the implications or consequences of the price for those who are asked to pay it (this need not be the actual user or consumer of the product) (Stanton et al., 1994: 304–16).

In general, most discussions of pricing by marketers focus on these kinds of issues and whether the goal for the price of the particular product is that of hitting a certain return (e.g. of profit maximization), maintaining or increasing market share or sales volume, simply meeting the competition, or stabilizing prices.

As so stated, these pricing goals raise general ethical questions about the purposes of business and marketing. However, they also raise more specific ethical questions about how those pricing goals are to be attained. This section concentrates on this latter set of issues. These pricing questions break down into four sub-areas as they pertain to:

(a)   individual customers and prices
(b)   pricing issues within companies
(c)   pricing issues with competitors, and
(d)   social issues

Individual customers and prices

The price of a product is an important (though far from the only) consideration for customers. Among the ethical issues regarding prices are the following: what knowledge the customer can have regarding the price; deceptive aspects of the price; and various special circumstances (e.g. natural disasters and new products) that may affect the price.

Customer knowledge of the price
Most of the ethical issues regarding what customers know about the prices of products have to do with deceptive practices marketers engage in. There are a few, however, that simply concern the customer's knowledge of the price.

What information regarding prices are customers entitled to and marketers responsible for providing? Should a business "provide full information on how prices are determined" (Kaufmann et al., 1991: 136)? In general, it does not seem plausible that customers have a right to know how prices have been determined – for example how Safeway arrives at the price of a bag of potatoes, or even how Ford arrived at its automobile prices. These determinations may involve confidential processes within a business to which customers cannot claim a right to access.

Instead, customers have a right to know what the true and total financial cost to them of a prospective purchase will be. This must be presented in a manner that reveals, rather than obscures, the full price to the customer. Marketers are concerned with the bottom line. So too are customers. Further, this information should be available to them in a timely manner, i.e., before they have had to decide whether or not to buy it. To learn what the price is at the check-out counter is to learn the price too late. Hence, the prices on products in a retail store should be clearly marked. A bar code that only machines can read does not suffice. A customer's right to know what they must pay is what is at stake here.

Once marketers have set the prices for their products, you might suppose that they would then simply communicate those prices to customers. Hence, when customers are buying a product on credit, or through time payments, they have a right to know what the monthly payments will be, but also what will be the total price to them, after the last payment is made. They have a right to know whether there will be extra fees or charges added to their purchase. Car buyers should know about various preparation charges, how much the taxes will be, as well as other fees. These are features of the total price to the customer which the marketer should reveal. Underlying these points and the customer's right to know is a concern with the role of knowledge and truth in the marketplace and people knowing into what situations they are putting themselves. Otherwise, they can hardly be said to have knowingly chosen to buy a particular product. The marketer who adds these charges at the last moment, after the customer is committed to buying the product, takes advantage of that customer.

Deception

Not all pricing issues have to do with what information is (or is not) provided to customers. Other pricing issues concern how that information is portrayed. Too often marketers play games with customers such that their customers may find it difficult to know what the (full) price of a product is, or to understand the significance of a particular price. The upshot is that customers are deceived regarding the price of the product. The general principle here is that efforts marketers make to disguise or hide the true price to the customer of a particular product are unethical. They can do this, of course, simply by not telling the customer what the total price is until after an agreement is reached. For example, a hotel might offer a room for a very reasonable price, but then hit the customer with "resort fees," "energy surcharges," "communication charges," and the like (see Perkins, 2003). Or a credit card may be offered at reasonable interest rates, but other hidden charges or special conditions added on to it that in effect raise the cost of its use. However, another way this may happen is when the details of the price are revealed in such a way that few can understand what is being said. When that is done, the revelation of the details is intended to obscure the reality, or deter those who might be interested in pricing details from gaining any insight into the pricing; this might happen, for example, with insurance policies. Sometimes this happens when important details that alter the price are published in minuscule print at the bottom of an advertisement. For example, tire dealers may announce a price for tires, but when you go to pay for the tires you learn that you must also pay for having them mounted, balanced, air stems placed in them, etc. Ethical marketing would be explicit and straightforward regarding the prices charged.

When marketers bury the information to which customers are entitled such that customers end up not knowing or misunderstanding what the real price is, they are, in fact, engaging in a form of deception. If what they do is simply not tell customers the full price, or reveal it in ways that are extremely difficult to understand or to detect, this may be a form of "soft" deception, but the result is the same. Customers don't know what it is they are committing themselves to spend when they buy a product.

There are other ways than withholding or disguising pricing information by which customers may be deceived when it comes to prices. Sometimes marketers prey on various psychological proclivities people have that also result in their not accurately grasping the price of a product. For example, customers may have some beliefs and impressions regarding pricing that do not correspond with the real price of a product. They tend to believe that if they buy larger quantities of various products they will pay a lower unit price for those goods. However, this is not necessarily true. A number of authors have pointed out that in some cases customers pay, in effect, a surcharge for buying the product that comes in the larger container (Gupta and Rominger, 1996). A variety of reasons for this have been given: greater demand for the larger sizes, larger packages stimulate buyers, etc. (Gupta and Rominger, 1996: 1300–2).

Similarly, customer beliefs tend to be misaligned with what they are actually getting in the case of "odd pricing." It has been shown that customers tend to believe that "an odd price is associated with value." And "when an odd price is associated with a larger quantity, that belief is strengthened. For example . . . the consumer response to changing the price of tomatoes from $0.33 a piece to $0.99 for three produced a 70 percent increase in sales" (Gupta and Rominger, 1996: 1302).

What we find, however, is that some marketers price their goods with these (mistaken) beliefs of customers in mind. The result is that customers end up misunderstanding or misinterpreting the price they are paying. And in some cases, they end up paying more for the products they buy, even though they may be thinking that they are paying less.

It might be responded, however, that customers have some responsibilities as well. The mathematics in the preceding case is pretty simple. Yet people also tend to impulsive buying and might, unreflectively, pick up the three tomatoes believing themselves to be getting a better price. Still, whose problem is this? Why shouldn't customers have the responsibility to check themselves, rather than have others look out for them?

However, if marketers really believed that their aim was to provide something of value to customers, would they continue this practice? Of course, we also know they are out to be profitable as well. Still, the question is how, or in what ways, marketers should be profitable. If customers become aware of such practices, are they likely to find their trust and their loyalty to the retailer strengthened? This is doubtful. Instead, the view of some customers that it is OK to retaliate against stores because of their practices becomes more understandable, even if not justifiable. A straight-up pricing strategy would avoid developing win-lose relations and show greater respect for customers. Practices that marketers know will deceive their customers should be rejected. They should compete on price (as well as product quality, service, etc.), but not on the deceptiveness of their marketing.

There are many other forms of deception that marketers should guard against. A rather different example occurs when the price of a product is kept constant, but the contents of the package are reduced. A candy bar of 5 ounces may be reduced to 4.5 ounces, while the "same" price is kept. And though this may be indicated in the small print on the side of the package, since it is kept in the same packaging, customers may not readily note the difference, at least at the time of purchase. Of course, in reality the price of the product has been raised, but this has been done under the cover of the continued use of the old packaging. Though the marketer may be literally telling the truth (in the small print) customers may not recognize what has happened and hence be deceived.

Now in the grand scheme of things this is fairly minor. Customers may not recognize the difference, or be mildly put out. Loyalty to the product may override. And customers have responsibilities to examine what they buy before purchasing it. Still, customers become accustomed to certain purchasing actions and assume that, unless something is clearly noted, the present product will be like the one they last bought. Hence, they end up buying something which is actually less good value than when they previously purchased it. Marketing in this manner is a form of soft deception. It does nothing to instill trust and confidence in the marketer, and may be part of a larger decline in trust and confidence in marketers. What is striking is that customers might really prefer the slightly larger candy bar and even be willing to pay the added premium that is now being charged in the case of the smaller product. On the other hand, if customers are really resistant to price increases, then a reduction in the size of the product may be in line. The important question is how to do this in a non-deceptive way. Different packaging or some clear indication (at least for a few months) of the "new size" would seem to be the minimum that is ethically required if customers are not to be deceived.

Special circumstances
The pricing of a product might be altered in any number of "special circumstances," for example during a natural disaster. If a hurricane has just blown through southern Florida, people might be willing to pay greatly inflated prices for water, gas-powered electric generators, or building materials. Is it legitimate to charge a higher price? If one is thinking of pricing simply on the basis of cost-plus, or on marginal bases, or the basis of what people are willing to pay, then no questions might be raised. Still, such practices in these kinds of circumstances do raise ethical questions of price gouging.

The response of some is that the high prices are simply a way to allocate scarce resources that are as good as any other, for example government price controls, restricting the amount each person may acquire, etc. However, in natural disasters the normal market is not functioning. Supply and demand are out of kilter. There are people who may be desperate for certain products; their safety and health may be at stake. If marketers can charge simply any amount such people are willing to pay, they are taking advantage of their desperation and weakened position. To do this is to exploit them, not to treat them as customers in the relationship that the integrated marketing concept has defended.

A different special circumstance arises when a new product is being introduced. One pricing strategy here is that of "market-skimming." This is the practice of charging a very high price for the new product at the outset. Among the justifications offered for this practice are that it will cover R&D, that it suggests high quality to customers, that the "newness" of the product is worth a premium to customers, that it will help match the levels of customer demand with those of the firm's production abilities, and that after time the business can lower prices on the product, thus making it seem desirable to more people.

In such circumstances, it is quite clear that marketers are seeking a premium price for the new product. For those customers willing to pay such a "premium" to have the latest computer watch, BMW, or flat-screen television, and for which there are no other relevant considerations, there isn't any obvious way in which they have been ethically wronged. The marketers are not ethically obligated to charge a high price for such goods; but they are ethically permitted to do so. Given no other relevant considerations, they have acted permissibly.

However, suppose again that the special circumstance involves not merely the newness of the product, but also an ongoing critical situation such as HIV/AIDS, where people's lives are at stake. Suppose your firm has developed a vital drug that is not available elsewhere – you have a lock on it. Should you merely appeal to the factors listed above? Should you simply use a marginal analysis to determine its price? Shouldn't the competition also be considered, since they will be trying to break into the same market and will be able to take some of your future sales?

Still, you have a product which can save people's lives, or at least delay their death. Should this be considered in the pricing of new drugs? In the U.S., pharmaceutical companies claim that higher prices are justified in order to engage in the research and development required to produce the wonder drugs that have been developed in recent years. Accordingly, Burroughs Wellcome appears to have employed a market-skimming strategy in setting the price of AZT at a very high level when it was first introduced. But the prices set were so high that many (even most) of those who needed the drug could not afford it.

Who is responsible for seeing that those people who are sick (and dying) get the drugs they need? If this were the sole responsibility of the drug manufacturer, and if fulfilling that responsibility would drive the drug manufacturer into bankruptcy, then there would be few drug manufacturers working to develop new drugs. That is undesirable for everyone. Accordingly, drug companies cannot be solely responsible in this kind of case. Governments, non-governmental groups, and international bodies also share in the responsibility, as do the victims and their families. There are multiple parties that are responsible.

The drug company must be able to recoup its expenses plus a certain level of profit, over its entire line of drugs, so as to stay in business.[5] If they possess a drug that uniquely can save lives, however, some consideration of this power is justified as part of their considerations. Further, to the extent that government agencies have been part of the development of these drugs, then the public has contributed financially to them and might expect some consideration in return.

The fundamental issue here, and in this entire section, concerns what constitutes a fair price. Is a pricing strategy unfair when it discriminates, based upon special circumstances, among those buying the product? Suppose, to alter the situation, a drug company charges poor people in Africa very little for their life-saving drug, but charges people in the U.S. much more. Is this discriminatory? Is it unfair? People in the U.S. will be, in effect, subsidizing the health of poor people in Africa. Do they have ethical grounds to complain?

Kaufmann et al. claim that the fair price is one that "would be just and both honestly and impartially determined and conveyed" (Kaufmann et al., 1991: 137). But we are not told what this means or how we would then determine the price of a product. Another suggestion is that the greater the benefit to the customer, the higher the price that a marketer might charge (Laczniak and Murphy, 1993: 128). An appeal to this "idea of proportionate reason" might make sense when we are dealing with products that are not necessary for one's health or life and people had abundant resources to buy such products. But this is not the case with many products, including food, drugs, and water. Such a view would justify imposing terrible burdens on the most vulnerable and most needy.

At the same time, we must recognize that not everything a firm can produce at a certain cost will be something that many (or perhaps any) people can buy. Further, not everyone can afford to pay the price of the products that they truly need. Marketers do not necessarily have the responsibility to provide those products at a price they could afford (if they can afford anything).

The guiding moral considerations must be that companies are entitled to price their goods such that they can continue in existence, assuming that they are doing this in an efficient and rational manner, and to compensate their investors at a level that takes into account that the greater their compensation the fewer will be those who benefit from any life-saving drugs they develop. Second, the more vital a product is to the well-being of an individual, the less justified is a pure market-skimming strategy. With drugs that can save people's lives, drug companies also should be working with the public sector to ensure that those who are most needy (both medically and financially) have access to the drugs they need. Drug companies are incorporated and licensed by governments to engage in making pharmaceutical products to protect the health of the community. They have a corresponding responsibility to participate in that aim. This may involve providing some drugs at sharply reduced prices to those who are most desperate.

Finally, the fair price of a product would be the price that must, from a marketer's standpoint, take account of the producer's costs, the competitive situation of the company, and the level of need of customers for that product. Marketers have responsibilities to make special efforts to ensure that the products they produce, and upon which people may rely for their lives, are made available to them to the maximum extent of the producing firm's abilities, compatible with the long-run, ethical sustainability of the firm.

Pricing issues within companies

The pricing of products and services between the various divisions of a company also raises ethical issues. Transfer pricing is one such issue that has received considerable attention due to the large amounts of money involved. And though transfer pricing occurs between divisions of the same company even within the same country, in this section it will be discussed as a technique transnational corporations (TNCs) use to price various tangible and intangible goods that flow back and forth between various divisions of the same company that are in different countries. The amount of money globally involved is in the billions of dollars (Mehafdi, 2000). This issue might appear, at first glance, to be simply a technical and internal matter to any particular TNC, but it is not.

Though the details are much too complex to go into here, consider a case in which a company prices, at a very low level, some resource it draws from one country which has high taxes. It moves that resource to another country which has much lower taxes, where, after certain modifications, it is now valued at a very high price. A TNC can manage to avoid the higher taxes in the first country by valuing the resource as low as possible, and yet can now reap for itself much higher profits in the second country due to its low taxes.

Is there an ethical issue here? It is claimed, by some, that this procedure is part of a legal method of tax avoidance, which is frequently distinguished from tax evasion. In this manner, company profits can be enhanced. But we also know that what is legal may not be what is ethical.

The legality of such actions will depend on whether the valuations placed upon products and processes in one country are truly acceptable according to the country's laws. Obviously it is possible for companies to assign values to both material goods and the work done on them in a country in ways that skirt (or even cross) the limits of the law. The ethics of such valuations will depend on whether the law has been violated, but also on the effects of the company's pricing policies on the people, the infrastructure, and the government of that country.

To what extent, we want to know, may the company be avoiding various tax liabilities in the first country that are part of its overall responsibilities to that country, for example helping to pay for roads, education, social security measures, and sewage? Host countries permit companies from other countries to do business within their borders with the expectation that they will contribute through their business transactions and taxes to the well-being of that country. Messaoud Mehafdi notes that, "through the manipulation of transfer prices, TNCs can add to a country's national debt, jeopardize its economic and social programmes and contribute to its population's misery" (Mehafdi, 2000: 374). The challenge, then, is for companies to pay their fair share of taxes in each country.

How is this to be determined? As before, we must look to a number of procedural ethical considerations. First, could this company openly broadcast the level of taxes it is paying? In short, transparency may shame some companies into avoiding certain legally permissible shenanigans. What is fair will depend upon what other companies are paying, what enforcement mechanisms the society has in place, and the extent to which that society and its government use them. In short, this is not simply a matter of this or that business, but also a social and political matter relating to a specific country. Of course, to the extent that businesses seek to intervene in those social and political processes so as to reduce their tax burdens they are engaged on at least two levels. This lobbying itself should be transparent.

A second, more specific, principle might be that products should be priced according to the market, and the value added in the countries in which they are produced, and not on the basis of external considerations. The attempt to reassign costs from one country to operations in another country so as to increase prices or reduce taxes runs afoul of this maxim (Hansen et al., 1992: 684–5).

Thirdly, it has been noted that transfer pricing takes control from local managers and centralizes it in the TNC. This lack of control may place local managers and executives under pressures that force them to cut corners and to engage in unethical acts (Mehafdi, 2000: 372).

Accordingly, pricing issues within companies, and particularly the form they take in transfer pricing, raise ethical issues of fairness and of the fulfillment of a business's responsibilities to the societies in which it operates. Many say, we have seen, that the law is the floor. Whether or not that is true, the law and what it permits does not answer these ethical issues that marketers must address.

Pricing issues with competitors

Marketers also face various ethical pricing issues that arise between themselves and other companies. One ethical issue arises here when a business sets it prices in such a way as to seek to do financial harm to a competitor. This may be done in a variety of ways and for different purposes. One purpose is said to be "educational," viz., to teach another business a lesson regarding prices the other firm has set that are too low (Nagle, 1987: 93–4). Or perhaps the firm simply wants to discourage other possible competitors from entering into a particular market. Entry into this market will no longer seem so lucrative.

However, one of the most blatant such examples of pricing in this manner is *predatory pricing*. This occurs when a business prices its goods below what they cost to produce (the business has ample reserves) or at unreasonably low levels, so that it can force other businesses to go out of business or to abandon a market. The reduced profits are accepted in the near term with the expectation that, having driven competitors from that market, the business may recoup its losses in the long term because there will be less competition. In short, the low-pricing firm can move in afterwards and capture its competitors' business.

There are several issues here. The first is that it may be difficult to determine whether a firm is engaging in predatory pricing. It may have lower prices because it is more efficient. But suppose we can determine that a firm is engaged in such a practice. Why isn't this something that a smart competitor would do? One reason is that such forms of pricing are illegal. The Robinson–Patman Act in the U.S. does not prohibit all forms of differentiating prices, but it does when the effect "may be to substantially injure competition" (Stanton et al., 1994: 339).

What about the ethical side of this issue? Some might argue that it is really a problem for governments, rather than for business. Businesses might see themselves, for example, as players in a game and the government as the referee. It is the referee's role to stop players from breaking the rules, assuming that a government has made predatory pricing illegal.

This is, however, a warped view of competition and the role of a competitor. Even in sports, it is the role of all players to play by the rules. Referees are present, among other things, to settle disputes, to make determinations about what players have (or have not) done (stepped outside the boundaries; thrown a strike or a ball), and to impose penalties on those who do not play by the rules. They are not there, in general, to make people follow the rules. If breaking the rules isn't the exception, then there are no rules. Unfortunately, increasingly athletes (and some businesses) do not seem to understand this.

Accordingly, businesses have a responsibility not to seek to eliminate the competition in ways that undermine the competitive system. By operating in a competitive market system a marketer undertakes certain commitments, among which is that conditions for the competitive market are not to be undermined. One of those conditions is that the price of goods is to be set in light of market conditions. There is a consistency principle operative here that is reminiscent of Kant's Categorical Imperative. If a business seeks to gain monopoly control, then it destroys the very basis upon which it may ethically offer its own products.[6] Certainly, if one business does its job well, its competitors may fail. This is part of a market system. But those competitors should fail through competition in the market, not through practices such as predatory pricing that seek to undermine the market. These considerations are part of a principle of fair pricing.

Social issues

It is clear that a single-minded focus on prices, and particularly on low prices, may be beneficial for the immediate customer in terms of dollars paid for products. But suppose we distinguish between the price and the cost of something. The price is simply the amount of money a person must give up to acquire a particular product or service. A person may pay a low price for some product and then have to do a great deal to fix it up to be the way he or she really wants it (e.g. an old wooden boat). The cost of that boat then, in terms of labor, working materials, time, etc., will be much greater than the price paid.

Now consider a business that sets its pricing goals so that it becomes the dominant business in its industry. Because of greater efficiencies, it can cut its prices to such a point that many other business in any community cannot compete with it. Suppose that it is not engaged in predatory pricing, so it cannot be faulted on those grounds. But suppose that it is able to offer products at a very low price because it pays its employees low wages, does not give them health benefits, and demands the cheapest prices from its overseas suppliers, while minimally monitoring their facilities. Further, suppose that its employees in the U.S. have to rely on community health clinics for their medical problems, and have to work more than one job to make ends meet, which has the effect that their children are unattended after school and require other social services. Though those who shop at this business pay low prices for its products, the costs of those products to the community are much greater. Through its policy of very low prices this business is externalizing some of the costs of its business and the products themselves onto the community. Its customers (as well as non-customers) have to subsidize, in effect, this business by paying for services for its employees through taxes.

Does this raise any ethical issues? In such a case, we have one firm whose employees are unable to care for themselves and their families without additional social support, and whose practices with suppliers may lead to poorer working and environmental conditions abroad. If this is the case, it would appear that this business is offloading some of its own ethical responsibilities onto others. A principle of fairness is relevant in this situation. This principle would state that one business ought not to undercut the prices of another business based upon other behaviors of that firm that involve its not meeting other responsibilities it has.

It is true, as some people say, that prices reveal information of various sorts. But they may also hide, cloak, and disguise. Prices are said to be important determinants of the market demand for some product, as well as a basic regulator of the economic system (Stanton et al., 1994: 297f). But to the extent that the basic factors of production are given a monetary value, that value may not itself reveal a great deal about the land or the labor that went into the product. The land could have been treated benignly or the labor could have been exploited. Of course prices can reveal something along these lines, particularly if we think that the costs of treating labor well or the land benignly are greater than the prices paid for each. Still, there is not a simple, one-to-one relation.

To the extent that the costs of a product are not, or cannot (presently) be included in the price, that price may be a deceptive indicator of the costs to individuals and society of consuming that product (e.g. the cost of cleaning up packaging discarded along roadsides, or caught up in ship propellers and hydro-electric plants, etc.). It may be excessive to demand that companies internalize all their costs. However, when the (effect of the) policy of a company is to externalize as much of its costs as possible, then there are surely questions of fairness and social justice that arise.

V Distribution

Any economic system must have a distribution system. Producers must have some way to get their goods to market and eventually to their customers. Whether it is due to inability or a lack of desire, few producers these days deal directly with their customers. Instead, they work through some sort of distribution system that will store their product, divide it into smaller lots, provide financial services, and make sure a final sale takes place. In this way, with variations, the product moves from producers through various intermediaries to the final customer.

A marketing distribution system then contains not only producers and suppliers, but also agents, wholesalers, retailers, and facilitators of various sorts who use their knowledge of the market to the benefit of supplier or purchaser. The role of such "middlemen" has been a rather disputed one in the past. Often accused of adding costs without adding value, their role has been considerably maligned. However, the importance of such members of a distribution system is now recognized. Any present disputes have to do with the number of those playing these roles, and the length of the supply chain, not whether the roles have to be played. In any case, this interconnected group of individuals and organizations forms a "channel of distribution," and this is the path that a product takes on its way to the customer.

In considering the types and numbers of intermediaries, as well as the conditions under which these relationships take place, we are faced with various ethical issues regarding the rights and responsibilities of members of the distribution channel. These may be considered on a general and on a particular level. In addition, there are social dimensions that relate to channels of distribution that also warrant marketers' attention.

General considerations regarding channels

The members of channels of distribution differ in number, interests, power, and influence. Some are independent firms, while others may be franchises, or even owned by other channel members. Accordingly, their interests and needs may either coincide or conflict. Some sort of coordination of the members of a channel is required so that products can move from one end of the channel to the other in an effective and efficient manner.

Accordingly, a general moral issue that surrounds channels is how the different and conflicting interests might be coordinated, if not resolved. What influence may one or another of the channel members exercise over the other members so that the channel operates in the best possible way? The answer to this question will, of course, depend on the nature of the legal and moral relations that channel members have to each other. For example, if one member has legal rights to determine how certain others in the channel behave, the answer will be different from the situation when other members voluntarily recognize the fitness of one of the channel members to become the channel leader. This fitness might depend upon certain expertise, experience, or financial benefits that that one member is able to provide. Questions related to moral fitness raise issues of the responsibilities and rights of the various members of the channel. Inasmuch as the form that a distribution system takes is alterable, particular channels of distribution are open to moral evaluation.

It follows that a morally acceptable answer to the question regarding which member should coordinate the different interests and activities of the channel members is not that member who has the greatest power or resources. Such a view that regards "justice as power" tends to be held by those who view marketing as a form of war (see chapter 1). For example, Ries and Trout hold that because marketing is warfare it is fundamentally driven by the principle of force (Ries and Trout, 1986: 19). Hence, they contend that "might is right" in marketing a product (1986: 29).

Of course, this might describe how some channel members actually treat each other, and some say that Microsoft has been a good example of this. However, such a view does not tell us how they ought to treat each other. Those with power may not, quite obviously, use it justly. If a franchiser uni-laterally decides to slow down bill-paying and payments of various kinds to its franchisees, thereby threatening their financial stability, it has, arguably, acted unjustly (see Laczniak and Murphy, 1993: 119). If a retailer demands impossible price cuts that force the supplier, in effect, to cease production or to use sweatshop techniques with employees, the retailer is acting unjustly. In such cases, and many others, it is clear that justice or morality is not simply whatever the most powerful desire.

Similarly, it is too simple to say that the just resolution of such conflicts and issues is the one that creates the greatest utility or the greatest good for the greatest number of participants in a channel. On this view, the morally justified course is the one which produces the greatest efficiency in the channel of distribution and in the economy more generally. This might be called "justice as utility." On this view, for example, one would consider the use of coercive demands for price concessions or slotting allowances by determining whether or not they produced the greatest utility for all. Or contrariwise, as some studies have maintained, one might conclude that "non-coercive sources of power increase satisfaction, while coercive sources of power reduce satisfac-tion within the marketing channel" (Gaski, 1984: 21). Still, whether the use of coercion is just or not would turn on the greatest utility being produced.

One weakness to this approach is that it is extremely difficult to determine what the particular effects of some action(s) will be. In a rough and ready manner we can gauge, in the most obvious cases, what the general effects might be. But the less obvious the case the more complex the effects, and the greater the distance of those effects the more difficult it is. In any case, the determination of those effects in any particular case is fraught with problems of bias, uncertainty, and measurement accuracy. Further, the justice-as-utility approach may not adequately take into account the rights which other members of a channel have, or the agreements which they have made with other members of the channel. Even if enforcing some price concession might maximize channel efficiency or utility, it may not be the just thing to do, since it may involve breaking an agreement which two members of the channel have made.

So what can be said generally about this coordination problem? As I have argued before, the quest for some single criterion is misguided. Instead, there are multiple moral criteria that have to be taken into account for there to be justice in channel relationships. These criteria are both substantive and procedural in nature. They arise out of the mutual interests, commitments, and dependencies of the various members of a channel of distribution. Among such criteria are the following: providing fair notice of actions and policies; keeping agreements one has made; respecting the rights of others in the channel (or those they employ); following justified rules governing competition; fulfilling one's overall social responsibilities with regard to the quality of the product and the means of production; and obeying to the law. This might be called justice as moral governance.

As an overall approach, the integrated marketing concept recommends these considerations as ways in which marketers may most fully integrate relevant norms and values with those individuals or organizations they deal with. Doing so should enhance the capacities of these members of the channels in which they operate. Such members are, in a real sense, customers of each other. As such it makes sense for marketers to treat each other like customers.

In short, the issues within the distribution channel must be approached in a manner similar to other questions that marketers face, albeit this context is one of leadership and governance. They may consider their own interests and rights, but must also consider those of others. They should do this not simply in consideration of only this or that exchange, but rather in an ongoing manner which would establish relationships that would involve the cooperation and coordination required by such a channel and its customers.

This approach does not suggest that all channels of distribution will be led or governed in the same manner. There is no one simple relation between marketers – some are intensely competitive; others are much more cooperative. Still, another background moral value that deserves mention here is that of trust, since each of these channels of distribution will require some level of trust to achieve its goals of effective and efficient coordination.

At the most basic level for there even to be a market, there must be cooperation at a certain minimal level. Basic trust refers to our trust of others within a social system, that they will follow normal and expected forms of competition. We trust that they will not harm us, such that we do not have to protect our buildings against competitors who would seek to burn them down. We trust that they will not bug our home telephones to learn private information about our business. Part of the problem with questionable forms of competitive intelligence-gathering is that they violate this trust, reducing its extent. This imposes greater costs on operations within the market. It may also lead to calls for greater regulation.

Accordingly, the role of trust in channels of distribution, as well as more generally in competitive market activities, has received increasing notice. The war metaphor detracts from this trusting relation. In fact, not all relations in the market must be marked by competition, let alone very aggressive forms of competition. Relations of cooperation and trust may also exist between and among marketers in general, as well as in channels of distribution.

There are additional forms of trust which are also prominent in the supply chain. Increasingly, due to the costs of technological development and setting up channels of distribution, some competitors decide to cooperate in order to compete against other opponents, i.e. they agree to work together towards joint ends or goals. There is any number of examples: Ford and Mazda, American Airlines and British Airways, etc. Such cooperation may itself take different forms. Two rather distrustful firms might agree to cooperate to act in certain mutually beneficial ways as long as each fulfills its side of the agreement. They would cease competing in certain respects or areas, so as to jointly attempt to bring about some mutually desirable result. In order for such cooperation to occur, another form of trust, guarded trust, may be necessary, which would permit them, on the basis of various contractual agreements, to engage in such cooperation. Guarded trust is the trust that parties to a contract share in each other living up to the contract. Since all the details of a mutual operation cannot be specified in a contract, trust of a heightened kind is required to participate in such contracts.

Finally, there is an even more developed form of trust which may exist between firms (and individuals) which agree to cooperate more fully. This extended trust occurs when individuals are willing to render themselves vulnerable to others in light of some common goods or goals those involved seek. In the basic and guarded forms of trust, trust is hemmed in with protections by the law or special contracts. Extended trust occurs when each partner to a relationship will not take advantage of certain weaknesses or vulnerabilities of the other in the relationship in spite of their ability to do so. The relationship may have been entered into in order to exploit or develop new technologies, to combine marketing forces so as to economize, etc. In any case, this last form of trust has been said to offer those marketing firms which engage in it a competitive advantage inasmuch as they can save on transaction costs (e.g. through reduced monitoring costs) in ways in which other firms that do not engage in such trusting relations cannot (Barney and Hansen, 1994; Brenkert, 1998).

Now, those who engage in extended trust are not thereby engaging in something that is of unrestricted moral value, since it is possible for criminals to trust each other in this way. Similarly, two firms might trust each other not to reveal that they are both dumping toxic chemicals in a local river. However, the more open and extensive trust is, the more it contributes to a channel of distribution that is moral and just. The reason is that in order to trust, as noted above, one must give up strictly or narrowly self-serving behavior; one must be prepared to allow another moral agent to make decisions over which one has little control. In this way, trust is both economically and morally important.

Accordingly, relations of extended trust presuppose that marketers seek to work out problems they face in a mutual manner. One does not seek to take advantage of the vulnerabilities of others. The implications may be significant with regard to some of the above issues, such as forcing price concessions, resale price agreements, and franchise systems. The development of trust in these relations may reduce other costs and promote greater flexibility in one's response to common problems. Still, this requires certain moral qualities such as an openness to others, a competency on one's own part, a consistency in one's behavior, and shared values.

The upshot is that the coordination of relations between members of a channel of distribution is susceptible to evaluation in light of questions of justice and trust. To approach them in this spirit is not simply to look to that member of the channel which exercises the greatest power over other members, even if that would be of the greatest utility. Instead, it is to look to a number of relevant considerations that are bound up with features of the integrated marketing concept and moral governance. Further, in acting in these ways, richer forms of trust may develop, which may permit reduced forms of monitoring and security. This can make the channel not only more effective but also more efficient and just.

Particular issues in the channel of distribution

There are many particular ethical issues within the channel of distribution that also deserve the attention of marketers. Some of the more important include those having to do with price concessions, tying and exclusivity arrangements, and areas of distribution. I can only consider the first two here.

Price concessions
In the idealized market, no single participant has any power over the price and cannot, as such, force price concessions. In real markets this is not the case. Large producers or retailers may have a significant amount of power which can be wielded to alter the price of products. Indeed, most of the major markets involve oligopolistic businesses which have significant economic power, even if it is limited in various important ways by other businesses and the government.

Some channel leaders have sought to use their economic power to specify "the minimum and the maximum prices the retailer or wholesaler, or both, may charge" (Ortmeyer, 1993: 392). Such demands have been called "resale price maintenance" or "vertical price fixing." Though they may do this for a variety of reasons, the general aim is to maintain a certain price level for a particular product, or line of products. Accordingly, sometimes it will be to keep prices down for the low-end consumer. At other times price maintenance arrangements are made so as to keep the price at a higher level that will project an image of quality. Discounters and price-cutters are then pressured to maintain the price level that the channel leader seeks.

Prior to 1975 such arrangements were permitted so as to protect smaller businesses. But in 1975 the U.S. Consumer Goods Pricing Act repealed legislation which had permitted this because it was viewed as inhibiting free competition. As a result, "explicit agreements between manufacturers and their intermediaries on resale price [are] . . . viewed as inhibiting free competition and, therefore, prohibited" (Ortmeyer, 1993: 392).[7]

Still, more powerful channel members may simply demand that others in the same channel reduce their prices. Here the concern is not to maintain certain price levels, but to reduce prices (and to reduce them as far as they can go). To enforce this, a channel leader might make clear to others in their channel that if they want to continue to receive certain goods from the channel leader, or to continue to supply various products to the channel leader, they must cut the prices they quote to the channel leader (see Trawick et al., 1991: 20).

A variety of methods may be used to achieve a lower price. Some of these are straightforward demands to reduce prices. Others are more indirect and nefarious. For example, a channel member may simply make an unauthorized invoice deduction (see Laczniak and Murphy, 1993: 113). And when Jose Ignacio Lopez was at General Motors, he was known for forcing suppliers to continue to cut the prices they charged GM for products they supplied to it. Wal-Mart is also famous for forcing its suppliers to reduce their prices, so that Wal-Mart, in turn, can charge its customers low prices. For customers, low (or lower) prices are usually desirable. However, such policies can also have effects, as I have noted, that are not themselves desirable.

Such price reduction demands neglect other aspects of the sale of a product, for example the knowledge and expertise that might be offered by suppliers offering a product at a higher price. The result is that concerns for the price of a product trump other considerations. Hence, these arguments on behalf of "free competition" have been a move in the direction of greater impersonality in the market, where the primary consideration is price (or those things for which customers are willing to pay directly).

Of course, it might be objected that if consumers really want better service, more knowledgeable retailers, they would pay for this service and someone would come forward to offer it. This objection runs into the difficulty of those consumers who shop with some retailers for information and then go to the discount retailer to actually buy the product. In short, this objection runs into the problem of free riders and the ethics of consumers. Marketers must make their decisions in this real context, not an idealized one. And clearly, in this case, they must also seek to protect themselves as well as act morally towards those with whom they do business.

There are other questions regarding the ethics of policies to wring price concessions from others in the channel of distribution. For example, in making demands for price concessions on other members in the channel, a marketing organization should consider its own needs and aims, as well as the effects of those demands on others in the channel of distribution. To do this, the marketer must know what is the other member's situation, what this will do to their relationship, how important that relationship is, whether the supplier has been cooperative or recalcitrant, etc. Knowledge of such information may also, of course, reveal that the other organization is, or has become, vulnerable. This may be due to changed circumstances over which that organization had no control; it may be due to changes that it actively undertook.

Suppose, for instance, a supplier has made a number of capital commitments so as to supply a specialized product and now depends upon the manufacturer for a significant part of its business. If the manufacturer now applies considerable pressure to lower prices and suggests that it may move to another supplier if those prices are not lowered, the supplier may find its very existence threatened. Would such a price concession demand pass moral muster?

Surely this is an instance in which any goodwill and/or trust between the two firms will be jeopardized. The manufacturer must also prudently consider to what extent it might need the help of the supplier in the future. If the manufacturer conceives of itself as engaging in discrete agreements, independent of any ongoing relationship, then those with whom it does business will normally respond in kind by attempting to protect themselves. In short, the self-interested advantages of an ongoing, longer-term relationship will be forgone.

In addition, moral questions may legitimately be raised as to whether the demands were simply imposed on the supplier with little notice; whether discussions were held as how to meet the problems or issues which the manufacturer was attempting to resolve through these demands; whether the manufacturer provided some transparency as to the issues the demands were supposed to resolve; whether the manufacturer offered to work with the supplier to meet the demands, etc. Giving positive responses to these questions will enable one member of the supply chain to treat another with respect. It may also be in that member's own interests.

It might be objected that the supplier placed itself in this vulnerable situation, and hence must now suffer the consequences. The supplier shouldn't have made such capital commitments, it might be said, without taking other steps to protect its independence. This is, however, implausible, since such small firms might not have any other effective choice. The model such an objection rests on is that every firm must be as fully independent as possible of others. And the reason for this would appear to be that otherwise they might be taken advantage of. There is some good prudential advice here. But also if firms could rely on each other, could trust each other, then some of these costs of independence might be reduced. Everyone might benefit as a result.

Accordingly, though the decision to seek price concessions will be made within a larger competitive context, it should still be a decision that is fair, reasonable, and just. It need not be intended simply to improve the well-being of the supplier, but it should not unjustly or unreasonably penalize that supplier, or do so in an arbitrary manner. These are among the conditions, as it were, of an ethically functioning distribution channel. Obviously, if a marketer is not worried about the channel operating in a smooth, non-rancorous manner, then such arguments will carry little weight. But if moral motivations tend to coincide with greater cooperativeness, then this is a reason to pay attention to such moral arguments.

An upshot of this approach is that, if one is seeking to develop a working relationship with another firm, the use of coercion to obtain price concessions is either not justifiable, or is justifiable only under limited conditions. Such coercion could only be used for certain specific ends that are themselves morally justifiable. But those would have to fit the above conditions.

Tying and exclusivity arrangements

A second area of ethical issues that arise in channels of distribution has to do with "tying arrangements." These occur when the leader within a channel demands that other members of that channel carry a product that they would not ordinarily carry, if they are to be allowed to carry some other product(s) they actually want to carry. Perhaps a manufacturer has a very popular toy that a retailer wants very much to stock. But the manufacturer demands that this retailer carry another toy that is much less popular, if the retailer is to get the popular one to sell.

Exclusivity arrangements occur when a channel leader demands that a distributor or retailer only carry its brands and not those of other, rival products. There are different forms of this situation. For example, a marketer might demand that others *not* carry a certain product. Microsoft demanded that its software not be placed on computers that also had Netscape since that would compete with its own Internet Explorer. Anheuser-Bush has sought to get its distributors to drop rival brands of beer (Ortega and Wilke, 1998). A different kind of example is when a franchise or channel member is told that it has to buy its ingredients, materials, etc. from a particular source, rather than go out into the open market to obtain them. This regularly happens with fast food franchises. At other times channel leaders will offer cash incentives to retailers, easier access to loans, and special access to new territories to distribute its products.

In these cases, the manufacturer is engaged in a form of quid pro quo. The retailer gets what it wants out of this deal (certain brands, products, promotions, distribution areas), but only if it agrees to something it does not want (selling other less popular products or not selling the popular products of other marketers). This is something most people have grown up with. If you want to go out tonight, do your homework earlier. If you want a new sweater, then be sure to clean your room this week. This can be seen as falling within the kind of bargaining that goes on in other contexts.

However, what about in a channel of distribution? The situation is different depending upon whether a franchise or an independent business is the object of these demands. If a franchise is told that it has to buy certain of its ingredients, materials, etc. from a particular source, this may be part of some original agreement. In that case, if the franchise has agreed to this, in full knowledge, the moral upshot is that it is bound to follow through.

However, if this happens in a conventional channel or even in an administered system, then the rationale for these limitations needs to be spelled out. If these demands take the form of threats or coercion from the channel leader doesn't the channel member have justified moral grounds to complain? Of course, it will be argued that this is taking place within a competitive situation. It might even be argued that this is not terribly different from the situation in which customers, seeking a particular song, are told they have to buy an entire album in order to get it. So isn't this kind of behavior something that is rampant in the market?

One ethical issue here has to do with the knowledge that a channel member has regarding such possible demands prior to becoming a member of the channel. If it is not aware that such demands might be made, then the channel member might object to them. But suppose such knowledge is general knowledge. A prospective channel member should know that such demands might be made. Is the practice then justified? Some contend that such practices seem to amount to a form of coercion. Hence, the difficulty here is that of drawing a line between coercion (which would be ethically unjustified) and making proposals or demands in a competitive situation (which might be ethically justified). One way to begin to draw this line would be to look at the effect of such demands on the channel member.

Accordingly, a related ethical question concerns the costs that are being imposed on this individual member to benefit the channel leader. If those costs are such that they undercut the economic viability of the individual channel member and absent those costs this would be a successful business, then that individual marketer should leave this system. However, that may not be possible. Further, these demands might be imposed in particularly ruthless and non-consultative ways that emphasize the instrumental relation that is being imposed on this individual marketer by the channel leader. If such marketers are also customers of the channel leader, then they are not being treated in accordance with the integrated marketing concept. Quite similarly, it might be noted, the AMA Statement requires that a marketer not exert undue influence over the reseller's choice to handle a product (see appendix I).

Finally, what about the costs to customers and to society? Does allowing such tying and exclusivity arrangements hurt competition and raise prices? This has been one of the main charges against Microsoft in the ways it has demanded that only its own products and not other internet programs be installed on computers using Windows. In the case of some products, for example beer, it may be that such tying and exclusivity arrangements will drive smaller brewers out of business. Thus, the marketplace becomes less diverse and offers less choice.

Social aspects of distribution channels

A distribution system may not only be long or short, but also may have a broad or narrow range, i.e. it may enlarge or restrict its contact points with consumers. Depending on its nature, it will have various impacts on different members of a society. Even individuals not in a distribution system may be affected by the currently available distribution system. Unfortunately, marketers do not sufficiently consider the social impacts of their distribution channels.

Consider the fact that various studies on determining optimal retail locations involve working with assumptions regarding whether the consumer makes single-purpose trips or multi-purpose trips (Ghosh and McLafferty, 1986). Such models involve components such as the following to capture consumer shopping costs: "(1) cost of travel; (2) cost of the goods to be purchased; and (3) cost of holding inventory" (Ghosh and McLafferty, 1986: 159).

What we do not see in such accounts are ethical questions raised about the environmental impacts of customers traveling to their retail outlets, the creation of large parking lots, or the transformation of rural and agricultural land into shopping areas. Decisions that marketers make shape the reality of our cities, rural areas, and environment for the present and the future. And though there are multiple levels of review boards, zoning commissions, etc., one would expect that the ethical marketer would look not simply to his or her own self-interests, but also to broader values and normative considerations.

Second, we also do not frequently hear discussions by distributors of their moral responsibilities to those who want or need their products. In the past (and still to a great extent) the ethical question here has taken the form of what responsibilities marketers have to maintain distribution points, shopping malls, etc. for customers in the inner city or in the downtown part of town (Zikmund and d'Amico, 1993: 61). In the 1980s and 1990s the number of supermarkets in the inner city in the U.S. dramatically declined (see Turque et al., 1992). Further, the number of other highly efficient, modern outlets also declined in this area. The result was that poor people in the inner city either had to travel considerable distances, at significant cost and inconvenience to them, or they had to pay higher prices for a narrower selection of goods that smaller local convenience stores offered. Further, often these stores were poorly maintained, and employed salespeople who used ethically questionable sales tactics. Accordingly, it has been claimed that the inhabitants of the inner city have been subjected to various injustices, including paying more for inferior-quality goods as well as being subject to disrespect in their shopping.[8]

More recently, with the rediscovery by many of the inner city and an increase in gentrification projects, this dynamic is being altered as the poor are being displaced by high-priced condominiums and apartment buildings. However, the underlying ethical issue remains the same. Wherever they might be found, urban and suburban dwellers cannot supply themselves with food by farming or hunting. As with others in today's society, they are dependent upon those who distribute food. Conversely, those who distribute the various necessities for daily life acquire a certain responsibility to place outlets such that all people can obtain food. This is particularly important when, as Sturdivant has noted, "the most direct contact between the poor and the business community is at the retail level" (Sturdivant, 1968: 131; emphasis omitted).

Now it is clear that the members of any channel of distribution cannot take all of society's burdens on themselves. There are limits to what any moral agent can justifiably be asked to do. However, if such agents cannot resolve

certain problems by themselves, they may also be obligated to seek the cooperation of others, for example government and community leaders, in resolving such problems. Accordingly, some have proposed investment credits,
tax breaks, etc. to encourage businesses to establish outlets in the inner city
(Sturdivant, 1968). Beyond that, working with community leaders to resolve
these problems – wherever they may occur – is another tactic retailers can
take to address these responsibilities.

A third issue that distributors should consider is the social and cultural
impact of their outlets. For example, when large retailers such as Wal-Mart
move into a small town, its local small stores may go out of business, thus
decimating the downtown and cultural area of the community. In Vermont
a considerable effort was made to prevent Wal-Mart from coming in and
destroying the small cities on whose outskirts it wished to locate. Marketers
must consider the harm which they will be doing in such cases. They may be
legally free to place their outlets in certain areas. The question they must also
ask concerns their moral freedom and the moral costs that arise in doing so.
It is true that change is inevitable. No business (small or large) has a guaranteed existence. Still, the ethical question is: What kind of change do we want?
What can we do to shape the nature of that change in directions that benefit
most people, respect crucial rights, and take into account relevant cultural
and environmental considerations?

What, they might ask, is the effect more generally on the city and its surroundings of distribution systems that concentrate in the suburbs and coun-
tryside? The last half-century has seen a considerable flight to the suburbs and
shopping malls. Do distributors or businesses have any responsibility to maintain the integrity of the downtown area? One businessman once quipped to
me that "they" could "bomb" the downtown area as far as he was concerned
– his business was tied up in shopping malls in the suburbs.

Why should these questions concern them? Part of the answer is that any
business relies on essential services from the cities in which they carry on their
business. Public roads bring customers to their businesses. Water lines, sewage,
trash collection – all generally run at public expense – facilitate business in
the suburbs or the city. Pollution caused by cars (exhaust, dripping oil, etc.)
add to the environmental problems of the city. Further, the continual expansion of distribution networks into surrounding areas necessitates the transformation of agricultural land into shopping malls, the reduction of habitat
for animals, and additional effects on water pollution.

Kotler suggests that in considering the design of a marketing channel one
should consider the "service output levels" to be offered customers (Kotler,
2000: 494). This involves the number of products they can buy on a single
occasion, the waiting time it takes to get the product, the distance they must

travel to obtain the product, the variety of products offered, and the number of services (repair, credit, installation, delivery, etc.) to be offered (Kotler, 2000: 494f). As such, the issue is situated primarily in terms of costs to the customer. In short, more service outputs involve higher costs, while the reduced service outputs of discount stores are taken to be an indication that customers wish to focus on prices and saving money (Kotler, 2000: 494f). But the preceding discussion indicates that more is involved than this. Issues of consolidation, decentralization, size, location with regard to city centers, kinds of employment, power with regard to employees, and power with regard to suppliers are all (ethical) questions that arise in these contexts. They are questions marketers also need to address.

VI Conclusion

The topics of this chapter, from product development to distribution, raise a number of crucial issues for ethical marketing. Though these issues are less "in your face" than advertising, they underlie the long-term and the daily relations marketers have with their customers. These ethical issues are not always recognized, let alone addressed. Nevertheless, they exist, and some sort of answer (however reflective or unwitting) must be given to them. Thought-ful answers will seek to engage the values and norms, such as freedom, justice, trust, transparency and the avoidance of harm, that are already embodied in these issues.

Finally, the integrity of marketers and marketing organizations is also crucial. This is clearly an issue when there are those who develop products that are harmful to individuals or the environment in ways that can be avoided, when packages are labeled and priced in deceptive or misleading ways, and when the effects of channels of distribution, both on their members and on society, are not taken into account in their design. Such situations undercut the thrust of the integrated marketing concept and set back the cause of ethical marketing.

Notes

1   This is not to say that each and every one of these products has harmed all those who used them. But these products have been identified as ones that have caused noteworthy harm to some consumers.
2   In the case of both guns and tobacco, one of the other major issues occurs when marketers are involved in selling amounts of guns and tobacco that far exceed

what the legal market can absorb. In these instances, a reasonable person might conclude that they are indirectly involved in some form of illicit trade in which individuals (e.g. youths or criminals) who are not supposed to have access to these products are readily obtaining them. Instead, they should better monitor the distribution of their products (see section V below). In such cases, their actions are morally deficient.

3   U.S. Environmental Protection Agency, 2006: 9.

4   The nature of the packaging itself and the safety it provides is largely a question that marketers must answer. When it comes to environmental consequences, customers can play a much larger role.

5   It appears that drug companies are among the most profitable of all industries. Consequently this raises questions about the sincerity of these companies when they respond to objections regarding their high prices.

6   Some believe that Microsoft and other such firms have tried to eliminate the competition, rather than to engage in straight-up competition.

7   It was viewed as per se illegal under §1 of the Sherman Act (see Zelek et al., 1980: 16n.; Nagle, 1987: 327).

8   One response has been that stores in the inner city are more subject to theft and damage, and have higher insurance rates (or cannot get insurance at all). Hence, the higher rates and inferior-quality merchandise simply reflect the realities of the market. While there is some truth to this response, it does not answer the objection.

Chapter Four

Promotion: Advertising, Retailing, and Customers

I Introduction

Product development, pricing, and distribution lay the basis for marketers' efforts to promote their products to customers. But with promotion activities (viewed broadly here to include sales promotions, advertising, personal sales, retailing, telemarketing, public relations, and publicity) we come to the heart of what most people consider to be marketing. Together these activities form a complex relationship between marketers and customers whose different components impact customers (and non-customers) in a variety of ways, not all of them welcome.

Some promotional activities are quite direct. Through advertisements, commercials, and flyers, marketers bring the product to the attention of customers, inform them about the product, and attempt to influence their attitudes so that they take steps to purchase the product. Similarly, retailers directly impact customers through the products they offer, their placement of the products, and their methods of selling them. More indirectly, marketers might place their products in movies and on television programs in ways that attract the attention of potential customers. In addition, marketers try through various media outlets to develop in people a favorable view of the producer, manufacturer, or marketer, and thereby to influence customer behavior towards that company and its products. In any case, promotion involves bringing both cognitive and motivational appeals to bear upon customers. In this chapter I consider both the marketing and customer sides of this complex relationship. On the marketing side, I will only consider promotional activities as they relate to advertising and retail sales.

Here is where marketers most frequently have contact with customers, either face to face, or by television, the internet, telephone, magazines, etc. More ethical complaints against marketing have been raised on account of promotional activities than any other area of marketing. Some of these ethical issues have to do with deception (honesty, truthfulness), while others pertain to offense, fairness (justice), well-being (harm), and manipulation (freedom). Respect for these values in accordance with the integrated marketing concept is what marketers must demand of themselves and what we should demand of them.

I begin with advertising. Advertising aims (ultimately) to move customers to seek out and buy their products. Given the vast sums of money spent on it, advertising is among the most visible aspects of marketing and subject to the most constant and sharpest criticisms. Among the most important are those involving deception, offense, and manipulation. These objections to advertising have both individual and social dimensions to them.

Retailing is discussed next, together with personal sales. These activities attempt to move the ultimate customer to make a purchase. Questions of honesty and manipulation arise here, as well as issues regarding privacy. In addition, retail ethics involve problems of product acquisition and placement in retail settings.

In facing these issues, we should think back to the framework in chapters 1 and 2. All these activities must fulfill the conditions of morality, which involve truthfulness, honesty, and not undercutting people's moral agency. I assume that it is not unethical, as such, to try to influence a person to do something, to change his or her views, or even to buy something. Whether it is unethical will depend on what it is that customers are asked to buy or to do, the ways in which that persuasion is carried out, who are the targets of such promotional activities, and the consequences. In any case, the attempt to influence people's views and behavior is not unique to business. It takes place in politics, education, and religion. It also takes place among friends.

I end the chapter with a brief discussion of the responsibilities of customers. Marketing ethics, I have maintained, is not simply the ethics of certain individual marketers, but refers more properly to the actions and relations of individuals and organizations engaged in marketing activities. This includes both marketers and customers. The clearest cases of customers violating their own responsibilities are ones involving shoplifting and fraud. However, we have all heard of instances in which a person buys a product for a particular purpose (e.g. a television to view a special sporting event) and then returns it for a full refund. Customers have moral responsibilities to marketers that also go beyond the law. In short, there are rights and responsibilities on both sides of the marketer–customer relationship. Marketing ethics is not simply the ethics of marketers.

II Advertising

The forms advertising can take are limited only by the imagination of marketers. They include everything from the print media, television, radio, internet, billboards, handbills and posters, point-of-purchase displays, school buses, bathroom doors, urinals to sky-writing and the banners pulled behind airplanes. In short, almost any place in which an advertising message can be displayed has been used to carry some advertisement. In addition, the range of advertisements is being extended by using commercial characters as the basis for television shows, and placing products within television shows and movies. Similarly, "advertorials" – stories in magazines or newspapers that look like articles, but are really advertisements[1] – are new forms of advertising designed to get around people's guard by disguising their aims. In most (market) societies, advertising is almost impossible to avoid.

Advertising is not only difficult to escape, it is also more cunning and subtle these days, based on extensive studies in consumer psychology and behavior. This doesn't mean that advertisements may not be brash and "in your face." But the understanding of what appeals to and can motivate people is much greater today than in past decades. Advertisers seek to use that knowledge to accomplish their purposes. The upshot is that advertisements have wide-ranging and significant impacts on individuals and society.

If the buying and selling of products is a morally permissible form of exchange relationship, then we must ask which of the ways marketers use to inform and to influence customers (and others in the supply chain) are morally permissible and which are not. Advertising is one area in particular in which this question must be raised. Do certain kinds of advertisements run afoul of important marketing values and norms? It is hardly surprising to find that most forms of advertising involve ethical issues of deception, manipulation, harm, and value integrity.

Truth in advertising

Producers are not required to advertise. In fact, if a producer decided not to use advertisements at all, it would be peculiar to say that this producer had failed some moral obligation. There are no customer rights, as such, to advertising and the information such ads might offer. Consequently, customers cannot complain under those circumstances that the producers haven't used advertisements to try to inform them about their products. In fact, some very successful marketing campaigns have relied on word of mouth rather than advertisements.

Nevertheless, the current economic system would suffer a significant decline if advertising were to stop; it would be considerably less efficient. In this sense, it is better for all involved that producers and marketers advertise. As such, the current system requires it. This is the economic argument that advertising is essential for the efficient functioning of the economy (see Pollay, 1986: 19). In any economic system but the most simple, some way of making known what is available, its price, features, how they relate to customer's lives, etc. is necessary. Advertising supplies, in part, this need for information.

By the nature of the case advertisements have multiple purposes. One purpose is the systemic one just noted of providing information about products, even if it only tells us of their existence and availability for purchase. As such, advertisements are the first wave (as seen by the public) in a proposal for an exchange.

However, in addition, marketers or advertisers seek to influence those targeted to buy, acquire, or act in some positive way with regard to the product in question. They may attempt to get customers to try some product they haven't tried, to get them to buy more of a product they ordinarily buy, to keep them buying a product when tempted by other products, to become more aware of some product line, to encourage customers to switch brands, or to return to a company more often in the future (loyalty programs). In short, important to the standpoint of advertisers is to sell products, to make them known, and to fix certain impressions, memories, attitudes, and beliefs in people's minds so that they will buy their products. Ads are interventions, as it were, in consumer buying behavior that seek to shape and direct that behavior towards an exchange with the producer.

It is in the balancing of these different purposes that many difficulties of advertising lie regarding the standards by which the truth (or deceptiveness) of advertisements is to be measured. Though marketers are seeking to influence behavior they cannot simply do this in any way that will accomplish that end, or with anyone whose behavior might be influenced. An ethical marketer will seek to make these distinctions in light of the integrated marketing concept.

There are three major issues that need to be addressed. First, what does truth in advertising require? Contrariwise, what constitutes falsity, deception, or lying in advertisements? Second, what standards are to be used to make those determinations? Third, (given the marketing aim of selling products, not simply informing customers) could deception ever be justified?

Advertisements that make factual claims about a product may make them with regard to their cost, availability, quality, construction, uses, etc. Issues of truth play an extremely prominent role here, as they did in marketing research. Now, if advertisements say something whose truth can be determined, it would seem that they should be truthful, since truth is a basic value. Customers may not have an absolute right that marketers tell them something by way of advertising, but if marketers do advertise to them, then they have a presumptive right that the ad be true. This is, after all, the first part of a proposed economic exchange.

An advertisement tells the truth if what it (or some part of it) asserts or portrays captures or reflects, in some substantive or materially relevant manner, the actual characteristics of the product advertised. These may include its qualities (composition, reliability, sturdiness), how it is used, its price, where it may be obtained, etc.

An advertiser who knowingly includes some false statement in an ad, when this false item is material to the understanding of the product, and who does so with the intention to deceive someone, would be lying about the product. In short, a lie is not simply anything false or mistaken that appears (for example) in some advertisement. A lie is some form of communication (usually verbal or in print, though it could be by pictures or sign language) that one presents to another person or persons with the intention of leading that other person(s) to be believe something that is not the case.[2] This is in accord with Bok's view that defines a lie as "any intentionally deceptive message which is *stated*" (Bok, 1978: 14).

As such a lie requires that the person, or advertiser, present some sort of statement to the viewer. If, however, an advertiser omits saying or presenting something about a product and thus misleads the customer, the advertiser has not lied. In such a case, the customer has been deceived.

There are many straightforward cases when advertisers have lied about a product. They have presented their products to customers in ways that are knowingly false. Producers of many diet pills, patches, and creams have been charged by the FTC with making "false and unsubstantiated claims" that have deceived customers. Years ago, Rapid Shave claimed, in a demonstration, that its razor could shave sandpaper with minimal soaking. It could not. The razor was actually scraping sand off of a piece of glass. It was said to have lied. When Volvo stated that its ordinary cars could stand up to monster trucks and not be crushed, they were lying since the cars in the ad had been specially strengthened. When there are outright false statements or claims in an advertisement these are unacceptable.

In each of these cases, I am assuming that what is false in the advertisement is, in some sense, *material* to the message of the advertisement. To say this is to say that if the claim were false, the product would be different, in important ways, from what the customer was led to believe and would want in that product. Hence, if there is some minor, irrelevant aspect of what a marketer presents (or fails to present) in an advertisement that is false, and that does not affect the overall impression of the product, then this is not a reason to claim that the advertisement itself is false and that, therefore, dishonesty is involved.

But when something false is stated or implied that is material to the product, the advertisers are dishonest. They engage in lying and attempted deception. These are, ethically, the simplest cases. However, though this is important, it also doesn't take us a great distance. There are lots of ways in which even the truth can be deceptive. For example, a true statement may be placed in a context which makes the overall impression deceptive. Ads for carpets or tires may state the correct price, but omit other charges and fees that run up the final price. Further, a true statement may only be partially the truth. What is omitted may be crucial for a correct impression of the product. Consequently, a (partially) true statement may also deceive people. Finally, even a true statement offered to people who are not sufficiently briefed to understand it may also mislead and deceive them.

Accordingly, truth is only a partial defense in advertising since there are ways in which the truth may be deceptive. Hence, even if advertisers tell the literal truth, if an ad misleads people then it is a bad ad. How are we to determine this? What constitutes deception?

It would be an endless task to try to catalogue all the ways in which advertisements have made false claims or given rise to misleading and deceptive impressions. Some of these involve simply false statements, partial truths, misleading impressions, false associations, unwarranted implications, omitted statements or facts, ambiguity, etc. Instead, we need a more general statement that will encompass these and other inventive examples some marketers might come up with.

At a minimum, deception will occur when customers are led by an advertisement to believe something will happen that does not happen, or that is unlikely to happen, or that something else not desired or sought by the customer will most likely occur if they actually purchase the product. Deception rarely takes the form (these days) of an outright falsehood. Instead, partial truths, misleading contexts, and false associations are used that give the consumer an impression different from what they actually experience with the product. Similarly, advertisers may rely on knowledge that is widely available (but not applied in the particular case), careless reasoning, inattention to the fine print, etc. in creating deceptive advertisements.

As such, deception also depends upon the person(s) looking at the advertisement. This emphasizes, once again, the relational nature of marketing. Deception is, in this sense, person-relative. An advertisement may be seen by people with vastly different factual understandings, appreciation of humor, or acceptance of exaggeration. Some are highly knowledgeable about the products they see advertised, while others are not. Hence, the viewers of advertisements may differ not only cognitively, but also emotionally. Some may be more vulnerable, innocent, or gullible than others. As such, deception depends upon what behaviors customers are likely (or unlikely) to engage in. This may involve naivety of some sort, or even foolish trust of what people tell one. Still, deception has taken place.

Now it is implausible to hold advertisers to a standard according to which they would have to avoid each and every case of deception. We are not searching here for a simple or abstract standard of deception, but one that could be used when marketers seek to advertise to some group of people. If an ad deceives a particular person, that is not, in itself, an indication that the ad is unethical. In this way, advertisements are different from what might happen between a particular salesperson and a customer. However, ethically we should wish to reduce the level of the deception from such ads to the lowest possible level.

Accordingly, suppose that an advertisement would not be deceptive if the customer exercised good reasoning and common sense, carefully examined the claims in the advertisement, was informed about the products advertised, etc. Such a standard might be called a "reasonable consumer" standard. Such "reasonable consumers" could distinguish many of the false claims. They would not be deceived. If such a customer would not be deceived, shouldn't we conclude that the ads that pass muster with this person are not deceptive? And aren't those customers who are deceived simply failing in what they should do? The customer is being incautious; the marketer is not being deceptive.

There are good reasons, however, to conclude that such a standard is too high a standard for deception in advertising. Increasingly individuals are at a disadvantage with marketers. The marketer knows what the relevant information is and where it is to be found. Placing it in small print means the customer has to hunt for the relevant information; there are opportunity costs here. In addition, marketers are keenly aware of customer psychological proclivities and shortcomings that render them more susceptible to missing important information.

Preston suggests that a "reasonable person" standard might end up with 51 percent who might see a false claim and be deceived (Preston: 1994: 14). This would be a society in which a significant number would be taken in by false claims. Would this also be a just or fair society? Goods would be produced, but large numbers would not buy the goods they thought they were buying, or buy them under conditions different from the ones they anticipated. They would have been hoodwinked. They would become cynical and little-trusting, though they might still be deceived again. Some other standard is ethically desirable.

A more sensible standard would be that the audience must fulfill conditions of the average competent consumer. This group would consist of persons who were aware of common knowledge, both explicit and tacit, and could make standard distinctions between fact and fiction. They would not be those who are least accomplished or most credulous, i.e. the deficiently competent. Those in this third group would not rise to the level of the averagely competent.

Now if advertisers deceived individuals in the averagely competent or reasonable consumer groups, then they are crossing the line. The rationale for this view rests in part on the broader position that seeks a society in which people may, as widely as possible, participate without being deceived. Accordingly, an ethical society might still be one in which the deficiently competent, i.e., those least accomplished or most credulous, might (unfortunately) still be deceived or misled. This is not to say that other marketers who note the deception of members of this group would not have a responsibility to try to fend off the negative consequences of those deceptions. Still, a just society would require that as few of its members as possible who approached advertising with average intelligence and inclination to examine the ads presented to them would be deceived.

Accordingly, advertisements must not be deceptive to anyone at or above this level. They must not carry claims that such individuals see and believe to be true, even though they are false and hence are deceived. Those below this level may see them as true and believe them; they may be deceived. But they have fallen below some average communication and competency level. If such individuals did not see these claims and were not, as a result, deceived then we (and they) could only be thankful. Still, if they saw them and were taken in, the advertisers could not be blamed.

If advertisers targeted groups of those without average competence, they would then have to make special efforts so that these individuals were not deceived. Consequently, an implication of the preceding concerns advertisements targeted at children. Previously, this discussion has assumed that advertisements are targeted at those who, at least in some minimal manner, can comprehend and evaluate their messages. Because there is such a range of abilities and given the importance of the market for people to fulfill their daily needs, I have argued that advertisers should aim at this minimal level of deception that might arise from their advertisements.

Those who fall below even the minimal levels noted above would be customers who are particularly vulnerable. They might be children, the senile, or those whose cognitive capacities are, in some manner, sufficiently undeveloped or diminished such that they cannot evaluate the advertisements they are presented with or that surround them. To head off problems of deception here, advertisers should seek to ensure that their ads do not contain materials that would specially attract those audiences while at the same time deceiving them.

Part of the problem here is that if young children do not understand ads and what they are seeking to do, then there is not a question of this or that ad deceiving them. They are, in effect, simply deceived by ads in general. Nevertheless, in the U.S. there is a long tradition of advertising to children, notwithstanding the above points and the many studies that have examined the beliefs and perceptions of children who view advertisements. It is clear that advertisers (and the public in general) have discounted the effects of ads on children. There is a sense that children can (or should) be able to handle them; that this can be a "learning experience" for children; that advertisers have a right to advertise to children; and that parents can simply turn off the television or the radio if they don't like the ads. Some of these claims are empirical, others normative. Each of them has been hotly disputed. And though some accommodations have been made by advertisers, it is doubtful that the above ethical standard for non-deception is met in the case of children. Other economic reasons have been allowed to take precedence.

Puffery and the desire for deception
A great deal of advertising does not make claims that could strictly be evaluated as true or false. Instead, it consists of exaggerated statements ("best burger in the world") or associations and implicit connections between products and various needs or desires people have (for acceptance, approval, security, etc.). These forms of puffery are viewed differently than assertions advertisements make about prices, durability, contents, etc.

Do these forms of advertising raise problems of deception and dishonesty? Certainly, if a perfume manufacturer markets its product in connection with some romantic or sexy suggestions, this is deceptive (if it is) in a very different way than if the price for this product is different than that advertised, or if the product claims not to contain certain dangerous chemicals even though it does contain them. But are these forms of puffery deceptive?

Some say they are not, but, rather, are embellishments and are recognized (or are recognizable) as such. According to Levitt, people desire to have puffery: "Whether we are aware of it or not, we in effect expect and demand that advertising create these symbols for us to show us what life *might* be, to bring out the possibilities that we cannot see before our eyes, and screen out the stark reality in which we must live" (Levitt, 1970: 91). On Levitt's view, customers want the puffery, the symbolism, and the visual and auditory embellishments that ads carry to make their lives a little less drab.

In this way, puffery (we are told) constitutes a form of embellishment that ties in with other parts of our lives: women wear makeup; men and women have cosmetic surgery; people dress in expensive clothes, drive expensive cars, and wear expensive jewelry. People do all these things in an effort to embellish the impression they make on other people. Similarly, we decorate our houses, wrap presents, polish our cars, mow our lawns, etc., etc. All this is intended to make ourselves and our possessions look as good as possible.

But should puffery be seen simply as part of this very human decorative desire? Certainly, if average competent customers were asked whether this perfume, beer, shirt, etc. would give them the properties associated with these products by advertisers, they would answer "No." But what we explicitly and consciously believe may vary from how we feel and are prepared to act. These advertisements work on levels that are both cognitive and emotional, as well as conscious and unconscious. They affect our self-perceptions and views of our own identity. To the extent that people come to measure themselves, their lives, society, and reality by these images and associations, to the extent that they are moved by the exaggerated claims, they accept the implicit messages in such advertisements as appropriate to these tasks.

Accordingly, since advertisements that engage in puffery do not make straightforward cognitive claims, as such, they cannot be directly evaluated as true or false. Hence, they cannot be directly deceptive. Still, their exaggerations ("the best pizza in the world") and associations (a sexy woman with a car, perfume, or almost anything) are intended to attach an emotional or symbolic glow to a product. In general, these emotional associations are effective in moving people to purchase the advertised products – otherwise they would not be used. But this means that people are prepared to view themselves and their lives in light of these associations through those products. Given that there is no rational or objective connection between the associated emotions and the products, this is (as others have argued) a form of soft or indirect deception. Not only the advertiser but also the customer takes part in this deception.

Some commentators, however, contend that these indirect or soft deceptions are not, as such, morally wrong, such as is deliberately lying to someone (Jackson, 1990: 60). Jackson refers to them as a form of non-lying deception that is similar to women using makeup, people smiling at each other's feeble jokes, or angry couples feigning harmony in public (Jackson, 1990: 54). These forms of behavior, we are told, enrich our lives; they provide benefits to us; and they may be used to protect our privacy (Jackson, 1990: 54). This is true, but irrelevant in this case.

Though it is obvious that deception does play an important part in everyday life, it does not follow that all such deception is morally desirable or acceptable. White lies are one thing, but out-and-out deceptions that harm people are another thing. Further, puffery on a single occasion is different from puffery that surrounds people with images and exaggerations that are created out of whole cloth by an advertiser. The ethical concerns that soft-deception puffery involves occur on this more general level. They involve the (false) association of important human emotions, values, and needs with various products and goods – something which may dilute the importance of these emotions and needs. If, for example, Southwest is "the symbol of freedom" then our view of freedom has itself been watered down in the process. Collectively the impact of such puffery is, arguably, not morally desirable.

And though some may like to have products presented in this manner, the purpose of these "embellishments" is not to enrich our lives or make them less drab, but to sell us a product which has little in itself to do with the puffery pronouncements. Consequently, such puffery will not reduce the stark reality of our lives – unless one is prepared to live the fantasy of the ads. This sets up, however, a contrast in our lives that is even sharper. Those who choose to live "the good life" on such bases have chosen to live in a world dependent on the images and associations of others which are created for their own purposes. Whether such a life can plausibly be called "a good life" is worthy of debate.

The free speech objection

Some contend that advertisements are a form of free speech and ought not to be curbed, even if they are mistaken or inaccurate in various ways. Deception and puffery are not outlawed in ordinary conversation or in political speech. Advertisers should not, it is said, have responsibilities to avoid deception and puffery imposed on them. Any attempt to impose them through regulation would violate the freedom of speech of advertisers and those they work for. In short, producers and advertisers have a right of free speech. They should be able to speak freely, even if what they say is false or deceptive.

This issue is, clearly, a particularly American one due to the existence of the First Amendment to the U.S. Constitution that guarantees the right of free speech. Those in other countries that do not have such constitutional guarantee may view free speech as permitting more control than do those in the U.S. Nevertheless, there is an ethical issue here as well with regard to the nature and extent of the freedom an advertiser should have to make claims that are false or deceptive, as well as the extent of government regulation of such speech.

Now even in daily life or in political speech, we might contend that people ought (at least ethically) to speak the truth or at least not engage in deceptive speech. Still, what about the advertising case? What justifies defending not only this ethical point, but also regulation of advertisers' speech? There are several justifying reasons.

First, the aim of advertisers is to sell a product. They are proposing, in effect, a commercial exchange. People may be injured quite directly by buying this or that product. Of course, it might be said that people may be injured also if a politician gets their vote, but the connection is much less direct (in fact it is so indirect that many people choose not to vote). So there is a *directness* that distinguishes the two.

Second, there are other forces and parts of a government that control the actions of politicians – other members of Parliament or Congress, a judiciary before whom cases of fraud, illegal behavior, etc. may be brought. Of course producers can be brought to court if their product injures someone (and is shown to be defective), but not simply because the person bought a product that was quite different than the one advertised. Without the possibility of government regulation, there is no *recourse* here (outside of letting the market act, which may result in many people being injured financially, even if not physically).

Third, in political speech there are others who will freely and openly criticize or evaluate the speech of opponents. In commercial speech, there are organizations that will evaluate the products of a company but generally one has to search them out, the evaluations are (many times) out of date, and one has anyway to buy these evaluations. This is different in political speech. Hence the *availability of evaluation* is greater in political speech.

Finally, though the traditional marketing concept speaks of fulfilling the wants of customers, this is only a means to the ends of the marketer groups. In political speech the aim of politicians, against which they are measured, is the public good. They are to do good things for their constituents, and not simply themselves. At least nominally, then, the *public good* is their end, whereas this is not directly the case for marketers (the point that Adam Smith made).

Consequently, there do seem to be good reasons for governments to regulate commercial speech. Of course, marketers (and marketing organizations as well) ought to look towards their own self-regulation of what they do. As Greenland (an advertising veteran) urged some time ago, they should "stop conning consumers" (Greenland, 1974).

Accordingly, advertising is not an instance of political speech. In political speech, a person or organization is seeking to persuade other persons (or organizations) to adopt, change, or maintain some public policy and/or course of action. They do not expect a direct return for this speech activity. They are not proposing a commercial contract. One does not buy their vote. In contrast, in advertising the advertiser is proposing, in effect, a commercial contract with a potential buyer. If a person misleads another person in this situation, they are engaged in fraud, misrepresentation, etc. that is ethically unacceptable.

Some try to muddy these distinctions by speaking of people voting with their dollars. But this is yet another instance (see chapter 1) of the extension of marketing to other realms. People do not vote with dollars; they buy goods and services with their dollars. People vote with ballots as part of a collective action that puts some one or other party into, or out of, office. Hence, though the political and economic realms are intertwined they are also distinguishable. What standards are appropriate in one need not be the same in the other.

Offensive advertisements

Advertisements may be criticized not simply for questions of truth, deception, or dishonesty, but also for their offensiveness. This may occur in a number of ways. Some are offensive because of what people do in the ads, or the situations they portray. Nike ran a "Horror" ad that involved a man with a chainsaw chasing a woman through the woods – she escapes because of her Nikes and her physical training. Midas presented an older woman coming into one of their shops and asking for some struts, not for her car but to support her sagging breasts, which she revealed to the clerks at the Midas store (but not the audience) by opening her coat. In these cases, the situation portrays a threat to or a violation of some important value or norm.

Ads can also be offensive by portraying people in various stereotypical and demeaning fashions or roles. This is said to occur when women are portrayed in a manner that emphasizes their sexuality, but de-emphasizes their intelligence or leadership qualities. Similarly black people may be portrayed in dismissive and stereotypical ways. Ads can also be offensive through the language they use, which might be particularly obscene, sexist, and/or racist. Even the name of a company, for example FCUK, has raised some eyebrows. And ads can be offensive by using certain images of things that some hold in high esteem or believe to be particularly sacred in ways that profane them. For example, an ad that purported to represent Mohammed would be offensive to many Muslims, even if Mohammed was represented in a positive manner. And though Jesus is frequently portrayed in churches and artwork, an advertiser who had Jesus endorsing the company product might well offend some.

The offense in these instances may be of different kinds. Ads may be morally offensive if they violate or contravene some moral value or principle that those offended hold. However, people may also be offended (non-morally) by things they perceive in other areas of life as well, for example aesthetics or religion. In such cases, something they encounter violates some non-moral value or norm that they subscribe to or a familiar way of doing things. The result is that people are irritated, annoyed, displeased, or even insulted. There is a felt or experienced violation, rather than simply the broaching of some indifferent or distant standard. The violation is, in this sense, taken "personally."

I have not said that the values or norms that are violated are ones that are "objectively" justified. All that is required for the offense at issue here is that some value or norm that someone holds is violated. It might or might not be an objectively justified value or norm. Hence, in the past, some people (in the U.S.) might have been viscerally offended by an ad that showed a black man walking hand in hand with a white woman. Today this offense may be felt by some with regard to homosexual couples. Or it may occur when matters that are believed properly private, for example sex, defecation, or various body parts, are portrayed publicly.

Accordingly what is offensive is not necessarily immoral, and what is immoral may not be offensive to some people. If some people still today are offended by seeing an interracial couple kiss, that is more a statement of their own personal views (or biases) rather than a reflection of the morality of interracial couples. People may be offended, even if nothing immoral has happened.

So how does it come about that advertisers end up producing something that is (morally) offensive, in the sense that it violates justified values and norms? If they set out to be morally offensive, then the problem we face is the same as if they set out to be immoral in some other way. They deserve condemnation. Customers should stay away from their products; trade associations should sanction them; media outlets should refuse to carry them; and possibly there should even be some form of government regulation.

A more interesting case to consider is one in which advertisers feel themselves under great pressure to push the envelope, to stand out, and thereby to attract the viewer's attention. The industry has the adage that "If you're not on the edge, you're taking up too much room" (Duke, 2000). Suppose the ads are intended to be "edgy," i.e., to push the boundaries of the acceptable. To do this can be startling, eye-catching, and attention-getting. But it can also be offensive.

This might happen in one of two ways. Some ads might be offensive wholly unintentionally. The advertisers simply didn't expect people to be offended. They didn't know that this kind of ad would be offensive to anyone. In short, they didn't identify what was (potentially) offensive in their ads. This might be because they use common or stereotypical images and don't think further about it. Or it might be because they think something will be funny,

eye-catching, but not offensive. On this alternative, the problem that advertisers face is to determine what will be offensive and to avoid giving offense
in unjustified ways.

On the other hand, suppose an advertiser knows, or has reason to believe,
that an ad may have the unintended secondary effect of offending some (but
not those they wish to target with their ads). To attract the attention of potential buyers, an ad portrays a situation that the potential buyers find amusing
or attention-getting, but that same ad may strongly offend others who are
highly unlikely to buy this product. Several years ago, Yves Saint Laurent
portrayed Sophie Dahl on her back, legs spread, completely naked, except for
high-heeled shoes. She was seemingly experiencing a kind of ecstasy to be
associated with a new perfume they were promoting. These pictures on posters
in London attracted considerable attention as well as causing offense. They
were withdrawn. In such cases, apparently the advertiser either doesn't care
about, or dismisses, the significance of the offense to others. They calculate
that the positive effect (customers purchasing their products) of the ads on
those they have targeted will outweigh any negative effect (offense) on those
they didn't target, but who see it anyway.

Now it would seem that since advertisers seek to sell various products, it
is in their self-interest to avoid offending potential customers. On the other
hand, if, to emerge from the clutter of other advertisements, an ad might have
to be edgy and those offended are not those targeted, one can see that advertisers are caught (or have placed themselves) between two very different
forces. It is a measure of our times that such a rationale on behalf of a commercial purpose seems almost reasonable. May such offense be discounted
due to the expected positive effects of the ad on the intended audience? The
contrary would seem to be the case. To the extent that an ad does cause any
group moral offense, when the underlying values and norms are justified, we
should reject it.

Further, given the self-interested aim of advertisers, one must wonder
whether such offense is necessary. It is possible to be "edgy" without being
offensive. A little moral imagination is needed. In fact, such offensiveness may
simply be an indication that the moral and creative imagination of the advertisers has failed.

Now sometimes it may not be possible to determine from outside an
advertising agency or campaign whether it intentionally or unintentionally
developed the offensive ad. Still, how advertisers navigate these tensions and
different situations will tell a great deal about their own character and moral
decision-making.

Consider again the television commercial, entitled "Horror," that Nike ran
during the 2000 Olympics, in which a chainsaw-wielding man in a hockey

mask breaks in on a woman in a remote cabin. She screams and runs. He chases her but can't keep up. As the ad concludes, the woman is shown panting for breath and a question flashes on the screen: "Why Sport?" The answer then appears: "You'll live longer." Not only if you engage in sport and stay fit, but also (apparently) if you wear Nike shoes (see Farhi, 2000). Interestingly, NBC, which was showing the Olympics and the advertisement, was the one that pulled the ad, not Nike.

Supposedly this ad was intended as funny and ironic. However, it was also tasteless because it provided comedy for some at the expense of the many women who fear attacks by men. Why was such an ad offensive? It was not offensive to everyone. The "Horror" video was played on ESPN and didn't occasion protests. So what made it offensive to some? Should it have been offensive to others? Part of the answer is that a commercial of this sort belittles by making fun of the situation in which real women have been attacked by men. In the year 2000, rape occurred 1,871 times a day in the U.S.; violent crimes against women occurred 2½ million times that year.[3] None of this is funny. Further, the ad suggests that the solution to the problem is to exercise and to buy a product from Nike to put on your feet, rather than to rid society of those who engage in violent attacks on women. A serious social issue is transformed into a commercial message. That is, or should be, morally offensive.

Now it is not obvious that Nike's advertisers had thought through these implications of this commercial. The offense appeared to be unintended. If so, this is an instance in which advertisers must reflect much more broadly on the consequences and implications of their ads not only for target audiences but also unintended audiences. Advertisements always appear in a social, historical, cultural, and moral context. This complex set of values and norms must be closely considered prior to releasing ads or commercials. And since those most closely connected with such ads may be biased by their own creative process, this argues for others, outside this immediate context, to review ads for potential offensiveness.

We might ask, however: Could it ever be justified for an advertisement to be offensive? We know that some lies are justifiable. Why not some forms of (moral) offense? It is conceivable, for example, that an ad might offend some, for example an interracial ad, or an ad about HIV/AIDS, and yet that ad be justifiable. However, if one of the main purposes of ads is also to sell a product or a service, then such offensive ads also have a self-interested purpose. Now advertisers are not moral managers, let alone moral guardians of a society. They do not have a moral responsibility to try to remake society morally. Yet they do have moral impact. And given the integrated marketing concept they must be particularly aware of these impacts on various constituencies. This is not to say that some advertisers or marketers might not choose to try to have a reformative impact on society. Benetton is an example of a marketer whose ads have sought to have positive social impact and which have been rather controversial, if not offensive, to some. They have had a social purpose, as well as a corporate purpose. But there is also a moral danger in the twinning of these two aspects, viz., the commercialization of important moral issues. As with the Nike ads, it may trivialize the social issue. Still, we know historically that at times some people must be "shaken up" and even offended in order for there to be change. How many people were offended during the civil rights era in the U.S., but to good effect in subsequent decades? This is clearly a consequentialist appeal. Such appeals seem justified if they promote some further justified moral end. However, if they are designed simply to promote a corporate end, such offense would not be justified. If it violated other values or norms, for example aesthetic or customary ones, it might be (morally) permissible, even if risky for the advertiser.

In short, there is no justification for an ad that morally offends, if that means simply violating a justified moral value or norm without any other morally redeeming feature. However, some people might perceive an ad as morally offensive even though it is not, since it does not violate a justified moral value or norm. And on some occasions creating such offense might be justified, but such occasions are rather infrequent. Much of this offense may occur because advertisers do not stop to think about the implications and symbolic effects of what they are doing. Hence, advertisers should carefully consider what value implications and statement(s) are conveyed by their advertisements and commercials. Are they morally justified? Do they promote a good society that people would, reflectively, wish to live in? Are they morally desirable portrayals of people? Answering these questions would warrant being particularly clear on what values they wish to portray. It would also justify having ads that are especially "edgy" in design reviewed by people independent of the creation of the ad itself. Both practically and morally advertisers should seek to avoid causing offense. Indeed, simply avoiding causing further offense may itself be an additional good.

Manipulation

Advertising must be evaluated not only for its truthfulness and offensiveness, but also, as we have seen, for the impact it may have on people's views of themselves and their behavior. Advertisements are not simply informational, but also motivational and perspectival. They seek to move people. In addition, they offer (wittingly or not) representations of the (or "a") world. It is not surprising, then, that advertising is often said to raise issues of manipulation.

In order to motivate people, advertising may appeal, among other things, to the desires, needs, emotions, wishes, etc. we have regarding, for example, our physical appearance or safety, acceptance by others, sexual interests, or patriotism. Thus, advertisements that relate to one's acceptance by others may feature bad breath (mouthwash), bodily smells (deodorants), or dandruff (special shampoos). They may also relate to protection of one's children or loved ones (special tires for one's car, life insurance policies, fire policies, etc.).

Other advertisements seek to establish a sexual aura around a product to influence the attitudes of the viewer. Given the greatly emphasized attention given to sex in modern society, advertisers who can establish a positive link between a product and people's desire to be sexually adequate (in whatever ways) will have a lever with which to work upon such people to get them to buy their products. Similarly, advertisements may also seek to influence people by portraying something in a way that appeals to nationalistic emotions. In so doing, advertisers appeal to important emotions, desires, and needs.

In each of the above cases, objections have been raised that marketers are not simply seeking to persuade or influence people, but are engaged in a form of manipulation that is ethically inappropriate.

What would constitute manipulation in these cases? Someone is manipulated when some other person (or organization) non-coercively creates or rearranges a set of conditions such that he or she can motivate a person to feel, believe, or act in certain ways that they would not otherwise have felt, believed, or acted in and that fulfill an aim of the person exercising this influence. There are, accordingly, both cognitive and emotional dimensions to manipulation.

Manipulation, then, is not directed simply at getting a person to do certain things (though, of course, this is the ultimate aim), but rather at getting people to feel, believe, and have certain attitudes towards particular products or product lines such that they later are more inclined to act in ways that the advertiser or marketer seeks.

In these cases, the person's own decision and motivational structures for acting are altered or overridden. The most serious charge is that advertisements are capable of manipulating people to do certain things that advertisers would like them to do. This may take place by their simply operating on wants and needs these people already have, or by creating new wants and needs in them which will lead them to act in ways that the advertisers desire.

Manipulation is different from coercion, which involves outright force, or the threat of force, to do harm to a person (or something that person values). To coerce a person is to bring sufficient force, whether physical or psychological, to induce a person, against his or her will, to do something that they wouldn't otherwise do. Coercion is something of which a person is aware and finds it impossible (or extremely difficult) to resist. Given the conditions of coercion, it is implausible to think that advertisements can be said to be coercive. Manipulation requires the person to use his or her own faculties, which are at the same time altered or undercut, while coercion simply circumvents those faculties except insofar as they are required for the person to engage in the coerced behavior.

Accordingly, manipulation is more subtle than coercion. In fact, people may be manipulated and not be aware of it. If a person does not know that they are being manipulated, it does not follow that they are not. It follows that questionnaires completed by viewers of advertisements which return the result that they are not being manipulated or that they could not be induced by such ads to buy or to do something are not terribly helpful. It still may be the case that they are being manipulated.

Consequently, manipulation can be overt, but it can also be concealed. We may recognize that we are being manipulated. Sometimes, on those occasions, we can resist the manipulation; at other times we cannot. Sometimes we might even accept it (for example, a person might recognize that a movie is attempting to manipulate his or her emotions and yet not resist that attempt). People can be manipulated for their own interests, but also for the interests of others. There is always a difference between what the person would do otherwise, and what someone else wants that person to do and through whose agency that person comes to do otherwise.

But isn't this what all business is about? My dictionary defines "manipulation" as "artful or skillful management." "To manipulate," this dictionary says, is "to manage or influence by artful skill" (Barnhart, 1956). It would follow that if advertisers manipulate their audiences, all they are doing is skillfully managing them. Are there any problems with this?

Certainly there are problems. First, "manipulation" has both a neutral and a negative sense. A person may be able to manipulate numbers or some objects and this not raise any concerns. Depending on their ends in doing so, we may even praise them. But when we speak of manipulating people, we appeal to a different sense of this term, since then we treat them as things. It is this equation of manipulation and (skillful) management that is mistaken. The reason is that manipulation also implies circumventing the ordinary decision-making or emotional responses of others. It may involve playing upon them to achieve the ends of the manipulator. In any case, the person's cognitive or emotional faculties are not engaged on their own terms, but are (in some manner or other) subverted or sidestepped. It is for this reason that "manipulation" is also said to involve controlling or playing upon "by artful, unfair, or insidious means especially to one's own advantage."[4]

Second, to the extent that advertising manipulates people and circumvents their ordinary decision-making, it subverts their role as moral agents. To use Kantian language, it treats people as things to be moved about, rather than as people to be respected. Accordingly, to the extent that advertising is manipulative it undercuts the integrated marketing concept. Nevertheless, on the present account, manipulation need not always be (all things considered) morally unjustified. In certain circumstances, it may be justified to manipulate some people to do things they would not otherwise do. For example, this might take place with children or with adults whose reasoning abilities are significantly underdeveloped or diminished. The justification of such manipulation will depend on the particular ends to be achieved.

Manipulation, then, differs in ethically dramatic ways from persuasion or efforts to (rationally) influence the behavior of others. The latter kinds of advertisements do not circumvent one's decision-making processes. Instead, they seek to engage them, though they may do so on grounds other than those that are purely cognitive.

It is to be expected that marketers will seek to portray a product in as attractive a fashion as possible. There isn't anything necessarily wrong with this, depending on the attractive features used to influence the potential customer's attitudes and views regarding the product. Oftentimes we try to identify some objective set of facts about a product which we distinguish from the influences that advertisers may also seek to bring to bear on behalf of the product. But this separation is a dubious one, inasmuch as even strictly factual accounts may be well or poorly portrayed, convincingly or haltingly stated, etc. Instead of criticizing advertisements for those aspects of them that seek to influence the customers, we should evaluate the nature of that influence and whether it amounts to manipulation.

In this case, everything will depend upon the means used to appeal to those targeted, who is targeted, and the narrowness or breadth of the appeal. In general, when marketers simply treat people as objects to be maneuvered or plied in certain directions for their own ends (even if those targeted thereby benefit), then there is manipulation and also reason for marketers to avoid these forms of marketing.

Forms of manipulation

Some forms of manipulation can be very blatant. For example, suppose an ad leads people to believe that a certain product is available at a store, but it isn't. When this is done with the intention that customers, after they have gone to the time and trouble to come into the store, may be willing to buy a higher-priced product, then they have not only been deceived but also manipulated. For example, ads might offer a great deal on a car, but when the customer shows up that car is not available – but the salesperson is only too eager to show the customer some other, more expensive, models (see Claiborne, 1998: 2–3).

This tactic of *bait and switch* is illegal in the U.S. It is also unethical. The advertiser has both lied to the customer and tried to construct a situation in which some of the customer's defenses have been reduced so that the retailer has a greater chance of selling a more expensive product. Though this practice is clearly manipulative, it is also sometimes successful. Nevertheless, the attempt itself is worthy of condemnation. The point here does not mean, of course, to imply that, in a buying situation that has not been deceptively designed in this manner, a salesperson may not, in good conscience, try to get a customer to buy a higher-priced item or to trade up.

A very different form of manipulation would be one in which advertisers could, through technology, infiltrate various beliefs and desires into a person's consciousness, but do so without the person's awareness of their origin. This might involve visual and/or auditory techniques to put messages before people that at a subconscious level they may perceive and process, even though not doing so consciously, let alone reflectively. What has been called *subliminal advertising* would fit this bill. Such advertising appeals are designed to circumvent a person's reflective processes. Whether this really can be done has been disputed, but the theoretical point remains relevant. It is hard to imagine that commercial use of such means could be justified, since they subvert a person's moral and practical agency. Even the use of such means for socially desirable ends, for example refraining from stealing, runs into the same moral objections.

A less dramatic example of manipulative advertising that is not up-front, but much more subtle is product placement in movies and television, for example, a can of Coke, or some other product, will appear in a program a person is watching. Even less obvious is, for example, the amount of smoking portrayed in Hollywood movies. This has greatly increased in recent years. And though this does not advertise any particular brand, it is viewed by many as an implicit (subliminal) message that smoking is OK; it is the "done thing." Certainly some people are influenced by such subtle forms of advertising. To the extent that these circumstances are intentionally designed to produce this result in viewers through altering the conditions of their beliefs, attitudes, and actions then this form of advertising would fit under the above meaning of manipulation.

What about advertisements of a kind we see under more normal circumstances? Here we find appeals to various desires, fears, and needs that people generally have. These advertisements must be viewed differently than those just mentioned. Suppose marketers use fear appeals to get people to buy safer cars, more durable tires, take care of their health, etc. If marketers remind customers that, for example, by using a certain product they can avoid getting sick, have they done anything unethical? In fact, haven't they done something commendable and helped people avoid a situation (e.g. getting sick) that they wish to avoid?

The answer is that some appeals to potential customers' fears might be justified in some cases, though not in others. So, simply a fear appeal need not be wrong. That needs to be decided on the basis of the particular appeal. We need to ask: Did the appeal to fear invoke objective considerations or did it simply seek to touch our raw emotions? There is a difference, we must assume, between being rationally persuaded that due to certain dangers you should buy a safer car, more durable tires, etc. and being unjustifiably manipulated into buying such products. In the latter case, the means used do not emphasize the factual, rational, or objective aspects of the issue, allowing the customer to make his or her own decision. Instead, they touch on emotional, non-rational, fears, desires, and needs that we have (and that do need addressing), but do so in a way that overrides the rational or objective evaluation of the means to satisfy those emotions, needs, and desires. The former does not raise ethical problems, while the latter does, especially when it is done for self-interested motives, rather than concerns for the well-being of those targeted.

The preceding examples suggest that manipulation exists over a range of interventions by advertisers that extend from what may hardly be resisted to that which could be resisted. The less that such manipulation can be resisted, and the less one is (or can be) aware of it, the greater is the ethical objection to it. As I noted earlier, this evaluation must not simply be made in the case of each ad, but must also be considered over multiple exposures to that ad, as well as in the context of an atmosphere in which such ads are pervasive. The greater frequency and pervasiveness of such advertisements adds to the threat of manipulation. This issue is the focus of the next subsection.

A cumulative effect

Particular advertisements may themselves manipulate people, though how often this occurs is difficult to say. In fact, it is a mistake to focus simply on this or that ad with regard to its manipulative force. Instead, a crucial aspect of the present issue is the repeated exposure to the same individual ads, to ads for the same products in different media (print, television, internet), as well as the constant presence of advertisements. If we focus just on this or that tree, we may miss the forest before us. Accordingly, living in an environment pervaded by advertising creates a climate of acceptability that is hard to resist. A climate that permits ads to constantly bombard people may itself be manipulative.

On this view, the manipulation may occur on an individual level, as well as on a more general, social level. Given its generality and extensive nature, manipulation on the social level may seem less obvious than on the level of this or that individual.

Of course, it will be objected that marketers do not really have the actual ability to manipulate and effect such changes in people's behavior. Some contend that customers have the ability to defend themselves. A survey of "green marketing" advertisements notes their failure to change people's behavior. If advertising is so powerful, why are there so many failed advertising campaigns? Numerous products do not succeed, even with massive advertising. In the past, the Edsel (a new car model Ford tried to market in the late 1950s) has been a favorite example. It was an advertising (and product) failure. Consumers do have choices.

Such counter-arguments tend to be hasty generalizations. It does not follow from the fact that this or that advertisement does not successfully move (or manipulate) people, that other ads do not do so, let alone advertisements in general. Advertisers make proud claims for how their ads positively affect certain social views: for example introducing black women as executives; showing interracial couples as they discuss buying furniture, etc. If these can be effective, then other advertisements can also be effective. Advertisers cannot claim impotence in the questionable ads, and potency in desirable ads.

Finally, the full impact of advertisements must be weighed not against this or that ad, but against their pervasive nature and how they fit into the larger economic and social organization of society. Particular ads offer people "a clear-cut impetus to a well-defined, individual action (the act of buying)." At the same time, they are "just one small piece of a major economic enterprise directed at getting consumers to buy" (Schudson, 2003: 3). In this manner, advertisements play a role in making a national culture; something that binds people in ways in which religion did in the past. The "argument" of these advertisements is not made rationally, objectively, or even explicitly. It happens in much more subtle ways that alter the conditions of one's behavior and direct it towards ends that marketers seek. To this extent they are manipulative. And to the extent that such manipulations do not have the well-being of those manipulated as part of their aim, they are ethically undesirable.

In short, the charge of manipulation is a serious charge brought against advertisers. Claims about the manipulative effect of specific advertisements seem overblown, but the cumulative effect is very real in promoting a consumer culture and acceptance of the importance of material goods, consumption, etc. in daily lives. In general, advertisements pass moral muster only when they engage people in ways in which they are capable of being aware of what is being presented to them and can evaluate it. When this does not happen, advertisements are rightfully the object of ethical criticism.

III Retailing

Retailing relates to the sale of products and services to the ultimate customer for personal, non-business use. It is generally done in various store buildings, but may also be done door to door, as well as through the mail and internet. Retailers come in all sizes, from giants like Wal-Mart, to small Mom-and-Pop stores. In addition, there are a variety of different ownership formats: corporate, independent, and franchise systems. Finally, different marketing strategies that are widely familiar are used by the different retail outlets, for example department stores, discount houses, specialty stores, factory outlets, supermarkets, convenience stores, and warehouse clubs.

There is a wide variety of ethical issues that pertain to retailing. Among these, two are of particular note. First, product acquisition and placement raise several important ethical questions such as: What is the permitted role of gifts and entertainment that retailers may receive from (or give to) producers in obtaining products to sell? What demands, such as slotting fees, may retailers impose on producers in order to stock and display their items? Second, product and personal sales raise other difficult questions: How are retailing techniques such as low-balling, resale price maintenance, and everyday low prices to be ethically evaluated? What ethical considerations are important in designing return policies, the monitoring of sale products, etc? What information may (or must) a salesperson give to a customer?

Product acquisition and placement

The means by which retailers acquire the products they sell raise a variety of ethical questions. So too, do the conditions under which they place them on their shelves. The next two subsections briefly represent some of the ethical issues that arise in this part of retailing.

Gifts and entertainment

Retailers acquire the products they sell to individual customers by purchasing them from other producers through various sales representatives, etc. What role may gifts and entertainment play in this process? Suppose that a sales representative, after a discussion of whether your retail chain will carry a particular product line he is touting, casually offers some tickets to the World Series, or to a local professional game. Does this raise any ethical questions?

Some argue that the answer depends on the intent of the gift-giver. It is wrong if the person intends to influence one's decision, but not wrong if the person is simply offering the gift as a nice gesture. The problem with this argument is that it is difficult (and perhaps impossible) to ascertain a person's intent in such cases. Further, even if the person has benign intentions, the gift may still be ethically inappropriate.

The fact is that gifts and entertainment we receive may alter our views of those giving the gifts and what they ask of us. Acceptance of such gifts may make us feel "obliged" to those who have given the gifts. After all, this is one of the traditional aspects of gift-giving – those receiving gifts do feel a certain obligation to respond in kind. And when, as a result, a purchaser makes an agreement that he or she would not otherwise have made, it appears that the person has been unduly influenced, if not bribed. Hence, gifts may raise questions of conflicts of interest.

An objection to this stance is that this presents a very impersonal view of business. Rather, business involves forming personal relationships such that one can trust the other, and this may involve developing bonds of friendship and commitment. Gifts and entertainment foster those relationships.

It is obvious that personal relationships are important in business, whether small or large. However, when these relationships are sought, and gifts given, simply to influence unduly a person's decision, this approach to others does not have ethical merit. But it may rest on a legitimate value or principle, viz., the importance of developing trust (and the confidence it may inspire) in doing business when one's interests might be harmed by another who could take advantage of one's position. Consequently, there may be a conflict of two respectable principles here: objective business decisions and trusting business relations.

Ultimately, the essential ethical question here regards the bases upon which business decisions are to be made. Can trusting relationships be built upon bases which might not involve undue influence and conflicts of interest? The danger that arises with the emphasis on personal relationships and the giving of gifts to foster them is that those decisions are not made on the merits of the case, but on the basis of the friendly relations between those making the decisions. This may result in higher prices to customers and products of lesser quality than might otherwise be agreed upon. This danger is exacerbated by the tendency individuals have to believe that they cannot, or will not, be influenced by gifts or entertainment that they receive. This is, however, false. If the customers of business are supposed to receive essential consideration in its determinations, then business policies regarding gifts and entertainment must constrain such gift-giving and entertainment so that they do not interfere with these decisions.

The upshot is that companies have adopted policies with regard to gifts and entertainment to try to forestall these dangers. However, these policies vary widely, since there is no one single bright shining line in this area. Some companies permit only gifts and entertainment with a value of less than $25; others put the limit at $100. However, when businesses operate in parts of Asia and Africa, giving gifts and entertaining may be expected. Policies may have to be modified. Nevertheless, though the various implementations may legitimately vary, the underlying moral dilemma is clear. How can objective business decisions be made while fostering cordial, trusting relations with one's business associates? How the principle of objective business decisions is realized will depend on the industry, the people involved, what local customs are, etc. And all these may vary. Simply having a policy or a set of rules in place regarding gifts and entertainment will not do what is needed. Not merely compliance, but an implementation with understanding is required. Since the crucial moral issues to be addressed have to do with undue influence and conflicts of interest within trusting relationships, new forms of business may be required. This will necessitate that ethical marketers have this moral aim in their sights.

Slotting fees

A very different retail ethics question arises when retailers charge monetary fees or demand free goods from distributors or manufacturers in order to place their products on store shelves. Such fees or free goods are called "slotting fees." The justification retailers have typically offered for these fees has been that they are needed to cover the costs of entering new items on their computer system, making space available on their shelves or in their distributor's warehouse, and later (if they fail to sell) removing them (see Quelch and Stern, 1993: 502). Particularly in light of the growing proliferation of products by manufacturers, retailers claim that they face significant costs in handling these products.

There is reason to believe, however, that the amount of these fees has grown beyond simply covering such costs and now are additional contributions to the retailer's bottom line (see Quelch and Stern, 1993). Accordingly, some other justification would seem to be required. One such justification has been the low profit margins which the retail industry has experienced. Slotting fees are a way of increasing these after-tax profit margins (Quelch and Stern, 1993: 505). But this is not an ethical justification. At best, it is in accord with the desire of retailers to maximize profits, which may be economically justified if it does not run afoul of other ethical requirements. In any case, no business or industry has a right to a certain level of profitability in comparison with other businesses or industries. And even if it did, how that level would be chosen would be considerably contentious.

Other objections have been raised against such fees. First, slotting fees raise the price of goods to customers. This is a factual claim that would have to be determined in each case, as well as in general. Clearly retailers do have costs associated with the multitude of products they carry. But since they do not publish what these fees are it is difficult to know how much of these costs is absorbed by the producer or the retailer, as opposed to how much is passed on to the customer. In any case, the mere fact that costs were passed on to customers would not necessarily constitute an ethical objection against them.

Second, slotting fees may keep some products from the shelves of retailers. In particular, many small businesses may not be able to pay the slotting fees and hence their products may be kept off retailers' shelves. If these products are innovative or superior to present products, customers will have less meaningful choices. But does this mean that customers are being denied anything to which they might rightfully claim they ought to have access? Are the retailers or distributors who demand such slotting fees then violating a customer's right? It is hard to see what right it might be.

Of course, if customers demand those products, retailers may be willing to forgo such fees in order to obtain those products for their shelves, but quite often customers do not know about those products and, hence, will not demand them. Accordingly, this issue is also sometimes framed in terms of customer welfare or an idealized market, rather than customer rights. Do slotting allowances impinge on, or reduce, customer welfare, by way of reducing competition or consumer choices (see Cespedes, 1993: 479)? If an ideal market permits a wide range of goods, slotting fees may be an obstacle to such markets which functions in a non-transparent manner.

Accordingly, the issue here is not one of the rights of customers, but of the justification underlying the market itself through what it supposedly accomplishes for customers. If markets are affected by various participants, for example retailers through slotting fees, in ways which reduce the number and quality of products available to customers, then those participants are potentially undercutting the rationale of the market. However, slotting fees do not mean that these products cannot appear in the market, only that they won't appear in certain retail outlets. Still, if access to those outlets is what is required to grow a business (smaller) businesses may be harmed, as well as consumer choice limited, when retailers use their market power to demand slotting fees. Hence the issue is also one of access to markets.

Still, just because a business produces some product, it would not thereby acquire a right to have it stocked on a retailer's shelves. There are simply too many products for this to be plausible. Some principle of selection is required. The troublesome feature of slotting fees is that the principle of selection does not necessarily relate to the quality of the product or its desirability by customers, but to the amount the producer is able (or willing) to pay to get the product on the shelves. Of course, there is not a total disconnection here between the products customers are willing to buy and what retailers are willing to stock, otherwise retailers would suffer. Still, a gap between the two may exist and this should be matter of concern to the ethical retailer.

Finally, the operation of slotting fees occurs, from the standpoint of customers, surreptitiously. Retailers are not open or transparent about the amount or the operation of those fees (see Quelch and Stern, 1993: 505). Hence, when customers find specific products on particular shelves in certain areas they may not realize (and certainly don't know) how much this is due to a fee the producer has paid to get those products placed there. Other, more desirable products (from the customer's standpoint) may be placed in less obvious places, or even not appear at all. As with other business arrangements, it does not seem that a retailer must make public the various economic deals it makes with producers. However, retailers, guided by the integrated marketing concept, cannot treat slotting fees simply as another source of income, without any consideration of their impact on the diversity of goods they display and the access to market that smaller producers may be denied.

As such, slotting fees may be justified by the costs of handling certain products, including removing them from the shelves and databanks if they fail to sell. However, the impact on customers with regard to diversity and quality of products, as well as on producer access to the market, must also be substantively factored into this determination. Retailers are not obligated to place any particular product on their shelves. However, if they treat producers differently in their demands for slotting fees, imposing the greatest burdens on small firms, then they also run the risk of being charged with an unjust use of channel power.

Retail sales

Retail selling occurs in a vast variety of different contexts. In all these contexts, retail sales raise ethical issues similar to those we have seen before, for example with regard to honesty, freedom, privacy, trust, and agency (vulnerability), but raise them in ways that make for their own difficulties. For example, if the retail salesperson is trained (more or less) to increase the chance of selling the store's products to customers, then one can imagine that without further training, any number of ethical problems might develop. This situation may be especially acute if the characteristics that make people effective salespeople are in tension with the ethical treatment of customers. For example, if the effective salesperson is one who has "abounding self-confidence, a chronic hunger for money, a well-established habit of industry, and a state of mind that regards each objection, resistance, or obstacle as a challenge" (McMurry, 1961: 118; see Kotler, 2000: 627), then there will inevitably be tensions with the ethical treatment of customers by such individuals. Guidelines, training, and monitoring will be necessary to have an effective, ethical sales force.

Honesty in sales

Several distinctions regarding the relevant moral values and principles will be initially helpful to sort through the ethical issues that retail sales raise. First, honesty may be viewed as both reactive and proactive. Frequently, questions of honesty arise when one person asks another a question and the second person must respond. But honesty can also require a person to tell another person something even if that person hasn't asked the appropriate question. Second, we might distinguish between honesty regarding the product (or service) to be exchanged and honesty regarding the current selling or exchange situation. It is one thing to be honest regarding the condition or nature of the product. It is another to be honest with regard to the conditions under which one is selling the product, what other competitors are doing, what other products are available, etc. – factors that constitute the selling or exchange situation. Third, we may distinguish between simple products (commodities) or services, and sophisticated ones. If the nature and quality of a product is relatively simple or easily understood by the customer, questions of honesty that the retail salesperson faces will be much less difficult than if the customer is considering a sophisticated product, whose features or condition are difficult to understand. Accordingly, salespeople should ask themselves what information is desirable, mandatory, or prohibited to reveal to customers about a product and the sale situation.

The product

What is the standard of honesty retail salespeople must meet with regard to the products or services they are selling to customers? The salesperson's responsibility is not (and cannot be) to tell literally everything about the product, goods, or service. The buyer would find such information overload unhelpful. Lawyers sometimes use this technique to bury the truth, rather than reveal it. If honesty involves portraying situations the way they are, telling someone everything might obscure important truths about the product or service in a mass of detail. In short, some pieces of information are more significant than others.

So what must a retail salesperson say about a product to a customer, and what is the justification for this? The various situations salespeople face are too numerous to list. But consider the following few.

Consider a sophisticated product regarding which the customer has little knowledge or understanding. In these situations, customers may fail to ask pertinent questions. Their "knowledge" about a product may be defective. In these cases, honesty requires not simply not deceiving or not lying to the customer, it also requires providing relevant information regarding the product. It would be morally ironic if a salesperson could, simply by remaining silent, insure his or her honesty. Instead, a salesperson must have some idea of the standard uses of such a product, as well as what the customer intends to do with the product.

However, it may be that salespeople themselves have little idea or understanding of some of the aspects of their products. The complexity of the product surpasses what it may reasonably be expected of a salesperson, who is not an expert in this kind of product, to understand. It is here that the producers and retailers must be forthcoming – either voluntarily or by being obliged by law and regulation – so that the consumer may be adequately informed. They place themselves and their salespeople at moral risk if the latter are not properly trained and do not have relevant materials with appropriate information.

What about a used product that a salesperson understands in terms of how it works, but regarding which he or she simply does not know whether this particular one has certain defects? Perhaps a car has a faulty water pump, but the problem has not shown up and the salesperson does not know about it. The salesperson can hardly reveal what he or she does not know. Not revealing this problem is not a question of his or her dishonesty.

If, however, the salesperson assures the buyer that the car is in top working order, even if a thorough check of the car has not been undertaken, then he or she is making an unsubstantiated claim. This claim may prove to be true, but if it turns out to be false (there was a faulty water pump), is the salesperson dishonest? In general, a person cannot be dishonest about that regarding which he or she is ignorant. In this case, it appears that the salesperson is trading on that fact. This is what suggests that this salesperson is dishonest. If the sellers of cars are supposed to have some knowledge of their cars, and this knowledge is supposed to be based on an examination of the car which was not in fact done – or which was done very inadequately – then the dishonesty here does not have to do with the specific case of the water pump, but with the basis upon which the person is selling the car. Hence, in a broad sense of "honest," it would seem that an honest person would either not make such unsubstantiated claims, or would indicate uncertainty – that he or she "*thought* that the car was in top working shape, but had not checked it out." In short, he or she would not make a categorical claim. To make such an all-inclusive claim while knowing that it has not been verified does suggest dishonesty.

The general moral consideration or principle here is that honesty requires providing accurate information, in response both to questions asked and to relevant questions not asked, in situations in which the legitimate expectations of the customer require that those questions be accurately answered. This principle does not refer to actual customer(s), but to legitimate or justified expectations that some (hypothetical) customer would have. "To determine exactly how much information needs to be provided is not always clear-cut. We must in general rely on our assessments of what a reasonable person would want to know" (Holley, 1986: 10). Certainly, any information that would materially affect the customer's decision should be disclosed.

Accordingly, we must avoid the intentional fallacy, i.e. the fallacy that a representation may be held to be morally justified only by looking to the intentions of the salesperson. A salesperson might not recognize that her well-intended acts nevertheless mislead or deceive some reasonable customers. Honest salespeople must also consider the state of the customer and his or her needs as well. They cannot simply look within themselves. They must consider the complex relation in which they stand with their customer.

If (part of) the point of morality is to prevent unjustified harm and to help resolve moral conflicts (chapter 1), then the greater the imbalance of power and knowledge between parties to an exchange, the greater will be the responsibility of the party in possession of the greater knowledge and power. Accordingly, in those cases in which customers may have little knowledge concerning the product or service (and where they are able to obtain such knowledge only with considerable difficulty), then retailers have greater responsibilities (whether or not they want them). In those cases, *caveat emptor*, which places the burden on the customer, will not be justified. Given the complexity of modern products, ordinary consumers cannot ascertain the nature or condition of important features of certain products by themselves. And yet these products are, in various ways, essential to their lives. Those who are in a position to make known the important and relevant features of these products have an obligation to do so. This obligation is the other side of the consumer's right to know or to have such information.

The selling situation

The selling situation raises different ethical issues regarding honesty. These may relate to the actual price at which a retailer is willing to sell some product, whether the product a customer is considering will soon be marked down as part of a sale, what price other competitors are charging, whether this item is really the last one they have in stock, etc.

Some of these questions are easier to answer than others. Whether some item is really the last one the store has is a factual matter. If there are others (or others are expected in a few days), then it is dishonest to say otherwise in an attempt to put pressure on a customer to buy a product. And for salespersons to say that they don't know exactly when more will be coming in, when this means they don't know the exact day or time, is also dishonest, if they do expect more to arrive in the near future.

Somewhat more difficult is the situation when a particular product a customer is interested in purchasing is going to go on sale the next day, or even the next week. A customer would want to know this, especially if the purchase was not time-critical. But this is not information that the buyer could obtain for himself by surveying the current market situation. This is a situation in which it would not be dishonest for the salesperson not to tell the customer (assuming the customer did not ask the question). Since the salesperson is the agent of the firm, revealing a new special sales date might not be permitted, even though it would be desirable for the customer to be informed of this upcoming sale. Furthermore, as argued above, since honesty does not require the salesperson to tell the customer everything that the salesperson might reasonably believe the customer would justifiably want to know about the sales situation, then honesty does not require telling the customer.

Still, customers may understandably feel that they have been unwitting victims of such a store policy. It is for this reason that many retailers offer customers a rebate if they buy a product within a certain time period before a sale takes place. Under those circumstances, customers feel less deceived. Again, this suggests that honesty requires more than simply not telling falsehoods or not engaging in deceptive actions. It may also require, even when not asked, various positive actions of providing information, which a salesperson may reasonably assume the buyer or the audience would want to know. Further, viewing honesty in this expanded manner may well have positive implications for an ongoing relationship of trust between customer and salesperson that may enhance this relationship and bring the customer back to the retailer.

A rather different question of honesty may seem to arise regarding the actual price at which a retailer might be willing to sell a product, especially when cars and houses are involved. Is it, for example, dishonest when a salesperson says that the absolute bottom price of the car is $25,000, and yet he is willing to take $23,500? Has he told a lie? A customer might think: "Well, if he were only honest he'd tell me what his bottom figure really is." But if this is a negotiated price then a customer may never know – and doesn't have a right to know – what that figure is.

How is this part of moral life? Wouldn't Kant be appalled? But here, as on other occasions, context is crucial. If this is a situation in which a negotiated price may be arrived at, the amount of dollars that a person or business would require to sell some product is not etched in bronze. That price may vary for a number of factors. Ultimately, it is what they are willing to take for it. But this can change as part of some negotiation. So a person might start out thinking "I must have $50,000," but end up thinking "I'll take $47,000." This would be indistinguishable from a person who began by thinking "I want $47,000, but let me see if I can get $50,000." So part of the problem here is the difficulty of ascertaining people's thoughts and beliefs.

Finally, consider a case regarding the price which some other store is charging. Suppose a salesperson has told a buyer the full technical details of a stereo she wants. Further, through this process the salesperson is also convinced that the customer knows what she wants and the product in question will nicely fulfill those wants. But now suppose that the salesperson knows that the same stereo is being sold by a competitor down the street for $50 less. Must the salesperson tell the customer this fact (see Ebejer and Morden, 1988: 338)?

Surely most customers would like to know this. However, it is plausible to think that the salesperson does *not* have to disclose this since this is not knowledge that he has in his expertise and role as a salesperson for the present business (see Ebejer and Morden, 1988: 338). Further, the buyer and anyone else could find out what other stores are charging for that stereo.

Assuming that a competitive market system is justified, the customer also has responsibilities to search out the best price on different items. One of the salesperson's responsibilities is to sell the products of store X, not those of store Y. Still, if store X does not have the product a customer wants, it may be permitted, though not required, for a salesperson to inform the customer about a product at some other store (even a competitor) that would meet that customer's needs/wants. This might even leave a positive memory in this customer about store X and lead to possible return visits. The level of confidence and trust in store X is increased.

It is important to remember that this retail salesperson relation with customers is a sales relationship. It is not the relation of two friends, of parent and child, or of a fiduciary to some group. In fact, salespeople are dishonest if they try to convince customers that they exist in one of these other relations. Of course, salespeople sometimes do this, by referring to a person as a "friend."

However, retail salespeople may also seek to form longer-term relationships with customers. In some cases, a retailer might inform a customer that he or she can get a product cheaper elsewhere. This is not demanded by honesty. Rather, it is a morally permissible, even morally admirable, step on the part of the retailer. Such candor, above and beyond the call of duty, may be rewarded by customers returning to the first retailer. Indeed, a television commercial for a car insurance company has focused on the willingness of this company to tell potential customers if they could get the insurance they wanted more cheaply at some other insurance company.

Accordingly, the general standard for honesty here is that the consumer ought to be adequately and accurately informed regarding information to which he or she may justifiably claim an interest. People may (and will) disagree over the extent of information, what "adequate" means, and how the person is to acquire that information. The salesperson has an important, proactive role to play here. Particular determinations regarding the fulfillment of this role depend on a host of factors. Our moral conclusions arise out of open discussions regarding these values and standards.

In general, "adequate information" means that the consumer has sufficient information to make a decision consistent with his or her best interests. This implies that in most situations involving complex products, a retail salesperson must disclose such information. Still, the extent of information depends upon the complexity of the product and the possibility that use (or misuse) of the product may harm the customer. However, the amount of information that honesty requires a salesperson to reveal is not the same as the requirement of honesty itself. This requirement, we have seen, depends upon the situation and the actor. Further, the honesty demands on marketers regarding the selling situation are less strong than those regarding the product.

Privacy in retailing

Depending on the locus of the sale, three major issues concerning privacy arise in retail sales. The first question pertains to what information retailers may gather on customers. The second regards how the information is collected. And the third concerns what use may be made of that information. Only the first and third issues are discussed here.

The information retailers gather on customers.   When a customer buys a product, retailers come to know certain things about the customer. For example, they know what products were bought, the means used to pay for those products, and where and when they were bought. Depending on the locus of the purchase, whether privately (online, by mail order) or in public, a retailer might also have access to other information, including a person's sex, race, religion, clothing preferences, marriage status, etc. In addition, if the purchase is made through a credit card or check, a retailer will acquire other information on a customer, for example the person's credit card number, home phone number, home address, and bank.

At the outset, information which does not pertain to the sale or the exchange itself should not be recorded or collected, even if it is available. In most cases, this would include information about parents' names, political preferences, or a customer's religion. Similarly, information about a person's health, whether they are married or not, their education, etc. are simply not relevant to most retail transactions. With regard to this relationship, those matters are private. Note that the standard here is not that information that might affect the transaction may be legitimately learned by the retailer. One's health might affect the purchase of a house. Similarly, one's sexual preferences or one's educational level might affect major purchases. But these are justifiably private. Customers have a right that such information remains private. Retailers have an obligation not to seek such information.

The point here is not that people will not give up this information. Some may be reluctant to do so, while others might comply. The point is that it is wrong for retailers to seek to collect it, even though it might benefit them. It follows that it is also wrong – even more so – for e-marketers to ask children or minors for such information. Privacy issues arise when marketers ask questions that are inappropriate, either to adults or to children. Hence, those e-marketers who have asked children for marketing information about their family's buying habits and interests have run afoul of marketing ethics.

In short, the collection of information about individual purchases that does not relate to those purchasing acts and the use of this information to build a profile of a customer violates that customer's privacy. Part of the reason is that it gives others the means to gain a form of access to them that no one else has and to which the customer either has not consented or ought not to consent. In this way, an unethical retailer would gain a certain form of control over the customer which would violate the latter's privacy.

The use of collected information.   What about the use of the information retailers collect? Let us assume that retailers only collect information to which they are entitled. Still, this does not mean that they can do anything with it. Just as physicians may collect private information about a patient, still they may not make any unauthorized use of that information.

First, retailers must make considerable efforts to ensure that private customer information remains private. With computer databases and the internet the dangers of the loss of confidential information have increased greatly. Stories of databases being "hacked" into, and of computers with confidential information on them being sold, lost, or stolen are increasingly frequent. Online commerce may involve private information of considerable significance regarding one's credit card numbers, social security numbers, income, and other private information. The possibility of identity theft or loss of information has become very real. Marketers must make special efforts (encrypted information, training of employees, firewalls, passwords, etc.) to ensure that private information with which they have been entrusted remains private.

Second, may such information be transferred or sold to some other group(s)? This is not always done for profit. For example, JetBlue Airlines shared its passenger information (names, phone numbers, and flight information) with a government defense contractor Torch Concepts, for use in a study on improving military base security called "Homeland Security: Airline Passenger Risk Assessment" (AMA, 2003). This was in violation of JetBlue's own privacy policy. They had told customers that the information would not be transferred, but it was. The Electronic Privacy Information Center filed a suit with the FTC accusing JetBlue of engaging in deceptive trade practices.

But suppose that the marketers inform customers that they intend to sell, share, or trade their information with other marketers. If customers have to deal with them, that gives them little recourse to privacy objections. Would it be sufficient, then, if retailers gave them the opportunity to request that such information not be included in these deals? In short, is it sufficient that customers are given the opportunity to opt out of having their information included in such deals? Or must e-marketers be required to get customers to permit (opt in to) such use of their information?

The danger with the former is that a customer may not see the opt-out opportunity, may not realize its importance, or may believe that if he or she opts out their current exchange with the e-marketer would be damaged. In short, there are features of this approach that will reduce the number of those who go ahead and opt out. On the other hand, if you require that retailers secure customer approval, i.e. that customers opt in, then we can be much more confident that customers will be clearly presented with this opportunity, that the importance of this decision may occur to them, though they may continue to believe that not opting in may affect their current exchange.

Does this place a special burden on the marketer? Perhaps, but not for anything that was rightfully theirs at the outset. This information is the private information of the customer. Hence, the customer should have an effective and failsafe means of determining how it should be used; it should not be used for the convenience or financial advantage of the marketer. Analogously, at grocery stores you may have to hand over a customer card to participate in any price savings they offer. Obviously you don't have to do this in order to buy groceries. In this sense, you must opt in.

A much more ethically desirable course of action is to render information retailers collect and transmit to others blind to specific individuals or customers. If the information that retailers collect and sell or trade to others cannot be used to identify individual customers, then the privacy rights of individuals would be protected.

Finally, beyond the information that retailers have stored on customers in their files and databases, they are also able to obtain, through other forms of technology, other kinds of information regarding customers which raise privacy concerns. Many retailers have access to video records of who visits a store. Security cameras could be used to compile a video record of a person's presence in a store and their purchasing behavior. Suppose that video record was then shared with the person's employer. Though the person is "out in public," the person is also in a private store. Our justified expectations of privacy vary from situation to situation. However, if we come to believe that any time we are outside of our own home, our behavior may be recorded without our being informed and our consent sought, and that this record may be turned over to others whose interests may not coincide with our own, then surely the area of our privacy will have shrunk considerably. People will have to become much more guarded in what they do and where they do it. This is not because what they may be recorded doing is unlawful or immoral. Not everything a person wishes to keep private is unlawful or immoral. Still, it may be personal, embarrassing, or simply nobody else's business.

In all these cases, how marketers respond to questions of privacy directly affects the levels of trust that customers have of marketers. A response that speaks to the privacy concerns of customers can affect the entire marketer–customer relation.

Retail sales pressures

Retailing also raises issues of freedom. Retailers can bring various pressures and forces to bear upon customers which may constrain or direct their decisions and behavior in ways such that we want to say that their freedom has been (negatively) affected. Conversely, they can do other things (provide more information, extend waiting periods before a contract becomes final) that expand people's freedoms. Rarely are the forces that constrain customers' freedom physical ones involving coercion. Rather, they are more subtle measures involving, for example, appeals to emotions (fear, self-regard), comments made to affect the perceptions of customers, store environments created to encourage buying, and efforts to alter customer risk assessments.

Such pressures may occur on both the particular and the general levels. With regard to the latter, it is obvious that retail shopping has become a "total experience" in which many retailers seek to leave nothing to chance. The light, sound, smells, and structure of the retail space have been carefully laid out. More than that, the shopping experience itself is something retailers are seeking to design and create. Skate parks, fishing ponds, and roller coasters are becoming part of the retail malls to which customers are drawn. Retailers have increasingly made a conscious effort to shape these locations so as to make the customer more open to, and eager to, engage in buying their products. To the extent that the excitement of entertainment is part of this experience people may linger while dropping their defensive mechanisms, and thus be more readily disposed to buy.

Do these aspects of retail selling place pressures on the customer that diminish their freedom or place them at an unfair disadvantage? On the one hand, customers can see the various things in front of them, hear the music, smell the air, etc. They have come to the mall themselves; they were not dragged there. Similar situations arise, some argue, when someone invites another person over for dinner, and puts on the "right music," lowers the lights, lights some candles, etc. Here the invited person supposedly willingly participates in this ritual. His or her freedom is not diminished, though certain choices may be encouraged. In both this case and that of retailers, it seems most plausible to see the situation as involving a relatively mild form of manipulation which does not, at such levels, constrain one's freedom.

But what about various particular cases? For example, a salesperson might play on one's emotions when he or she says that "These cars are going fast; this one may not be around much longer." Of course this could be true, and if true the salesperson is not the one placing pressure on the customer. Instead, the situation itself is a pressure-filled situation. But if the salesperson does *not* have reason to believe this, if the pressure is something he or she conjures up, is this still acceptable? Well, if this is a competitive situation, then in competitions one player is permitted to increase the pressure on others (though only in certain ways). This cannot be done (or it shouldn't be done) in tennis by talking or yelling at the other player. Nor should it happen in chess. But in football and baseball it is permitted. What about retailing?

Warning that a certain product may be sold if the customer doesn't buy it now is only one way of many to put pressure on customers to buy. Salespeople have also used guilt, as when, a salesperson encourages a bereaved son or daughter to buy an expensive coffin by saying "Surely you want to buy the very best coffin for your mother!" Again, by appealing to the notion of friendship, a salesperson might try to get someone to buy something to strengthen the bonds that friendship suggests. Or when salespeople have a number of customers together they can try to use peer pressure or embarrassment to get a person to buy certain things (e.g. time shares).

Are there any general guidelines here? Retail salespeople have an obligation to their employers to act in accord with the justified directives of the store. In short, they may not do anything qua employee of a store that contravenes these. Under this, however, they may reasonably be expected to represent the store and its products in their best light, while doing so without placing undo pressure upon the customer. Since customers and situations will differ, what is "undue pressure" in one circumstance will be reasonable pressure in another circumstance. Those who are vulnerable will be more susceptible to certain pressures than others. However, one form of "undue pressure" will be that which exists only in the representation of the salesperson. Hence, if a retailer knows that a product will not disappear quickly, then it is false and brings unjustified pressure on a customer to say that it will – or to give rise to that belief in the customer.

Salespeople can seek to persuade people to buy the products they sell by truthful and accurate reference to the qualities of the product. But the attempt to arouse fear by misrepresenting the situation is an ethically inappropriate form of pressure.

Finally, the use of pressures upon customers that are particularly vulnerable raises special ethical problems. Those customers who have suffered a death in the family, have a family member who is very sick, who are themselves underage, or perhaps aged (and uncertain of themselves) are not people who are "ripe for picking," but people who require special consideration. Salespeople ought not to take advantage of these vulnerabilities to sell their products or services. Indeed, they need, in advance, to make special arrangements as how to treat such individuals. Since he or she is older, a salesperson can bring great pressure to bear on children, for example. They must be keenly aware of the greater knowledge and power they have, with the consequent implications of potential for manipulation and exerting inappropriate pressures that this may bring.

In short, there is a background relation within which we recognize that salespeople may, in their effort to do their job, place pressures on people, but only in a manner that is within certain limits. Classes for salespeople on "how to close a sale" ought to discuss what these ethical limits are with regard to the pressures they can place on potential customers.

IV Customer Responsibilities

Previous discussions in this book have focused on how marketers should relate to customers. This is the standard approach of most marketing ethics discussions. Some have suggested that this emphasis is due (in part) to the emphasis in marketing on the marketing concept (see Polonsky et al., 2001: 118–19). I do not find this persuasive. Instead, marketing ethics can best be understood as a two-way relationship. What more generally should be said about customer responsibilities with regard to marketers?

Customers have various rights against marketers. These include a right to relevant information regarding the product or service a customer is considering buying, and rights with regard to product safety, non-deception in advertising, etc. These rights imply correlative obligations of marketers. But customers also have responsibilities, and correspondingly marketers have rights.

Among the more obvious responsibilities customers have regarding marketers are the following: acquiring the products and services they do in a legal and ethical manner; paying bills on time; informing themselves about their intended purchases; using the products they purchase in a manner that respects the safety limitations producers identify; and not purchasing goods they know have been produced in an illegal or unethical manner. Just as not all marketing responsibilities can be subsumed under the law, nor can those of customers.

Space does not permit consideration of all of these responsibilities (or others that have been identified or linked with special marketing situations). In the following, I will briefly consider a customer's responsibility regarding acquiring products in a legal and ethical manner, and their responsibility concerning products produced in unethical and illegal situations. The first responsibility is a broad one encompassing everything from shoplifting to dishonest dealing. Underlying each of these is a view of how this relationship should, more generally, be seen. Here too some contend that forms of warfare or gamesmanship play a role, even though these claims are susceptible to the same criticisms as those made in early chapters.

Customers and the law

As with marketers, it might seem that the law is at least a prima facie floor for customers. And one of the floor-level considerations is not taking what is not yours or what you are not entitled to. However, as is the case with marketers, customers also sometimes sink below this floor. Shoplifting is illegal, and yet marketers lose a great deal of merchandise to shoplifting every year.[5] When customers take things off the shelves and put them in their pockets, or handbags, or when they put on a dress or a shirt under their own clothing and walk out they are simply stealing products. Motel "guests" have taken towels, phone books, Bibles, blankets, light bulbs, etc. A more subtle form of this occurs when some customers change price tags on products in a store and try to buy the item they want under the cheaper price tag. The shirt for $75 is now $55, or the CD for $14.99 is now $9.99.

There are few ethical issues here. These acts are simply wrong. The ethical issue that can arise is whether a person is ever justified in engaging in illegal actions if they feel that they are being exploited or mistreated themselves. Though shoplifting is a form of theft, some customers feel "justified or "entitled" to do so since they also feel that they are being "ripped off" by the retailer. This is seen as simply the chance to "get even." Indeed, there is a great deal of anger and skepticism that many people feel against business. They feel that large businesses are exploiting them. They believe that they are not listened to or cared about. After all, some retail clerks express indifference to what a customer wants; many times the attempt to reach a business by telephone and to get service seems almost impossible (and when it is possible still requires a lengthy period of responding to computers telling one to press this or that number on the telephone); airlines bump people from flights, etc., etc.

These feelings of anger appear to some to justify theft, from significant items down to petty ones from retail stores. Clearly, however, these feelings and emotions do not justify such retaliatory actions. A person may feel aggrieved and not have been wronged. But even if wronged by a store, it does not follow that theft of that store's merchandise is the remedy. Further, people may take out their feelings of injustice on stores or marketers that did not wrong them. They are responding to other, more general, wrongs from business that they perceive themselves to have suffered.

At other times, the sense that people have is that businesses have a lot of money. They won't miss this item. Especially this is true when we are talking about very small items. For example, some people load up on ketchup and mustard packets at fast food stores. In some locations this has occurred to such an extent that stores have had to place these packets behind the counter, rather than leave them out for customers to help themselves. Again, such actions are not justified, though people use these rationalizations anyway.

There is a yet broader rationalization that customers sometimes have regarding business and that they also use to justify such actions. This is that marketing is a form of war (as some marketers have claimed) or a ruthlessly competitive game (see chapter 1). Some customers then adopt these metaphors and greatly admire those who respond in kind. To take advantage of a business's weaknesses is only doing what that business does to them. Given such general views they claim that the above actions are justified.

However, just as I argued previously that these war and game metaphors are unjustified when held by marketers, so too they are unjustified when held by customers. Neither they nor customer feelings of mistreatment by business justify customers in breaking the law. There is a form of rationalization that is going on here to justify what is simply in the self-interest of those customers. It is not an ethical justification.

Soft theft

Not all cases of illegality are so clear on the face of it, at least to those involved. One area in which this is true and in which new technologies such as the internet, etc. have had a profound effect is the downloading of music (and software) from other people on the internet.

The sense of many who do this is that what they are doing is not wrong – technically, they say, that they are simply sharing files with other people. If I lend you my shirt to wear for an evening, have I run afoul of any responsibility that I have to the Gap? That's unlikely. What if I let you have that shirt? Not so then too? Well, aren't music files the same?!

Not exactly. There are significant differences. One's music files can be shared with tens of thousands of other people, not just your best friend. They can then be used by all those people at the same time (in effect, my shirt has had multiple copies made). Suppose in the future scientists develop "replicators."[6] Then I could place my shirt in a "replicator" and you could then download a copy of my shirt at your house and wear it as long as you want, as I continue to do the same thing with the original. At that point, the ideas of sales, patenting, copyrighting, etc. would come into serious question. Accordingly, the assumptions we have made in the past about these notions are slowly (sometimes not so slowly) being changed. Napster was just one of the first cracks in the wall. With the ability to download books, music, newspaper and journal articles, etc., the notion of intellectual property rights is seriously challenged. People are getting something for nothing.

The argument of the intellectual property rights holders (the music companies etc.) is that people downloading music without paying for it are stealing. Their primary response seems to be to arrive at some way to scare customers enough so that they do not do this and yet come into the stores (or shop online with legitimate music sources) to buy the music they want. In short, they seek to force those downloading music (and other copyrighted materials) back into some format that respects the tradition of property rights.

The interesting ethical issues here have to do with what is property and what are the rights one (a marketer or a business) can be said to have when one is said to own something. We have two conflicting traditions here. On the one hand, there is the lending tradition, of books, and even of clothes and other items. Public libraries lend books and music, but are not accused of stealing from publishers, authors, and musicians. On the other hand, there is the tradition of property rights and the controls over the usage of one's own property. If I make something for sale and then sell it to you, I may assume that you won't replicate it and begin selling it to all my other potential customers, in effect "stealing" my property.

Due to the developments of the digital era our views of property are changing, but at the same time we seek to protect and guarantee property rights. We have few other examples like this in our other moral experiences. This makes thinking about such cases more intuitively difficult. However, consider people who buy pirated forms of music and videos on the black market. This can easily be done in most countries around the world. Is there anything wrong with this? Obviously large numbers of people do it, without a trace of remorse or guilt. The price is too good to pass up! Similarly, what about the buying of cheap knock-offs of brand goods, for example bags, pants, etc.? Since customers frequently do this knowingly, they are admitting that the illusion of the brand product is enough. So long as it looks "good enough" then they have the advantages of the brand name, without the costs. Still, in each of these cases a person is buying something that has been taken, or copied, from a producer without paying that producer/owner a fee of some sort. Though this is widely done and tempting to do, it is hard to see the ethical justification for it. The ethical customer would not do it. If this is the case, then by analogy it would seem such sharing of music and other copy-righted files is also unethical.

Some, of course, engage in a form of rationalization here when they note that Microsoft, or this or that record label, makes so much money, that it's OK to go ahead. But this form of consequential reasoning doesn't justify this, or else it would justify many other similar actions as I have argued above. If the present system is unjust in its distribution of wealth, that needs to be attacked directly and openly, rather than quietly and simply for individual benefit.

Dishonest dealing

There is an even softer form of "theft" that occurs. Some consumers have hit upon the idea of going to local stores, often rather small ones, and pumping the owner or clerks for information regarding particular products, for example cameras, computers, jewelry, etc. Armed with such knowledge, they then turn to the internet to buy the product for a lower price. Of course this means that the time the shop owner or clerk gave that customer was wholly lost. In effect, the customer acquired information from the shop in a costless manner (free to the customer, but not the shop) and then used it to reduce the purchase price from an outfit on the internet. Perfectly legal, but morally suspect. They have taken the retailer's time, drawn on his or her expertise, and given rise to false expectations or hopes (see Mills, 1998). But they "forget" the cost of these items to the retailer. Also to whom will they turn when the product they buy on the internet has problems or needs repairs? To the small retailer? Will he or she still be in business? The point here emphasizes the importance of seeing ourselves as living within an interdependent web of relations.

Mills refers to an ancient code of conduct in the Talmud known as the "Shopkeeper Law" which says that "One is not permitted to ask the storekeeper the price of an item if he knows he will not purchase it" (Mills, 1998: C4). As it stands this is too simple. One might not know whether he would or would not purchase something if he didn't ask the price (assuming that the price is not already displayed on the item). Epstein gives this a better interpretation by noting that this "law" means "you should be serious about intending to buy" (Mills, 1998: C4). "The rule is aimed at people who have no intention of buying, but who spend time learning in detail about a product from the storekeeper" (1998: C4).

Exploiting marketers' return policies

Retail companies have a variety of return policies with regard to customers and the products they purchase. Some of these may be exploited by customers to their own advantage. For example, some customers may return products which they themselves broke, but which they say were defective. Other customers may use the products they bought over a weekend or short period of time and then try to get their money back. The return rate on newly purchased large-screen televisions shortly after the football championship Super Bowl jumps sharply. Customers may lie about the reasons why they are returning a product. They may claim that it is unsatisfactory in some way, when in fact they simply wanted to purchase it for a single use. In short, problems of honesty are not simply one-sided.

Now it might be said that if stores have return policies that permit these behaviors, then they can't be wrong. And, of course, it isn't legally wrong. But neither did the stores, when they instituted such policies, believe or intend that they were engaged in a lending program for no money at all. There is a certain amount of tacit background knowledge that is part of this situation of which the customer is taking advantage, viz., that stores have policies which are not so discerning as to catch those who wish to "borrow" rather than "buy" the product. Normally, if one buys a product, then unless it is defective in some manner, it is now the property of the customer.

However, suppose a customer decides that he or she no longer likes or wants the product because of what it is or how it operates. Then it is up to the store to decide whether that is a sufficient reason to allow a customer to return it. The customer does not have a right to such a return. If, however, a customer no longer likes or wants the product because they only wanted it for a single occasion, and now seek to return it, they are themselves headed down a road of deception. They are treating the retailer as simply a means to their own ends. In short, they are mistreating the retailer.

In the past, stores such as Target, Nordstrom, etc. have had liberal policies of returning products. However, customers who have engaged in the above kinds of actions have taken (unfair, dishonest) advantage of these return policies. In doing so, they have undercut those policies. The universalization principle seems applicable here. The upshot is that many of these stores have begun to tighten their return policies. Unfortunately, those people who have a genuine reason to return a product might be negatively affected as a result.

Sourcing of products

What responsibilities do consumers have with regard to the sources of the products they buy and consume? If the goods are produced by workers who are badly exploited in some other country is that a problem? What if the diamonds are from a conflict zone, or clothing is from terrible sweatshops, or goods have been produced in totalitarian regimes? Should this make any difference to a customer? Does the marketplace wash away these unseemly aspects of the products we consume?

A first issue here is the extent to which a customer can know about the source(s) of the products he or she buys. Further, given globalization even such mundane items as tee-shirts may well be produced in more than one country. Certainly this is true with more complex products, for example cars, computers, etc. Perhaps some of the sources involved are benign, though others are not. What is one to do then? If one refuses to buy a product because some part of it comes from an unethical source, even though other parts of its sourcing are ethical, isn't one being unfair to the latter innocent source?

Labeling laws make it possible to know, in general, where one's clothing is made. Still, it is difficult to know the details of where other products come from, for example food, cars, furniture. Nevertheless, one can find out a great deal, if one tries, about the sources of the products one buys. Products that are made with cheap labor are products that save the customer money, but this possibility arises, of course, only on the back of the poorly paid laborer.

It may be asked: "What can I do about it?" The suggestion is a kind of consequentialist ethic in which unless the results are significant one need not do anything. However, if we think of our acts as revealing who we are, then even a single act may be important. The oft-told story of the young child who throws back a single crab into the ocean comes to mind. The beach is covered with crabs, dying from exposure. The worldly wise adult challenges the child on the point of throwing back a single crab. The answer is that to that crab it makes all the difference in the world. Often our perspective needs to be changed. Hence one argument is that an ethical customer does not purchase those kinds of goods simply because they are produced in ways they disapprove of, not that he or she doesn't purchase them because it will cause the producers to change their ways.

Of course, a further, stronger response is the consumer boycott. This can be done in a variety of ways. A customer can simply stop buying the products of a company. This would be a form of a silent boycott. Customers may also publicly stop buying those products through writing letters to the producer or to the local paper. More aggressively they may join groups protesting or lobbying against those practices, carrying placards outside a store, etc. The last response is a rather extreme measure for most customers. Whether it would be an obligation on the customer or simply morally permissible may be debated.

The strongest obligation here requires not purchasing or using goods that are produced through unethical or even illegal activities. To do so is to support or to take part (vicariously, at least) in those activities. In buying a product that was illegally or unethically produced, one is making oneself a member of a supply chain that permits the illegality to exist. The response that such proactive responsibilities are fairly limited because one cannot (individually) do much is emblematic of the difference between appealing to consequences and focusing on the principles themselves that define who a person is.

In short, customers have a host of responsibilities when it comes to their interactions with marketers. These responsibilities emphasize the fact that we can understand the marketer–customer relationship and marketing ethics only if we consider both sides of this relationship. If marketing ethics is to be a reality both sides of this relationship must acknowledge their own responsibilities. Only this will fully capture the integrated marketing concept.

V   Conclusion

This chapter has examined the promotional aspects of marketing that reach the public most directly, viz., advertisements and retailing. If marketers had a clean ethical bill of health in these areas it is safe to say that the complaints against marketing would fall considerably. At the same time, the level of confidence in marketers would rise greatly.

I have maintained that marketers and customers exist within a system of relationships such that we should view marketing ethics as encompassing both marketers and customers. Both members to this relationship have rights and responsibilities. Under the headings of "Advertising" and "Retailing" I have considered responsibilities and rights that marketers have with regard to customers. Though the responsibilities of customers to marketers are not frequently emphasized, they too deserve our attention. They are part of this relationship. In some of the instances I have briefly noted, customers cannot portray themselves simply as unwitting victims. They too must fulfill the values and norms identified in previous chapters. Still, marketers must shoulder the great part of the burden of setting high ethical standards when it comes to advertising and retailing. When they do, everyone is better off.

Notes

1   One might consider how similar this situation is to the issue, noted in chapter 2, regarding marketers falsely portraying themselves as market researchers while seeking to make a sale or to solicit donations.

2   Jackson also holds that "lies can be acted as well as spoken" (Jackson, 1990: 53). Hence a person can lie through a nod of the head or a gesture, so long as the acted deceit is also a communication to the person lied to.

3   See U.S. Department of Health and Human Services: <http://pathwayscourses. samhsa.gov/vawc/vawc_supps_pg12.htm>, accessed March 5, 2005.

4   Merriam-Webster Online Dictionary, <http://www.m-w.com/>, accessed August 23, 2006.

5   According to the 15th Annual Retail Theft Survey, "over $4.7 billion was lost to shoplifting and employee theft in just 25 U.S. retail companies in 2002, with only 2.43 percent of those losses resulting in a recovery": <http://retailindustry.about. com/cs/lp_retailstore/a/bl_jlh100603.html>, accessed June 27, 2006.

6   With apologies (and thanks for the idea) to Star Trek.

Chapter Five

Marketing in a Global Society

I Introduction

The preceding chapters focused on marketing and those it directly affects with little regard for more global aspects of marketing. Looking at ethical issues bound up with product development, pricing, distribution, advertising, and retailing is crucial for developing a marketing ethics.

However, marketing's ethical implications extend far beyond those particular customers it directly impacts in local and national commercial contexts. Over the past half-century a global extension of marketing has taken place in two very different ways. On the one hand, marketing has been employed in communities and places around the world that it had not previously touched. On the other hand, marketing has been applied within each society to areas heretofore not its object. Both of these extensions of marketing are considered in this chapter.

With regard to marketing's employment in other societies, marketers not only face different customs and moral rules, but they are also challenged to consider the cultural impact of the goods and services they bring to those countries. The topic of ethical relativism arises naturally here. What are the ethical responsibilities of marketing in other societies? Specific issues arise with regard to bribery, gift-giving, and corruption, as well as doing business in cultures with values seemingly opposed to one's own basic moral values.[1] In addition, marketers may be charged with employing sweatshops and child labor to produce their goods, marketing various controversial products (tobacco, chemicals and drugs not approved in their home country, etc.), and altering traditional channels of distribution in ways that harm local and societal traditions. Given that growing numbers of marketing firms receive major portions of their profits from overseas, this area of marketing ethics is of considerable importance (see Singhapakdi and Vitell, 1999).

The extension of marketing within (each) society has impacted all areas of our lives. In addition to all the usual commercial places, we find marketing's presence in schools, churches, textbooks, bathrooms, political campaigns, social causes, and environmental movements. The ethical implications of this extended use of marketing deserve close study. Of course, some maintain that if you have a great product (be it a political candidate, religious cause, or social problem in need of treatment), there is nothing better than bringing the powers of marketing to bear. However, others argue that viewing politicians, religious doctrines, or environmental concerns as "products" and the object of marketing is to adopt inappropriate commercial assumptions and world-views. This extension of marketing, they say, runs afoul of important ethical values and views about the good life.

This chapter concludes by looking at a third extension marketing faces, viz., how ethical marketing can be fostered. If marketing is to be ethical, we cannot simply place the responsibility on individuals, but must look more generally at the firms and societies in which marketers work. To focus simply on the former and not look at broader, social dimensions of marketing is to miss the forest for the trees. Given the wide variety of ethical issues in marketing, what steps can marketing take to be ethical? Does ethical marketing require changes in the mindset of marketers, as well as codes of ethics, the involvement of professional associations, and changes in various background institutions (such as the law and government regulations)? The answer to these questions is, I believe, "Yes." Sometimes marketers have to work together (and with others) to solve problems that their individual behaviors foster or create. Marketers are, at one and the same time, citizens, and fellow human beings. They cannot consistently or morally go to work and create a society in which harm is done, or a society less good than could otherwise have existed, and then go home and deplore that situation.

II Marketing and Other Societies

"The globalization of the economy" is a well-worn phrase, but one that reflects the fact that the economies of all nations, with very few exceptions, are now significantly interconnected. In addition, the collapse in the early 1990s of the bipolar world has led to much greater acceptance of market-based econo-mies and, consequently, the important role that marketing plays. With this there has been a steady increase in the internationalization of marketing, even though there have been considerable disputes over the nature and desir-ability of this global extension of marketing. Still, in a time during which corporations such as Gillette, Coca-Cola, and Johnson and Johnson earn over 50 percent of their profits overseas, marketers can hardly avoid the moral dimensions of marketing internationally.[2]

The globalization of marketing has been characterized by marketers placing their branded products in markets in many, if not most, countries around the world. For some marketers their primary growth markets are outside North America and Europe. For others, the developing world simply offers significant access to new and important markets. The upshot is the availability of Coca-Cola in small Indian villages, music CDs in the villages and towns of South America, and Toyota vehicles in remote areas of Africa. In addition, due to technological advances, fewer regulations, and the desire for financial investments by developing countries, marketing companies have been able to extend their distribution and promotion networks through advertisements, billboards, networking, entertainment, gifts, etc. in ways unimaginable 50 years ago. Finally, many companies, for example Nike, have simply constituted themselves as international marketing companies dependent on less expensive natural resources and cheap (though sometimes highly skilled) labor from around the world as part of their business plan. They themselves don't manufacture anything. They simply focus on the marketing of products. Hence, questions of the sourcing of products, and the conditions under which this takes place, are crucially part of global marketing.

In each of these cases, the products, promotions, and outsourcing are not ethically "neutral." They carry with them, both explicitly and implicitly, values, norms, assumptions, and expectations regarding human behavior. In the case of the products themselves, marketers have explicitly sought to associate certain values and attitudes with these products through branding. The use of factories in developing countries that have limited health and safety protections for workers also signals certain values and attitudes regarding employees. One shouldn't be surprised when some people in various countries complain that these products and forms of marketing are exploitative or part of a value imperialism. Whether or not either of these is involved, certainly there is the implicit transfer (if not the imposition) of the values associated with these products and forms of labor. Of course, sometimes this isn't bad. Some values and behaviors in most countries (including the U.S. and European nations as well) should be changed. But how that happens, who makes it happen, and for what reasons is the basic set of questions that needs to be answered.

There is, then, a host of ethical issues that arise for international marketing. Among them are: bribery, kickbacks and corruption; gifts and entertainment; different product standards between countries – for example selling products that are deemed harmful in a developed country to those in developing countries; respect for different cultures and ways of life; intellectual property rights; problems with pricing, for example dumping products in another country at below-cost prices; misuse of products sold in developing countries (e.g. Resistol, infant formula); respect of human rights; and environmental standards and regulations.

Behind each of these issues lie questions regarding the use or application of value and normative standards in different countries and parts of the world. The basic issue here is whether marketers can look to underlying global ethical standards that can be applied in different countries, or whether they must seek out different ethical standards for each of the countries in which they operate. After this basic question is addressed, each of the above ethical issues itself deserves particular consideration. Since it is impossible to treat all the previously listed issues in this book, I will first examine the underlying question regarding general global ethical standards and then select a few of the above topics to discuss as examples of the ways in which marketers need to proceed.

Global ethical standards or ethical relativism?

The most basic issue here has to do with the apparently different values and norms that define different societies and the people within them, as well as the implications of these differences for global marketing. These different ethical stances seem to point in the direction of the relativism of values. If this is true, the significance of such relativism would mean that marketers morally ought to follow the local (or societal) standards of the countries they operate in. They would have to act as the Romans act, at least when they are in Rome. They could not appraise the values or behaviors of another society from a perspective not linked to some particular society. But is ethical relativism the correct view?

It is very clear to anyone who has lived in another country that other countries have different cultures, sights, sounds, smells, rhythms, expectations, and values than one's own home country. This doesn't mean that these are all incompatible with one's home values, though many seem to be. But different they are. And depending on the country one lives and works in, they may be extraordinarily different.

To discuss how marketers ought to respond to the different morals and normative situations of other societies, it will be helpful to distinguish among values and norms in three different ways: first, the values and principles according to which people (individually and as groups) *do* in fact live; second, those they *believe* they ought to live by; and third, those by which they *ought* (all things considered) to live.

For almost everyone, there is, typically, some discrepancy between the first two. Suppose that we described the values and principles in a society both in terms of how people do in fact act, and in terms of how they believe they ought to act. These two related (we may assume) sets of values and principles would each constitute a *descriptive ethics*. The further apart they are, the greater the hypocrisy and disconnect within a society. The closer they are, the greater the moral consistency and integrity of people in that society. Anthropologists and sociologists might be quite adept at developing such accounts. Thus, their descriptions of the moral values and principles of Buddhists in Tibet or Sunni Muslims in Egypt would most likely reveal that people in these societies actually live by different values and principles than those they profess. This will be true of any society.

We might also distinguish between values or norms that are basic (e.g. to do good, be just), and those that may be derived from them (e.g. care for children, defend a non-corrupt system of justice). Now if the most basic values that one group of people lives by differ from those that other groups of people live by then we would have an instance of *cultural* (or *descriptive*) *relativism*. What is believed to be right in Romania is not believed to be right in Rwanda. In this case, it is often supposed there could be no rational appeal when the two systems conflict.

However, there is a gap between affirming that different societies believe different things are morally right or wrong (even with regard to their basic moral beliefs) and maintaining that, all things considered, different things are morally right or wrong for these different societies. The former (as was just noted above) is an instance of descriptive ethical relativism. The latter is a case of *normative ethical relativism* that holds that what is really right in one society is not (or may not be) right in another society.

For normative ethical relativism to be a significant view, it must apply to a society's *basic* values and principles, not ones that are *derived from* basic values and principles. The reason is that due to different factual conditions and other non-moral beliefs that people in one society may have, they may come to have moral beliefs and judgments that systematically differ from those of other societies even though they hold the same basic moral beliefs. They differ, then, not because of their underlying moral beliefs but because of the different factual situations in which they find themselves. It is the situations that differ, not the basic moral values and principles. In short, it is possible to have universal values and principles which are applied in different situations with different results. Their situational application does not render them non-universal.

There have been strong objections against normative ethical relativist views. If societies have different basic moral views, then it appears that there is not a common basis that could be invoked for the rational resolution of disputes between societies. Such disputes could not be resolved so much as won through the use of power, emotional appeals, or the eradication of those who differ. In addition, if what is right is simply what one's society says is right, then it would not be possible for members of that society to morally criticize their own society for anything other than hypocrisy or the failure to live by the society's standards. In short, ethical relativism seems to imply that any fundamental ethical criticisms of moral behavior in that society would be impossible. Such an implication seems contrary to fact, counter-intuitive, and ethically troublesome.

Further, the descriptive ethical relativism which many take to be a significant argument in defense of normative ethical relativism has not been conclusively established. There is considerable dispute among anthropologists and sociologists over whether the basic values and norms do differ among different groups of people. A number of anthropologists and sociologists have argued that there are various ethical values and principles that are universally common. Some hold, for example, that principles like the Golden Rule are recognized and accepted by all societies. Similarly, courage, love, friendship, integrity, and reciprocity are also recognized by all human societies. These may be interpreted variously by different societies, but this does not mean that there isn't some commonality with regard to these values and norms across societies. Hence, one must be wary of those who hold that "because of the range of societal values (be they religious, philosophical, or cultural), there are no absolute, universally accepted ethical standards" (Schollhammer, 1977: 54). Finally, the mere fact that a group of people sincerely hold a certain value or norm, and even act by it, does not imply that that value or norm is one according to which they should act. It may involve prejudice, bias, or discrimination. It is not for lack of sincerity that racists and Nazis have been ethically criticized, but for their views themselves.

Consequently, there are strong reasons to look beyond cultural and ethical relativism. Even if cultural and ethical relativism were true, the significance of this view is a matter of some debate because its truth does not, by itself, demonstrate how people *ought* to act. In short, the fact that people in different societies act on different values and principles, and even that they believe that they ought to act on those values and principles that differ basically among societies, does *not* show that those are the principles and values by which they *ought* to act. People in some societies have sincerely believed in slavery as well as the destruction or domination of various religious or minority groups. It surely is ethically questionable whether anyone ought to live by these values, regardless of how sincere they are. In short, sincerity of belief is not an acceptable justification of a person's or a society's moral beliefs.

Alternatives to relativism

Moral absolutism

If ethical relativism should be rejected, what are the alternatives? One response has been to maintain that there is a set of absolute principles that hold for all times and all places. These standards require virtually the same kinds of behavior in all societies. Thus, men and women should treat each other the same in all countries. Similar forms of behavior are required when it comes to gift-giving, employee–employer relations, product standards, treatment of animals, and the environment.

While this view may satisfy some people's need for sameness and consistency, it undercuts the importance of the contexts of different societies. It imposes a numbing sameness on all cultures. And though it may recognize various ways in which cultures, personal identities, and moralities are bound up, it does so, in effect, to reject them. Rules are rules; norms are norms; and there is essentially one way of going about things.

There is a marketing view analogous to such absolutism that appears in the arguments of those who defend the standardization of products across all societies (Levitt, 1983). For example, Levitt distinguished the multinational corporation that makes efforts to accommodate its products to the local culture from the global corporation that "operates with resolute constancy . . . as if the entire world (or major regions of it) were a single entity; it sells the same things in the same way everywhere" (Levitt, 1983: 92–3). Part of his justification for supporting such a view is that "the world's needs and desires have been irrevocably homogenized" (Levitt, 1983: 93). The upshot, he claims, is that "this makes the multinational corporation obsolete and the global corporation absolute" (Levitt, 1983: 93).

The problem with Levitt's argument (and such absolutist views) is several-fold. First, the fact that people in different societies all enjoy Coke, listen to transistor radios, or watch television does not mean that they all have the same homogenized desires. They will hear and see different things on their electronic devices. And the fact that they drink Coke doesn't mean that they don't have a host of other non-homogenized desires. Second, contrary to Levitt, marketers have in fact adapted their products and continue to do so. The Coke sold round the world may be exactly the same everywhere, but McDonald's and other global marketers adapt or vary their products depending on local tastes and situations.

Third, as noted above, it is mistaken to think that these products are simply value-neutral or culturally neutral. Most of them are branded products and, as such, carry some very definite value and attitudinal associations encouraged by their owners. At the most general level, they carry value implications having to do with, for example, the speed of communication, preparation, and design by others who may have a considerable reputation for taste, individual access to and control of such products and their uses, mobility, etc. Fourth, marketers are not simply responding to homogenized tastes, but fostering such tastes through their products and marketing programs. The absolutist marketing approach does this explicitly. Finally, even homogenized products may be put to uses tied to cultures which have very different values and aims, for example television programs used to spread Islamic jihad movements. At best, then, standardized products respond to a common desire to spread or realize one's own values and desires, which may be distinctly different from those of other societies (see Johansson, 2004: 96–103, and also 63–5).

I don't deny that there has been greater homogenization of tastes, wants, and behavior around the world as the result of the global business and international marketing of the last 50 years. Still, this doesn't resolve the issue of the importance of context in morality, as well as in marketing. And since context and reasons are bound up, it should be clear that context does matter when it comes to morality (Donaldson, 1996). For example, someone who maintains that one should always tell the truth, regardless of the context, is clearly an absolutist. But while such rigidity may "honor" the norm of truth-telling by defending it without regard to circumstance, it actually undercuts morality, since truth-telling is simply one of many norms that we should live by. Those who insist on a single norm of this type will find that people will have to reject or deny all other norms, for example saving lives. They will protect truth at the cost of acting morally. On the contrary, which norms rise to the top in our moral deliberations depends on what the circumstances are within which we must act. Moral absolutism must be rejected as an alternative to relativism.

Constructive pluralism

A more reasonable approach neither ties morality simply to different individual societies and the differences that exist among them, nor identifies it with a set of unyielding, context-insensitive absolute norms and values. Instead, it allows for the importance of context, recognizes commonalities among societies, identifies more specific norms or values that have action-guiding potential to them, and speaks to the process by which that action-guidance is obtained. This "middle" view I have called "constructive pluralism" (see chapter 1). For present purposes, its relevant features can be captured by the following several points.

First, values and norms can be identified at different levels of abstraction. The most universal and general are taken to be the most basic since they are supposed to encompass all others. These have included the principle of utility and Kant's Categorical Imperative. They are arrived at through a process of abstraction from more substantive values and norms. How much direct or practical guidance they can provide has been a matter of considerable dispute. Further, as I argued in chapter 1, it is doubtful that they can be reduced to a single ultimate principle applicable to everyone.

Second, substantive or action-guiding values and norms are less abstract and general. Examples might include justice, freedom, trust, truth, well-being, honesty, love, courage, fidelity, beneficence, the Golden Rule, etc. Still, at both this level of abstraction and the most general, these values and norms are shared around the world. However, the route by which we move from these substantive values and norms to more particular ones, and the resulting actions and policies, is through a path involving explicit and implicit knowledge, contextualization, and moral interpretation. It is not a simple process of deduction through conjoining such moral principles with particular factual contexts.

Third, this process takes several forms. It includes formulating various lower-level rules that are compatible with more general values and norms. They may be expressed by more specific rights, for example to life, property, health services, and privacy. Further, it involves distinguishing between (minimal) moral values and norms that are crucial to prevent conflict – what some have referred to as the worsening of the human predicament (Warnock, 1971) – and more maximal values that pertain to different forms of a good life (Walzer, 1994). This distinction is important, since what is required to prevent conflict is more restricted in scope and more universal than is what is part of a good life.

With regard to the former, moral injunctions against physically and psychologically harming other people are crucial. Similarly, moral norms related to keeping one's word, treatment of guests, and reciprocity are all important. In addition, the important role of trust has received considerable discussion in recent years. And though Fukuyama has characterized different societies in terms of being high- or low-trust, the importance of some form of trust is clearly crucial to all societies and to morality itself (Fukuyama, 1995).

With regard to the broader realm of the good life, this can plausibly take different forms. These will be framed, in part, through other significant, though non-moral, personal or individual characteristics and values that will be embedded in the psyche of those living in the different societies. Accordingly, our motivations may be different. For example, McClelland has described the important role that the desire or need to achieve plays in the West.[3] Along these lines, Terpstra has pointed out that early disciples of Hinduism were taught that concern with earthly achievement was a snare and a delusion, while St. Benedict, a dedicated Christian, said that to work was to pray (see Lee, 1981: 59).

Likewise, Hofstede has identified a number of different value continua by which he has distinguished different societies. They include:

(a) power distance
(b) uncertainty avoidance
(c) individualism–collectivism
(d) masculinity–femininity (Hofstede and Hofstede, 2005)

More recently he added (e): long term–short term orientation. For example, according to the masculinity–femininity category, some societies might value performance, independence, and ambition more highly than quality of life, interdependence, and service. Other societies tend to do the opposite. These value continua relate to various capabilities people have that can be developed in different ways. Still, they are subject to a twofold evaluation. First, they are not acceptable "choices" if they run afoul of the minimal moral norms. Second, they may be faulted if the forms they take, in light of the development of their other capabilities as well, are less complete than they could be (see Nussbaum, 2000).

Fourth, the obvious implication is that people in different societies will continue to disagree over the various (moral) judgments they make. Yet these conflicting judgments will not arise because people have wholly different basic values. Instead, they occur because (among other things) people weigh moral and non-moral values on a number of common continua in different ways. They interpret common substantive norms involving justice and freedom in different ways based, in part, on different historical experiences, economic conditions, and religious beliefs.

Accordingly, when we look at any ethical situation in which a moral value or principle is invoked or a judgment is made, we must look at the surrounding meanings, context, and interpretations in order to understand why any particular action was performed. Whatever principles and values are identified, their meaning, significance, and application will be affected by the society in which they are operative. For example, "in many Arabic countries, a handshake is worth more than a written contract, and Arab business executives may be insulted if a contract is suggested" (Zikmund and d'Amico, 1993: 467). The idea that one must ask for a written contract is viewed, not as a willingness to consummate a deal, but as an indication of a lack of trust or an unwillingness to trust. It is against this background context that we might have a potential (ethical) problem if a non-Arab businessperson insists on a contract.[4] Both businesspeople value trust and commitments, but they believe in different ways of securing them.[5] Surely, these differences might affect the distribution system which one wished to set up. At the least, it would influence how one went about setting it up.

The important point is that there is not simply one way of doing things that is ethically justified for all societies. Or, rather, that doing the "same" thing in different countries may have very different ethical implications because of different background meanings and understandings. Any marketer worth his or her moral salt must understand this. Within broad limits, it is the idea or the meaning that is important, not this or that particular form of behavior.

Consequently, disagreement among people from different cultures will oftentimes be over factual or customary matters rather than moral ones. Under factual disagreements may also fall different assessments of the danger of a product and hence different willingness to allow certain products to be produce or distributed. Sometimes disagreements will be over theological or metaphysical matters rather than moral ones. For example, people in different societies may experience time differently. In Western society, people are said to follow a monochronic order, scheduling one thing at a time, with no overlapping. In Asian societies, it is claimed that people follow a polychronic order (Hall, 1983). Other researchers say that, in Africa, time is experienced in terms of a basic distinction between things that have happened and things that have not happened (see Morello and Van der Reis, 1990; Morello, 1993: 307).

In any case, it is crucial for marketers to determine exactly what the bases of these differences are, for example, factual, moral, metaphysical, historical, or developmental. The means of addressing these differences will differ depending upon their nature. If the differences are factual, scientific means may be brought to resolve them. This is not possible where the differences are metaphysical. If they are developmental, only time or additional aid may help. And if they are moral a variety of techniques, as noted in chapter 1, may be required, for example identifying the nature and contours of the basic concepts involved, examining the arguments for and against their present interpretations, determining the centrality of such values or norms, etc.

Finally, the upshot is that neither normative relativism nor absolutism is correct. Instead, we see that all human societies exist within certain common moral bounds, even though those bounds themselves do not have sharp borders and may be variously related to each other. Still, they are real as well as plural.

Interpretation and recognition of context are important to resolving moral disputes, both within as well as between cultures. In approaching moral issues in this manner, it is important to recognize spheres of moral centrality. At the very center lie the most crucial moral norms and values regarding not harming, in various gratuitous or unjustified ways, other people and living beings. Hence, the use of slave labor to produce products or the willful distribution of products that will inevitably harm their users (without their knowledge) may be justifiably condemned wherever it occurs. Matters of fundamental justice and the most basic human rights are also found here. Further out lie matters of doing good to other people, helping them, and less basic human rights (e.g. to leisure). And on the periphery lie matters that are voluntary, questions of style, and idiosyncratic aspects of the good life. This means that the principles of morality are not simply "given" for all time. They are open to (and require) constant interpretation, contextualization, etc. These distinctions and differences, however, do not imply, as relativists suggest, that we cannot criticize ourselves or other societies.

Marketing implications

Several important implications follow regarding international marketing ethics and the impact that marketing may have on different societies. First, marketers must recognize the differences between themselves and those they deal with. If they fail to recognize these differences they will, at best, manage to escape difficulties. At worst they will offend and make missteps which will harm them and possibly those they deal with. There are endless examples of instances in which marketers have not taken account of such cultural differences. Some of these are simple cases of foolishness or carelessness that don't morally offend. Thus, when Kentucky Fried Chicken attempted to use its well-known phrase "finger-lickin' good" in China, the translation came out "eat your fingers off" (Ricks, 1993: 73). Similarly the Sunbeam Corporation ran into problems when it sought to introduce its "Mist-Stick" into the German market, not realizing that "mist" in German means "excrement" (Ricks, 1993: 36). In these cases we can laugh at the mistake, though for those involved it was surely no joke and might have been career-ending. However, in other cases, questions of morality and moral offense do arise. A Japanese whiskey was to be sold in the U.S. as "Black Nikka," until some black Americans indicated that they found the new name to be demeaning (Ricks, 1993: 41). And people in Britain resented the use of American ads featuring children and messages directed at children. They were deemed an improper way to try to influence children (Ricks, 1993: 62). These blunders and blindness to local conditions result in failed business projects as well as the creation of moral disputes. They remind us that context matters.

Second, part of recognizing cultural and ethical differences is that marketers must recognize their own *ethnocentrism*, i.e., the tendency to view one's own culture and traditions as superior to those of others. Marketers, like other people, are tempted to see others different from themselves as having not only different, but lower standards. Thus, there are many studies which show that people tend to view other people and those in other societies as acting in ways that are less fair and less moral or reputable than themselves (Messick and Bazerman, 1996). For example, a study by Fritzsche and Becker surveyed marketers in three countries – the U.S., France, and Germany – asking them to evaluate the ethical standards in marketing in ten countries (Fritzsche and Becker, 1984). The results were strikingly different. Marketers from the U.S. rated the ethical standards of U.S. marketers the highest, while those in Germany ranked U.S. ethical standards seventh, and those in France rated them third. Overall, Germany was perceived to have the highest ethical standards, followed by the United Kingdom, the U.S., and then France. Of the countries surveyed, those seen as having the lowest ethical standards were Mexico, India, and Italy (Fritzsche, 1985: 86–7). Similarly, a Touche Ross survey showed that US executives placed the ethical standards or behavior of the U.S. far above those of other countries (Touche Ross, 1989: 6; see Laczniak and Murphy, 1993: 212).

It is possible, however, when the values of one's own society differ from those of another society, that the other society's values are the correct ones, not one's own. But this is very infrequently considered to be the case when people confront these differences. The other side of this point is that those from roughly the same traditions can be expected to have more similar values than those from very different traditions. For example, Armstrong et al. conclude that "Australians and Americans have similar perceptions of the ethical problems normally encountered in international marketing, and differ very little with regard to ethical issues and management practices related to ethical problems" (Armstrong et al., 1990: 14; see Lee and Sirgy, 1999).

Third, in order to operate effectively and ethically in other countries marketers must be clear on what their own underlying values and norms are and the ways in which acting upon them can be reasonably defended when operating in other countries. In short, how extensive is the scope of those values and norms? Can they be reasonably defended as universal in scope? Marketers must also be knowledgeable of the contexts in which they are operating so that their interpretations of these values and norms in those contexts are justifiable. They must also have an effective strategy that links their marketing with their values and norms, as well as with the real situations in which they do business. Some of the implications regarding this last point are taken up in the last part of this chapter, where we look at fostering ethical marketing. It remains, then, to consider some of the more specific ethical issues these points raise for marketers.

Four more specific issues (there are many others) that marketers face in international markets include: gifts; bribery and corruption; controversial products; and the conditions surrounding the source(s) of one's products.

Gifts

In the previous chapter, the role of gifts within retailing was briefly considered. When the topic of gifts arises in an international context, the issue is even more complicated. As in the earlier discussion, the underlying ethical issue concerns when a person may (or even should) give another person something of value in a business relationship, and when they should not do so. By "giving something of value" I refer to things such as money, entertainment, various kinds of objects (e.g. televisions, cars, horses, or even chickens[6]), discounts on products, as well as services (even prostitutes). One of the central underlying moral issues here (as noted in chapter 4) is whether business activities should be based on merit considerations alone, or whether personal factors may or should enter in. Those who defend a meritarian view assume that a business relationship can (and should) be strictly separated from personal and friendly relationships.

The practice of gift-giving differs according to whether it occurs between close friends and relatives or in more official contexts such as in business (of course this presupposes that we draw a distinction between personal life and business life). In private contexts, to give a gift is to give something one values with the expectation that the person receiving it will also value and appreciate the gift. Ideally, gifts are given as an expression of one's friendship or relationship, but may also be given for any number of other reasons, including etiquette, social pressure, gratitude for having received a gift oneself, a wish to curry favor, or a desire to impress someone. However, gifts are also seen, quite generally, to bring with them obligations of gratitude on the part of the gift receiver and even of reciprocity with regard to a return gift. Some societies, for example the Kwakiutl, developed gift-giving into elaborate displays of power and influence. In any case, gifts typically are part of reaffirming or fostering a relationship between people in which different forms of future reciprocity are anticipated.

In business contexts gifts may also be given for various motives: to show esteem, reaffirm friendship, impress others, win attention, influence others in the relationship, as well as influence others in their decisions regarding the relationship. When the last motive is the operative one, gift-giving may become a form of bribery (which is discussed below).

To avoid charges that gifts are given (or received) in order to influence official decisions to be made on a basis other than the merits of the case, many companies have instituted policies forbidding the receipt of any but the most minimal gifts. Some limit gifts received to $25; others place a $100 limit; and some simply speak of gifts of moderate value. Similarly, restrictions have been placed upon the kind of entertainment one may accept or provide to business clients. Ironically, some companies restrict the gifts its employees may receive, but do not limit the dollar amount of the gifts its employees can give!

Policies that limit gifts may come into conflict with the business and cultural practices of other countries in which gift-giving plays an important role in creating and maintaining reciprocal relationships. As I have argued before, marketers must evaluate occasions of gift-giving by considering the nature of the situations they face. A rigid, hidebound approach to morality and moral codes without looking to the meanings and situations is not appropriate. Thus, it matters a great deal whether the value of the gift is relatively minor or something approaching millions of dollars. It matters whether the gift can be given publicly or whether it can only be given privately and secretly. It is important if the point of the gift is to create or reaffirm a relationship, or it is to persuade an official not to execute the responsibilities he or she would otherwise fulfill.

Within the individualist context of the U.S. this may seem rather straightforward. However, in more communal societies, people may view themselves as part of an inner circle "devoted to mutual protection and prosperity" (Fadiman, 1986: 7). The mutually supporting relationships that define such groups may be maintained through the continuous exchange of gifts (Fadiman, 1986: 8). One of the roles of gifts in such settings is to reaffirm important obligations and relationships between members of the inner circle. They may also seek to use gifts to bring others within this network. "The point . . . is not the exchanges themselves but the relationships they engender. The gifts are simply catalysts. Under ideal circumstances the process should be unending, with visits, gifts, gestures, and services flowing back and forth among participants throughout their lives" (Fadiman, 1986: 8). In such contexts, gift-giving is part of a system of "future favors" in which "any individual under obligation to another has entered a relationship in which the first favor must be repaid in the future, when convenient to all sides" (Fadiman, 1986: 7). Consequently, in these settings, marketers face very different situations when they engage (or feel pressured to engage) in gift-giving. In individualist situations, gift-giving in business may raise questions of inappropriate influence, conflicts of interest, non-merit-based business, and possibly even bribery. In more communal settings, these questions may also arise, but they are placed within a more complex setting of inner- and outer-circle relationships, which define their members, delimit areas of trust, and create expectations of future favors.

Increasingly, people around the world are aware of these cultural differences and make efforts to accommodate them. A variety of ways to avoid compromising one's own values of merit-based decisions while exhibiting respect for gift-giving practices have been found. One way is to accept the gifts on behalf of one's company, rather than for oneself. Or one might suggest some other recipient to receive the gift, for example some worthy social cause. Some may excuse themselves because the laws of one's country or policies of one's company forbid certain kinds of gifts. If the businessmen of one country expect that part of a business negotiation will be that they are provided with the services of a prostitute during an evening, then one will have to explain that one's company does not provide that form of gift or entertainment. The guiding principle here would be that marketers do not provide gifts or forms of entertainment which are themselves unethical or which tend to promote unethical practices. And, even if this is not viewed as unethical in the host country, the fact that it violates one's own ethical standards should still count when one goes abroad.

In short, ethical marketing requires that one maintain those ethical standards one believes justified wherever one engages in marketing. In the case of gifts, there is nothing that necessitates this or that limit. What is crucial are the (potential) implications for the decisions and relationships that may be affected by gift-giving. In those cases, however, where the gifts themselves are arguably unethical, for example the services of prostitutes, then a marketing ethics would reject either accepting or giving such gifts.

Bribery and corruption

Marketers face other difficult cases when a business or public official (whether in one's own or another country) either demands or expects a bribe. As so often, the theoretical answers are much easier than the practical actions when confronted with real cases. In an international context, one theoretical escape, viz., that bribery is what is acceptable in some other country, is less and less plausible. In fact all countries have laws against bribery (Noonan, 1984; Donaldson and Dunfee, 1999). And though bribery may be widespread in many countries, the general response is not that it is morally right, but that there seems little that can be done to stop it. It is the way things are done (Donaldson and Dunfee, 1999: 226).

Marketers must be clear on just what bribery is. It is the offer of something of value that is intended to influence a person in a position (public or private) to make a decision within their official capacity in a direction favorable to the person (or organization) making the offer. Bribery is different from extortion or blackmail. Each of these involves placing pressure upon another person (or organization) to offer the person imposing the pressure something of value, while at the same time implicitly (or explicitly) indicating that if this is not done either something the other person wishes not to happen, will happen, or some harm that the demander could impose on the person will be imposed. Even though, at times, the two may be confused, the moral difference is important since the initiative in the case of bribery lies with the person offering the bribe, whereas in extortion or blackmail it lies with the person demanding something of value. The upshot is that the moral evaluation of the person offering something of value may change depending on whether bribery or extortion (or blackmail) is involved.

In the case of bribery, it is common to distinguish between minor or facilitating bribery and grand bribery. The former takes place when something of value is offered in a relatively minor instance; indeed, it may be simply to get a person to do what their position or office calls on them to do, for example bribing a customs official to allow one to pass by the border in an expeditious manner, rather than being delayed for hours. Grand bribery occurs when officials of higher offices are bribed to make important decisions regarding purchasing various products or services. In a notorious case, Lockheed was accused of grand bribery when its CEO offered Japanese government officials a large sum to buy the Lockheed 1011. More recently the CEO of an American consulting company was indicted on charges of bribing oil officials in Kazakhstan on behalf of Mobil Oil and other oil companies. Such examples can be easily multiplied.

In the U.S. the Foreign Corrupt Practices Act was passed in 1977 and amended in 1988. It forbade bribery by U.S. corporations, but permitted forms of "grease" payments, or facilitating payments. Further, it pertained to government officials, not to businesses executives or employees. After considerable lobbying by the U.S. government, the Organization for Economic Cooperation and Development (OECD) also adopted, in 1998, guidelines for its members that forbade bribery. This required a number of nations to change their own laws, since previously those laws had permitted bribery (outside their own borders), and had, indeed, even permitted their own national corporations to deduct the costs of international bribes when paying their income taxes in their home countries.

Such laws have legally resolved, in part, the issue of bribery – at least for businesses whose governments are members of OECD or the U.S., and which seek to obey the law. However, as noted above, these laws permit facilitating bribes and apply only to government officials. And even if almost every country around the world has laws against bribery, still, many of these laws are not enforced and bribery is widespread.

What is the moral case? Assuming the above definition of bribery, then to offer a bribe is to try to get an official to do something the bribe-payer wants for reasons extraneous to those that his or her official position permits or requires. It is an attempt to corrupt the person and the position. It is for this reason that bribery is said to be morally wrong and not something condoned by marketing ethics. Admittedly, some bribes may involve attempting to induce an official to do something that is relatively benign, for example permitting the traveler to pass by the border. Some may even be on behalf of products of superior quality. The justification, then, is that if a bribe is not given, the promoter of some lesser-quality product will win the contract because he or she does pay a bribe. Still, other bribes may result in substandard materials being used in building projects or inferior machinery being purchased. Dams in China have collapsed after corrupt dealings resulted in inferior materials being used to construct them. Similarly, buildings in Turkey have collapsed that were poorly constructed such that they could not resist even low-intensity earthquakes. However, even in the minor cases, we must also consider the cumulative and symbolic effects of such minor harms and wrongs. The marketer must ask at what point he or she has become part of the problem, rather than a person seeking to resolve or avoid a problem.

It may be objected that this assumes that the holders of such offices are not morally permitted to demand such payments that are referred to here as "bribes." If, on the contrary, demanding such payments were something that was widely recognized and approved in that society, then this would no longer be a bribe, but some sort of additional fee that the official is permitted to demand (see Velasquez, 2004). Such might be the case if an office were viewed as one which is supported, in part, by those who use that office. Then the office-holder might, as a result, receive payments as part of his or her compensation. However, in such cases, the fee schedule (as it were) for dealing with that office would be something that could be public and widely accepted. Most often, however, this is not the case with such payments. They are not publicly or officially approved. They remain forms of extortion.

Another objection might be that the present argument presupposes that those in an official position are to make decisions based on independent and objective considerations, rather than influenced by personal connections and private networks. On the contrary, in much of the world, a position is viewed as something that is to be used by the office-holder for his or her benefit and the benefit of those towards whom that person (official) is well disposed.

The appropriate response to this "personal use" view is that there is little doubt but that the factual claim here is correct. However, such a view, if openly espoused by those in a country, is quite different from one in which the demands that people make in those roles and positions is kept quiet and out of public view. Since the latter stance tends to be the case, this strongly suggests that this is part of a corrupt view of those positions, rather than one that is widely approved. However, if this "personal use" view of offices were widely acknowledged in a society, then the notion of each office having its own duties and responsibilities would have disappeared and been replaced by simply the desires of the "office-holder." This would be the end of impartiality, fairness, objectivity, and merit in the exercise of such offices. A society so designed would pay an unreasonably high price, both morally and practically.

But what are marketers to do if they operate within a country in which it is widely understood that, in order to get a phone connected or secure a major contract, the office-holders involved must be given something of value (viz., a bribe)? These situations arise much more frequently than marketers would like. They test the moral imagination and stamina of marketers.

There are several responses. One answer that some businesses (such as Motorola) have given, in the case of grand bribery, is that they simply will not pay such bribes and will forgo such business (Donaldson, 1996). They announce, in advance, that they do not give bribes as a matter of policy. Many have found that this reduces the number of instances in which bribes are expected from them. Such an approach works particularly well, of course, with prominent businesses offering rather unique or specialized products.

A different response has been for businesses to do something publicly that can be associated with the official or office. This might involve building a community center, planting trees, or the like. In short, something is done which benefits other people, even though the official may still take (some) credit for it. The advantage of this approach is that it is public and that others who may be truly needy may be aided in the process.

There are, however, a number of excuses that marketers may draw upon to justify, in some cases, relatively minor bribes. The more minor the bribe and the official, and the more pressing the situation that demands the bribe, the more justified (and excused) marketers would be for engaging in such actions. The more significant the bribe and the official, the less excused would be the offering of such a bribe. What about a bribe to a major public official that would save thousands of jobs in one's home country? The problem with such consequentialist justifications is that they do not take into account other jobs that are lost by other companies involved, nor the system of corruption that they foster or help maintain in place. These excuses are failed excuses and do not justify the bribes involved.

Finally, it is also important for marketers to determine the source of the corruption that leads to expectations of bribery. Does it stem from those in the business community or in the government, or does it flow from the entire social system? One's responses would have to be different depending upon the source. Thus, if one is approached for a major bribe by a company, and yet the relevant government is one of integrity, a person's moral situation and possibilities of redress are different than if both government and business are corrupt. In the latter case, a business would have to decide whether it can do business in that country at all, and, if it can, what its responsibilities are to help nationals of that country address the systemic problems they face. Lacking any attempt to address a corrupt system but participating in it anyway makes marketers complicit and leaves them with dirty hands.

Controversial products

Controversial products can take a wide variety of forms. They include: products declared unsafe in one's home country, but sold in another (drugs, pesticides such as DDT, etc.); products that can be used safely in one country, but not in others due to local conditions (infant formula); products accepted in one country, but offensive in others (magazines, books, videos portraying explicit sex, criticisms of religion, local culture, politics), and so on. In short, with such products, marketers may be accused of harming or causing offense to people in another country. The harm or offense may come from the product's own characteristics, the way in which it is used, or the response that people have to it. When, if ever, should this be ethically acceptable? If all people's lives are equally valuable, how is such behavior ethically possible for marketers?

Even though we must, ethically, assume that all people's lives are equally valuable, we also know that not everyone, or every country, has the same level of resources, the same environmental conditions, or the same cultural values. Thus, in the case of products that may be harmful due to their constitutive properties (chemicals, conditions for proper use, etc.), countries with different levels of resources and environmental conditions may decide to use them in different ways. A chemical whose dangers are judged unacceptably high in the U.S. may be deemed acceptable in another country with environmental conditions that render that chemical more desirable or necessary. Thus, the chemical, EDB (a soil fungicide), that is banned in the U.S., might ethically be used in tropical countries where increased solar radiation and high soil temperatures render it relatively harmless (Donaldson, 1996: 51). In developed countries there has been a conscious decision, oftentimes involving considerable public debate, over the levels of safety that they wish to impose on themselves. If products excluded as a result of these processes are simply sold to developing countries without any warning to those who might be employing them, and without public consideration of the pros, cons, and risks of using such products, then marketers may be charged with dumping dangerous products on people and countries. However, if people are aware of the risks and are willing to run them for other reasons, then marketers should not be morally criticized.

The implication is that products with fewer safety features might be sold in developing countries, not out of disrespect for customers, but because customers in those countries cannot afford more expensive products with additional safety features. For example, lawn mowers with cut-off switches and lathes with protective devices are products that, a few decades ago, were not considered necessary even in the West, though now they are. Assuming that such products are more expensive, people in different countries might rationally decide to use machinery without the same safety equipment. It would not be unethical, under those circumstances, to sell them such products.

Part of the difficulty here may rest upon who, in developing countries, makes such decisions. If those who will benefit, but bear none of the risk, are those who make the decisions, and if the voice and interests of those who will bear the risks are not heard, then marketers cannot simply disclaim the responsibilities that they have towards those people. In short, to ethically market such products, marketers must have some sense that the processes that have led to the acceptance of them are processes that are ethically appropriate. Too often, however, those who make the decisions in such situations are not those who will bear any risk.

Products can also threaten people in some countries not because the products themselves are harmful, but because of the conditions in which they are used, or the level of knowledge and experience of those who will be using those products. In fact, in some cases the products themselves, if properly used, are very valuable and beneficial. For example, infant formula may be helpful to mothers for a variety of reasons, for example a physical inability to nurse, or because the mother must be away from the child for lengthy periods.

Still, if marketers provide free samples to mothers in hospitals to encourage the use of infant formula, if they market infant formula as the modern, scientific way to raise infants, then they may persuade numbers of mothers not to nurse their children but to turn to infant formula, even though breast-feeding is widely recognized as the much better way to care for infants. In addition, if the economic and physical circumstances of the new mother and infant are such that unclean water is used to prepare the formula and the amount of formula used is reduced to make each package go further, then infants may suffer from diarrhea and/or malnutrition.

Are marketers responsible for such problems? Are they guiltless if they simply give the infant formula away while presenting it as the modern, medically approved way to feed newborn children? Aren't they simply doing what good marketers would do who are trying to create a consumer and to move a product? On the contrary, marketers must take into account the circumstances of their customers. Some are more vulnerable than others. As before, context matters. As a matter of fact, the circumstances in which infant formula has been marketed have led to infants being harmed. The general guideline must be that marketers ought not to market products in circumstances in which they have good reason to know (or where they have learned) that the end users will be harmed by them. This does not mean that such products cannot be marketed. But it does mean that they must take effective steps to prevent such harm from occurring as a result of any actions that they undertake in the marketing of those products.

Though the example here relates to one widely known case, the principle behind it can be applied to much more complicated cases when businesses seek to transfer sophisticated forms of technology to other countries, but where the workers, the local plants, or the conditions in those countries are not prepared to handle that technology safely. The ghastly forms this may take were witnessed in 1984 in a toxic gas leak from a Union Carbide plant in Bhopal, India, where between 15,000 and 30,000 people died as a result.

Finally, some products may not cause harm as much as offense in the countries in which they are marketed. This offense may occur, for example, in response to products that involve sexually explicit materials or perceived religious or cultural affronts, or contain a high level of violence. Obviously there is little market for products if they are marketed to those who find them offensive. So the problem (for marketers) arises when there are some people in a society who are interested in such products even though others find them offensive. Those who take offense may be a small but vocal (and threatening) minority or they may constitute a large percentage of the population.

If a government prohibits such offensive materials from being sold in its country, then marketers should abide by these constraints, even though they may use legitimate channels to try to change that government's mind. However, if the government does not prohibit such materials, then marketers must decide whether they wish to offend a portion of the population. Should novels be sold that criticize some religion, or movies distributed that have brutal sex scenes in them? Are some materials so pornographic or violent that they ought not to be marketed at all? Obviously there will be a wide variety of answers to such questions, but they must be answers to the right questions. Does the marketing of these materials violate any ethical values or norms? If it does, are there other overriding values and norms that may be appealed to that would justify the marketing of such materials? To whom are such materials being marketed? Can those people who are offended easily avoid being confronted with those materials? Are the grounds upon which they experience offense regarding such materials basic or peripheral to the value structure of their society? If marketers can satisfactorily answer the above questions they may be able to justify marketing materials that cause offense to some people in another society – just as happens within any society.

Conditions surrounding the source of one's products

With globalization, the offshoring of products and services has greatly expanded. Increasingly, marketers have sought to obtain the products they design from production facilities in other (developing) countries. The reasons for this move include cheaper conditions of production, closer proximity to important markets, nearness to important natural resources, and reliable sources of (skilled) labor.

An important ethical issue that has dogged marketers has been not only the cheapness of the labor but also the conditions under which that labor has been employed. Claims that employees are being paid insufficient wages – an exploitative wage – have been made time and again, not to mention the questions that have been raised regarding the age as well as the health and safety conditions of those workers. In addition, in some of the cases, the factories are in countries with authoritarian governments which do not permit the organization of labor (except that controlled by the state) or other social and political freedoms. Finally, all too often, lax environmental regulations and monitoring also characterize these production facilities.

What ethical responsibilities or considerations must marketers take into account in these situations? Clearly they ought not simply to consider the fact that it is inexpensive to produce goods in such countries. And as Nike found out, in the early 1990s, it is not sufficient to disclaim any responsibility by maintaining that the factories involved are not owned by one's company and that, therefore, it is not responsible for what happens in them.

Consider the following two major ethical issues here. First, may marketers ethically operate in any country, regardless of its social and political order? Clearly there are practical questions that will influence whether marketers operate in authoritarian societies, for example if the rule of law is shaky, protection of their investments may be too risky; and violent (government) treatment of workers may jeopardize a stable and productive workforce. But there are also other ethical issues. Suppose a business could operate profitably, as many do, in an authoritarian society. Because people are oppressed and do not have various social or political rights, there may be few disruptions of production. Employees live lives of fear or intimidation, but still produce goods a marketer might want.

One argument has been that it is morally permissible, though not required, to operate in such countries, because doing so will improve the economy, put more money in people's pockets, expose them to Western ways of doing business, and thereby act as a force for reform and change. In short, a consequentialist argument is offered. Generally this is done with little supporting evidence regarding whether these changes will happen in the particular country or what the time frame might be – is it 5 years, or 50 years? Would that difference make a moral difference? Certainly an entire generation or two might suffer as a result.

A second argument has been that other marketers will operate in those countries, thereby obtaining a competitive advantage, due to (for example) the cheapness of the labor, and (possibly) proximity to important markets. If one is not to be out-competed, one has little choice but to enter into such markets as well. This is another consequentialist argument; in short, operate in those countries, or lose one's business. Again, little direct or concrete evidence is produced to substantiate such arguments, though anecdotal evidence is often given. However, the example of China after the millennium does provide rather strong evidence for at least some of those who rely on this argument. This is one of the reasons that Google has given for operating in China, even though this has required it to censor its search engine in accord with the Chinese government's demands.

How one evaluates such arguments will depend on what responsibilities marketers have to operate only in countries with morally acceptable levels of social and political life. With regard to sourcing issues, what if the raw materials only exist in that country? Crucial to answering this question will be some determination of the extremity of the situation in the country being considered. Is this North Korea or is it Columbia? And are there morally positive changes taking place in that country? What is the realistic prospect for such changes?

The rationale for the objection to marketers operating in authoritarian countries is that through their activities they lend support to that country. This takes an economic form (the injection of hard currency from outside) as well as a moral and political one inasmuch as associating with that country lends it some legitimacy. Of course, a problem of the one and the many also arises at this point, since if one marketer operates in such a country the effects are likely rather small, whereas if many do so, the effects will be much greater and more significant. And since each marketer may fear that others will decide to operate there, they too may so decide (pre-emptively). Unless there are United Nations sanctions or an international boycott (such as there was of South Africa years ago), there are likely few legal or economic constraints to operating in such countries.

In the end, marketers must decide how dirty or clean they want their hands to be. To what extent does the country engage in a systematic suppression of human rights? Of course, particular companies cannot be responsible for the protection of all human rights in a country. Though all countries of the world have endorsed the UN Universal Declaration of Human Rights, countries may interpret these rights differently and assign them different priorities. Thus, in some countries rights regarding health care, housing, and work are assigned higher priority than rights regarding political activities and freedom of the press, speech, and religion. The appropriate role for marketers is not to make these decisions for the countries involved.

Surely, however, they are responsible for their own actions and the violations of human rights they might occasion. And, arguably, they are also responsible for creating conditions whereby others violate the human rights of citizens in a country. If they choose to operate in an authoritarian country, then they have negative responsibilities not to do anything that would permit or encourage further repression of people. And within the limits of their powers and influence, they have a positive responsibility to encourage the development of fewer authoritarian controls, and greater respect of human rights.

May (or should) a marketer seek, then, to work (with other foreign nationals and locals) to change the moral views of a nation? Of course, the very presence of the foreign marketer in a country is itself a force for change. Still, a company might back the efforts of the citizens of the country to change its background conditions (i.e. the laws, customs, and expectations of people) so that the moral problems they face might be reduced or limited. Thus, a multinational might support laws against bribery in the country it seeks to do business in; or it might seek to promote efforts through regional trade associations, or world bodies, to counteract some of the situations which raise moral problems. This would be to invoke what De George has called the "principle of displacement" (De George, 1993: 97f). That is, some problems can only be solved by addressing other background conditions and systems.

Overt attempts to change another society by outsiders may, of course, backfire; they may be viewed as imperialistic. On the other hand, covert attempts to do so may produce worse results. Further, as a foreign "guest" a multinational's prerogatives may be more limited than those of a national business. Finally, the responsibilities of the multinational to its own shareholders and employees place limits on the extent to which it can try to act as moral intervener. This is not, however, to say that it should not do anything. It also has stakeholders in the country in which it is the guest. It owes these stakeholders responsibilities as well.

The immediately preceding comments relate to the conditions over which marketers have some direct control, for example wages and working conditions, the products they produce. Too many marketers have been charged with fostering sweatshop conditions. Of course, some have argued in response that, actually, what these countries need are more sweatshops, since such production facilities provide jobs that usually pay more than the minimum wage, and offer working conditions less hazardous than other production facilities in those countries (Maitland, 1997). This is demonstrated, it is said, because those jobs are greatly sought after rather than avoided by citizens of those countries.

The responsibilities of marketers regarding wages cannot be discharged by simply referring to the legal minimum wage. This may have been set very low for any number of reasons not having to do with the well-being of the worker. Nor can one appeal simply to what the market dictates to provide a satisfactory answer either, since there is generally an over-abundance of available labor and few jobs. Supply and demand will force workers' wages to levels determined by the minimum that the most desperate will be willing to accept. These levels will often be morally too low. The market should serve human ends, not be the sole determinant of those ends.

Instead, marketers must look to the level of a just wage (as well as just working conditions) that takes into account not only market conditions but also the well-being and needs of employees, as well as social and environmental conditions. How this is determined has been the subject of considerable discussion. One method would be through negotiations between free labor unions and the production facilities. However, since independent unions may not be permitted in some countries, marketers may have to determine what the constituents of a just wage would be through other procedures. One such technique looks to what is required to provide for the physical, social, and psychological needs of employees and their families. Hence, just levels of wages will consider the appropriate levels of such needs as food, clothing, transportation, health care, education, and housing for employees and their families. There are no magic formulas here. There may be multiple and different answers that, morally, are equally correct or justifiable. Circumstances or contexts will differ from society to society that must also be taken into account.

Summary

The upshot of this section is that marketing is today unavoidably international. Marketers must be aware of the differences they confront, as well as understand the common values and norms that hold for all people. Marketers have an impact on the economic, social, and political development of the countries in which they operate. It is important that they recognize these impacts and seek to ensure that they can be justified not only to members of that country but also to other stakeholders in today's global society.

Marketers have also had any number of other (beneficent) impacts internationally in areas that overlap with the moral arena. For example, marketing companies have set new standards of cleanliness and efficiency in developing countries (e.g. bread-making in Central America). They also set various specifications for the nature and quality of the products, for example, shoes, clothing, coffee beans, for which they contract. Some of the standards relate to the treatment of employees, while others regard production itself or the environment. Marketing firms such as Nike have learned that they are responsible for the ways in which plants producing their products are run. Thus they have also set standards for the plants with which they work (Toys-R-Us is another example). These are direct ways in which the marketers of one country may be intervening to modify values and norms in other countries.

If the argument above is correct, viz., that important and basic values do cross national and cultural boundaries, then this need not be an instance of moral imperialism or ethnocentrism. It is true that we are seeing the development of a more unified, more homogenized world. Still, diversity remains an important (and in itself desirable) part of that world.

The conclusion is that marketers have multiple responsibilities to their customers, to the social and political realms of the countries in which they operate, as well as to the environment. They are not responsible for everything. But their international responsibilities extend far beyond simple profitability and the physical products they deliver to their customers.

III The Expansion of Marketing within Society: Social and Political Marketing

In the past half-century, marketing has not only significantly expanded around the world, it has also extended itself within each society to areas formerly foreign to it (Hunt, 1976: 18). For example, marketing techniques and forms of thought have been applied to social and political causes. Part of the criticism of marketing in chapters 1 and 2 had to do with the inappropriate extension of marketing techniques, attitudes, and modes of behavior to other areas of life. Social and political marketing raise many of those same concerns.

Social and political marketing involve the application of various techniques (as well as assumptions and background views) developed by marketers within the commercial realm to accomplish social or political aims. Among the reasons marketing has moved into these areas has been considerable evidence that commercial use of these techniques has been successful in modifying people's behavior to buy certain products. The thought naturally occurs that if marketing works in the commercial area, why not with regard to political or social causes? Other factors playing a role have been the desires of market-ers to make marketing more socially relevant (Andreasen, 1994: 109), the view that traditional institutions have failed to solve a wide variety of increasingly pressing social problems (e.g. drug use, AIDS, teenage pregnancies), and the greater acceptance by political systems of the open receipt of money to support political causes, together with the collapse of political machines and party discipline (at least in the U.S.).

The preceding reasons for this expansion of marketing are both self-interested and ethical. However, they must be weighed against other ethical considerations that arise from the ways in which, and the ends to which, marketing techniques are applied.

On the positive side it must be conceded that techniques involving market research, advertising, organizing channels of distribution, etc. may help non-governmental groups to confront social and environmental problems, as well as political organizations to organize more effectively around political issues. This is the positive side of social and political marketing.

The negative side of this extension of marketing is that, since the home metaphor of marketing is the market, these techniques are viewed as ways to "sell" certain "products" or forms of behavior that will solve social problems or aid political causes. However, it seems ethically inappropriate, some argue, to treat potential solutions in the social and political realm as being something "up for sale." Underlying this objection is that marketing techniques are not neutral but carry some of the assumptions and values of commercial market-ing and the market with them. When they are applied in the social and politi-cal areas, they may imply that these causes and candidates are something that may be accepted only if enough money is spent to "package" and promote them. In short, it suggests an attitude that views people and causes as things that can be "sold," that are exchangeable and even interchangeable, and the problem is to find the right price. This, some argue, is a corrupt way of viewing potential means to change. As the familiar saying goes, people may know the price of everything, but the value of nothing.

Social marketing[7]

Social marketing is the use of marketing techniques to solve social problems or issues. This view is compatible with Kotler and Zaltman's definition of social marketing as "the explicit use of marketing skills to help translate present social action efforts into more effectively designed and communicated programs that elicit desired audience response" (Kotler and Zaltman, 1971: 5). Social marketing should be distinguished from *societal marketing*. Andreasen says that the latter deals with regulatory issues and various efforts to protect consumers from problems in the marketplace (see Andreasen, 1994: 109). This is too narrow a view, since societal or socially responsible marketing is something that all marketers should engage in and includes most of the topics of this book. In contrast, social marketing focuses simply on addressing current social issues, such as the use of drugs, the physical abuse of women and children by men, leprosy, HIV/AIDS, and forest fires. These are issues with which commercial marketers (even socially responsible ones) may not be ordinarily involved.

Social marketing has greatly increased over the past several decades. For example, marketing techniques have been used to try to dissuade teenagers from using drugs, to prevent adults from drinking and driving, to encourage sexually active people to avoid unsafe sex, to stop people from smoking, to promote the use of seat belts, and to promote blood donations among the adult population. In addition, various groups and institutions that wish to increase their membership or influence have also turned to marketing. Educational institutions, churches, and non-governmental organizations have drawn on the techniques developed in marketing to foster the ends they espouse. These are non-profit organizations in any traditional sense. Still, the ends they seek are not necessarily simply for themselves. They may regard the social problems and issues that these groups perceive society to face. Accordingly, social marketing has been used to market a wide variety of social causes.

Among the many ethical issues that social marketing raises, three deserve special mention. The first one has to do with the ends or aims that a social marketer is asked to undertake. These are not simply neutral ends, but ones that carry significant value implications. For example, there is nothing in the definition of social marketing that would exclude a social marketer being asked to promote white supremacy or fascism. Similarly, Andreasen notes that social marketing technology may be used by "the Ku Klux Klan, the German National Socialist (Nazi) Party, Mother Teresa, and both pro-life and pro-choice forces" (Andreasen, 1994: 113). Yet some of these projects are morally repugnant and a social marketer ought to refuse to undertake them.

Accordingly, social marketers require a theory of ends which would tell them which of these ends they may (or should) undertake, and which they should reject. Clearly there will be differences over some of the ends social marketers have promoted, for example handgun control or abortion. How should social marketers seek to resolve these issues when they must choose which ends to aim for?

Andreasen suggests that, after building the best social marketing technology that can be devised, "we [as social marketers] also owe it to ourselves and our communities to see that it is used for what a broad consensus of society agrees is its own social good" (Andreasen, 1994: 113). In short, social marketers need some theory of the social good. This is especially obvious when they are asked to engage in social marketing in other countries, and where the causes identified may have to do with the treatment of women, children, and minority groups.

Andreasen suggests (as just noted) that the social good be identified through a broad social consensus. But this faces problems when such a social consensus opposes the education of young girls, or believes that religion requires the ostracism of leprosy victims. Another proposal is that social marketing may pursue those social goods or ends that are determined by "some sort of societally representative collective. This collective could be a legislature or a government ministry, or it could be a board of directors or an advisory board made up of citizens of diverse backgrounds and interests" (Andreasen, 1995: 31). Similarly, others claim that "most government-sponsored social marketing efforts are likely to be fairly uncontroversial when used to increase the effectiveness of legislatively mandated social programs" (Fox and Kotler, 1980: 30). However, these suggestions are neither necessary nor sufficient as an answer to the present issue. On the one hand, not all attempts to resolve social problems need be part of legislatively mandated programs. On the other hand, there must be reasons to believe that legislatively mandated programs are also ethically justified, and not simply imposed by a political elite through a legislature or parliament. Only under these conditions could this be an ethically appealing approach to social change (Fox and Kotler, 1980: 27).

The problem with such views is that governments, legislatures, and boards of directors may be corrupt, biased, or prejudiced. The implication is that their identification of the individual and social welfare to serve as the aim of social marketers may be skewed. Accordingly, social marketers must develop criteria and standards for individual and social welfare which such bodies should use. This is different, it should be noted, from commercial marketing, in which the desires and wants of customers are taken as authoritative, though even commercial marketers may seek to modify those desires and wants to fulfill their own private ends. However, even in these cases, the final touchstone is the non-coerced willingness of customers to buy their products or services. In the case of social marketing, on the other hand, the desires and wants of those who are targeted may be the problem, for example desires to use drugs, get pregnant, act in environmentally harmful ways, or discriminate against women or minorities. These must be altered so as to align with rationally justified views of individual and social welfare. And though social marketing seeks to bring such people willingly to adopt different views, it is those views on individual and social welfare that are the touchstone in this case. Accordingly, social marketers face a different ethical challenge here than do commercial marketers.

Consequently, social marketers require a theory of individual and social welfare according to which they may justifiably act on behalf of the individuals they seek to benefit. Currently, social marketing lacks such a theory.

Second, social marketers tend to draw on theories of consumer behavior for their analyses regarding how to approach and treat those who are subject to social problems. In this way, they retain their marketing roots. These theories, however, view the behavior of individuals as resulting from various causal factors, with self-centered calculations a matter of primary concern. Accordingly, values or moral norms are regarded only with respect to their causal effectiveness (or ineffectiveness) in altering people's behavior. For example, a social marketer might ask whether, in a promotional campaign, a reference to or portrayal of some injustice or harm to others actually moves people to act in the way they want them to act.

The problem with this is that to treat moral and value considerations as causal factors in people's behavior is to significantly alter any reasoned, and potentially rational, approach which engages people in discussion and rational decision-making. On this consumer-based approach, the criterion of success is that of effectiveness, not rational justification. In contrast, on a reasoned approach, the appropriate standard is not causal, but that of rationally justified agreement. The former uses values "externally," as it were. The latter engages those values internally.

Hirschman has made a similar point. She has argued that the marketing concept does not apply in the case of aesthetics and ideologies since these activities and disciplines are and must be judged by norms from within the activity and by the peers involved, rather than by those who partake of those activities, i.e. by "consumers" (see Hirschman, 1983: 47). In short, not all these activities can be understood on the basis of an exchange or transaction model.

Third, a final danger of social marketing is that of transforming what are non-market relationships into market relationships. Billy Graham once commented that he saw nothing wrong with selling Jesus as one might sell a bar of soap (see Fromm, 1955). As such, the extension of marketing to social causes threatens to overturn and confuse a variety of different kinds of relationships, transforming them all into one kind. In contrast, for example, the relationship of religious leader and follower, doctor and patient, or social leader and constituent is not – or ought not to be – the same as the business-man (marketer)–consumer relationship. The doctor, religious leader, or social leader is not – or ought not to be – offering a product to those consumers who can pay the highest dollar or offer the best terms. Instead, those relationships should be centered on common values such as spiritual truth or patient health. To the extent that these relationships all become the same, we must speak of the commercialization of religious or medical relationships. The same holds true of art, law, or education. Each of these areas has held special, unique relationships between those involved. Put in different words, we see in the expansion of marketing a reflection of the extension of market relationships to new areas. Morality requires that we recognize the different kinds of relationships involved and with this the different values, norms, and perspectives. If, indeed, a marketing approach is to be used in these areas, those who do so must recognize that they are replacing the values and standards which have historically characterized them. As such, they are engaged in a process of moral substitution. Clearly this is (or should be) a significant moral issue.[8]

Political marketing

Political marketing takes aim at a wide variety of political causes, including getting particular laws passed by legislatures, creating demands through public referenda for governmental action, arranging for special provisions to be inserted in pending legislation, and electing officials to the full range of political bodies, from the presidency to local city councils. Huge amounts of money are spent in the U.S. on these kinds of activities. In addition, politicians take polls to determine what the voters favor, and buy television advertisements or "messages" to influence public opinion. Some politicians are significantly influenced by their "handlers" who only let them be exposed to situations that will promote their candidacy. Public relations experts appear after the politician to explain (away) various comments he or she may have made. Indeed, political marketing has developed beyond the aim of achieving this or that political end (the election of some person or the passage of a particular legislative bill) to something used by many politicians on an ongoing basis to maintain parties and individuals in office.

This use of marketing techniques in this arena raises many of the same questions we have noted previously. When is such marketing deceptive, and when is it manipulative? What is the ethical nature of a particular political marketing campaign as opposed to the ethical impact of political marketing on society in general? However, there are two ethical issues that specially arise in political contexts that are worthy of attention in this section: the effect of political marketing on democratic processes and the relation between political marketing and free speech.

Political marketing and democracy

Of course, if political marketing "merely" amounts to efforts to find out what voters want, to design programs, laws, regulations, etc. that will address voters' concerns, and to articulate the rationale for such measures in ways that will be understandable and appealing to constituents, then political marketing can hardly be faulted. However, the evidence of the past few decades is that while political marketing may be involved in these activities, it has tended in other less savory directions as well.

If democratic processes are desirably held to involve discussion, reason-giving, and the evaluation of the diverse positions different candidates or parties represent, then certain forms of political marketing may be accused of undercutting democracy. Just as advertisements for products give less and less information, so too advertisements for political candidates dwell less on their views and more on what will move voters to vote for them. When the aim of political marketing is to convince or persuade potential voters to act in certain ways (Andreasen, 1994: 110f) the means need not be cognitive or informational, so much as persuasive or emotional. This implies that complex issues are simplified; grey tones are sharpened into black and white; subtleties and difficulties are left unarticulated. This is an implication of the view of some that marketing is neither communication nor education, but is, rather, the attempt to change people's attitudes and beliefs, and ultimately their behavior (Andreasen, 1994: 111).[9] There are two ethically troublesome implications of this approach to politics. First, it may mean that the real issues get submerged and even transformed. Worse yet, various "attack ads" focus on aspects of a candidate's previous record that may be irrelevant, as well as distorting the truth regarding other relevant parts of that candidate's views. It is highly ironical that at least some of these advertisements would never be accepted (in the U.S.) in commercial marketing, but they regularly are displayed in political marketing. Such marketing may help foster greater polarization within the body politic, rather than contribute to an appreciation of common bonds and problems. Second, these forms of political marketing may encourage individuals to see themselves more as consumers of politics, rather than as citizens who partake in political processes. The collapse of this difference between our role as consumers and our role as citizens impoverishes the latter. Accordingly, some commentators speak of the ethical losses and "erosion of loyalties and ties [resulting from] . . . being taught at the aggregate level to be consumers in everything we do" (O'Shaughnessy, 2002: 1086).

The upshot is that political marketing may be ethically criticized when it reduces, rather than enlarges, real political discourse. On those occasions, it may be charged with attempting to "sell" politicians and various positions through campaigns that lead to distorted views of these "products." In this manner political marketers do not rely on the practices of social and political discourse that involve open discussion, rights of participation, political parties, grassroots action, negotiation, and compromise. Instead, they seek to bring about political (and social) change through marketing techniques. The indifference (or hostility) of some of these procedures to democracy appears when they are used to get people to stay at home and not to vote or participate in the political process (see Banker, 1992: 844). It is hardly surprising, then, that members of the public have responded rather negatively, with cynicism and apathy, to much of the political marketing of candidates and political issues. Partly as a result, they have tended to withdraw from political campaigns, rather than be drawn to engage in them (see Banker, 1992).

In this context those with great wealth and resources will be more readily heard and their influence will be much greater, than that of those with scant resources and wealth. Of course, this has always been true, even if it has been recognized as undesirable. However, political marketing simply increases this division, by giving those who already have great economic power more effective means to use that power to overwhelm their opponents. Still, if democratic countries are based upon political discourse, exploration of the issues, and citizen participation through voting, then political marketing appears to add to the forces that undercut, rather than advance, that fundamental democratic premise.

In addition, if marketing is portrayed as giving customers what they want, then political marketing involving polling etc. may lead citizens to view candidates as simply "pandering" to them, rather than being leaders who are willing to set out their own values, beliefs, and vision in light of the underlying values and interests of the members of their constituencies and society. There are (or should be) important differences between customers and citizens, as well as between the "products" of marketers and those of politicians.

It may be objected to the preceding that the development of the internet has greatly opened up the political process, both in terms of acquiring information about candidates, parties, and issues, and in terms of the collective power of small contributors. There is a great deal to be said for this objection. However, this is different from saying that these are the results of political marketing. The internet may be used in a wide variety of ways. It remains to be seen whether it will enhance the positive characteristics of political marketing or whether political marketing will undercut the potential of the internet. In any case, the internet has also changed the political process into a much more brawling, competitive affair.

Finally, some claim that the preceding objections to political marketing unrealistically presuppose a view of political decision-making that is objective and based on full information. In contrast, they argue, "voters are not in the end particularly rational decision makers, but respond to gut feel and emotion . . . [T]herefore they use the cognitive shortcuts and cues provided by political advertising, journalism, etc., in order to facilitate a decision"

(O'Shaughnessy, 2002: 1081). While this may be descriptively true, this ought not to be taken as a license to offer base, irrelevant, but emotionally charged cues to voters. Such "facts" are not normative licenses. The fact that a political marketing campaign may motivate voters tells us little about the ethical nature of that campaign. And though some people are moved by such appeals, it appears that many voters are also disenchanted. Quite correctly, they conclude that when political marketing turns to these means to accomplish its purposes it undercuts democratic processes. On the other hand, when it provides insight into issues and candidates that reaches voters, and does this in meaningful and ethically defensible ways, it can enhance democracy.

Political marketing and free speech
If people are entitled to free speech, then we must recognize, at the same time, the difficulties of stopping the expansion of marketing into the political arena. If a person or a group has a right to free speech and wants to promote their views through advertisements or lobbying the legislature, it would seem that efforts to curtail these activities would restrict this important right. Nevertheless, politicians sometimes admit that, in order to win political office, they are "forced" to use various marketing techniques that raise ethical issues. In the United States, at least, legislative efforts to restrict the amount of money that can be expended for campaigning and lobbying have had only slight success.

Further, the use of television, radio, the print media, and the internet for political advertising is protected, in the U.S., by the First Amendment. The right to free speech is, in short, the major (legal) argument in the defense of political marketing. Since the form of speech promoted in these cases has been viewed as "political" speech, it has not been brought under the standards of commercial speech.[10] Nevertheless, at some point, such marketing becomes simply a form of propaganda issued by those with sufficient financial resources. At that point, the ends that a good society should embrace are being undercut.

However, since what is legal is not necessarily moral, ethical marketers must think beyond the minimal levels that the law permits. For example, the use of television clearly carries the greatest ethical dangers since negative advertisements can have significant influence before an opponent has a chance to respond. Further, once certain images are implanted in the public mind (the Willy Horton ad used against Michael Dukakis, the Swift boat ads against John Kerry), it may be almost impossible for the person against whom they were directed to remove those images. In addition, the use of the internet has grown exponentially in recent years as a means to reach specific groups of people with messages tailored to advance this or that political campaign. This new ability only heightens the dangers of political marketing.

Accordingly, marketers have a special responsibility to monitor (and restrict) forms of marketing that ethically cheapen current political and social processes. The challenges here are, at least in part, those of establishing a set of guidelines and expectations that will produce responsible marketing, rather than permitting (or even promoting) irresponsible political marketing. The criterion to be used should not be simply that of effectively influencing large numbers of voters. Nor should it be how negatively one can portray one's opponent, without incurring a public backlash. Instead, political marketers must develop guidelines that can be derived from a theory of the good political order. In short, neither political nor social marketing can be undertaken without additional normative theories. Hence, in the case of political marketing, the use of ethnic, racial, or gender stereotypes, of misleading information (however factual it might be), the portrayal of others as unpatriotic, the morphing of opponents' faces into those of other (disreputable) opponents, etc. are devices that are all too often used, but which are ethically inappropriate for marketers of integrity. The sole criterion here is not job creation for marketers.

Still, not everything that needs to be done in this area can be done by individual marketers. Instead, governments and professional associations must also establish rules and guidelines regarding elections. For example, if each candidate (suitably circumscribed for party membership, or votes received by his or her party in the last election, etc.) were allotted an equal amount of time on television, this might mute some of the ill effects of large sums of money being used to dominate the media. If editors of newspapers and television would reject (or require revisions to) advertisements that violate the above criteria, the tone and effects of political marketing would change. If marketing associations would develop standards by which to evaluate the actions of their members who engage in political marketing, this too might move the discussion in healthy directions. The current code of ethics of the AMA is clearly aimed at commercial, rather than political, marketing. However, suppose parts of it were applied to political marketing. For example, the AMA Statement of Ethics (see appendix I) enjoins that in the area of product management marketers are to disclose "all substantial risks associated with product or service usage." What if political marketers then were called to disclose such risks with regard to the candidates they were advertising and their practices in office? The AMA Statement also requires, in the area of promotions, that marketers avoid "false and misleading advertising" and reject "high-pressure manipulations, or misleading sales tactics." If this were applied to political marketing, political campaigns might be quite different. Much of this is unlikely, to be sure. There is too much money and power involved. But the point emphasizes the ethical distance between the AMA Statement and the practices of political marketers. Such great distances can be covered by taking small steps. But marketers must commit to the journey. Finally, another important step would be that the major sources of funding for political advertisements be publicly acknowledged so that the public would know who stood behind them. These are among many proposals made to try to channel political marketing into healthy forms of political discourse and competition.

IV Fostering Ethical Marketing

The earlier chapters, and most of this one, have discussed ethical guidelines, principles, and ways of approaching ethical issues that are available to marketers. If there is nothing that can be done to encourage or foster the use of these resources in marketing, then the preceding will have been merely an intellectual outing rather than a preparation for practical changes. What can be done to encourage ethical marketing?

No single answer or action, of course, will respond adequately to this question. Many different things must be done. Some have already been mentioned in the preceding chapters. We know, for example, that if people do not recognize moral issues, they may well act unethically. We also know that if people are not held accountable or if others do not trust them, people will tend, in general, to behave less well, ethically, than otherwise. Similarly, if people do not understand the notion of acting on the basis of principles or general characteristics such as virtues, but simply focus on short-term gains, their level of ethical behavior will decline. Accordingly, it is quite clear that, at the least, ethical marketing requires:

(a) the recognition of ethical problems;
(b) an awareness of relevant concepts, tools, and models to address those ethical problems;
(c) an appreciation that ethical problems are not simply individual in nature; and
(d) some notion of accountability for one's actions.

The first three in this list are part of the adoption of the integrated marketing concept. However, the underlying question here has to do with the practical conditions that would promote and sustain these features of ethical marketing. Given the preceding chapters, the effort to foster ethical marketing is part of a larger endeavor that involves both marketers and customers. Due to space limitations I will discuss only marketers in the following, rather than ways to foster the ethics of customers as well.

In attempting to address these problems, it would be unreasonable to demand that the standard of success be that all marketers always act ethically. In marketing ethics, as in everyday life, there are degrees of better and worse. The aim must be to move marketing behavior as far along as we possibly can towards agreed-upon forms of ethical behavior. Still, the desired end is one in which everyone acts ethically.

There are three levels we must consider: the individual, the organizational, and the societal (both national and international). Far from being discrete or separate, these three levels are intimately bound up. Although some marketers have focused on only one or two of these levels, all three require significant attention if marketing is to be ethical.

The individual level

Ethical marketing requires that individual marketers have the necessary cognitive, practical, and motivational resources. Cognitively, they must be able to recognize when they (or their organizations) face ethical problems. This is easily said, but much less easily done. It is striking how often it does not happen. Sometimes people simply don't see the ethical issue confronting them. The lenses through which they see the world filter out the ethical issues. Some call these filters "schemas," i.e., "cognitive framework[s] that people use to impose structure upon information, situations, and expectations to facilitate understanding" (Gioia, 1992: 386). Unfortunately, often these schemas exclude ethically relevant details and transform morally important considerations. In these ways, descriptions of events may be altered terms that cloak the moral questions of those events.

Moral blindness also arises because we are much too inclined to think that we are not, and cannot be, influenced by external pressures or influences, such as potential conflicts of interest. In short, we are inclined to view ourselves as secure against outside, ethically questionable influences, even though this is not the case. This may reflect naivety on our part, or (worse) a form of arrogance. Marketers need a reality check when it comes to these behaviors. The implication is that it is "clear that neither simple conviction nor sincere intention is enough to ensure that you are the ethical practitioner you imagine yourself to be" (Banaji et al., 2003: 63).

The belief that ethics is simply a matter of personal opinion also tends to undercut, ironically, individual efforts to address ethical issues in marketing. If ethics is simply a personal matter, there are no inter-subjective, interpersonal truths that we might draw upon. One can only be judged by one's own standards (outside the law). But if public and collective discussion of general principles and values is unavailable, individuals will experience greater moral stress since they will find it difficult, as isolated moral decision-makers, to know what they morally ought to do (see Waters and Bird, 1987). The argument of this book is that this purely subjectivist view is mistaken. In fact, it is a rather radical view at odds with a great deal of human moral history. The road to recovery, as it were, must begin with recognizing the deficiencies of the subjectivist view, as well as our moral limitations, noted above.

Finally, another ethical obstacle is the mindset that some individuals bring to marketing that seeks to accomplish its aims without duly considering the implications and/or consequences. One form this short-sightedness takes is the particularly competitive, if not combative, stance that characterizes some in marketing. This is used to justify a host of behaviors that would not otherwise be viewed as acceptable. Sometimes this view is captured in comments such as "Anything you can get by the law goes," or "You have to be on the edge." It is always about pushing boundaries. If this is what a person is thinking, then it is not surprising that they step over the edge.

These features of individual decision-making shape the moral behavior of marketers. Some individual marketers can, on some occasions, overcome them by themselves. But there is a tendency of too many ethicists to look simply to the individual and his or her own resources. For them, ethics is linked to the individual and his or her decisions. The role of marketing ethics is to inform people about relevant norms and values and encourage their application in marketing. However, this neglects the inconvenient fact that the above challenges to ethical marketing are not simply individual choices or stances people have adopted in light of their own knowledge. Instead, marketers are socialized into the individuals they are through a (moral) language they did not invent and in organizations over which they may have little control. They tend to hold values and norms that derive from their surroundings. We can identify cognitive mistakes and deficiencies that influence individuals in the decisions they individually make. But we forget, at the risk of being irrelevant, the social (psychological, genetic) embeddedness of individuals in the organizations, institutions, and societies about them.

Consequently, those who seek to foster ethical marketing must work with individuals as informed and influenced by the contexts in which they have been educated and socialized and in which they work. It is true that these individuals require the cognitive abilities to make appropriate ethical distinctions, to know when questions of justice, coercion, manipulation, honesty, etc. are present, and to understand the moral implications of different policies. But though this knowledge of ethical concepts, basic moral tools, and theories is important in confronting the ethical problems of marketing, it is also of limited help. Otherwise all ethically knowledgeable people would be ethical – something that is, unfortunately, not the case. Properly viewed, the ethical knowledge in question is not simply an abstract knowledge that certain things about ethics and ourselves are true, but also a practical knowledge of how to apply them when we must make decisions. However, the ability to do so must be fostered through training programs that involve case studies, role-playing, the recounting of stories about successful (and unsuccessful) market-ers, and the presence of moral mentors who can provide guidance as to what people in their roles and organizations should do (see Gioia, 1992: 388).

These conditions for moral decision-making introduce a motivational dimension to this issue. Oftentimes it takes courage to apply ethical knowl-edge. Considerable strength of character may be demanded to recognize and acknowledge what is difficult, inconvenient, opposed to the common wisdom, or at odds with one's own present views or immediate interests. Nevertheless, our own larger interests are bound up with morality and ethical marketing. And part of this motivational structure is that individuals are punished for their misdeeds, even if it is only through the social disapproval of their peers. In any case, they are, or ought to be, held accountable.

These are not, however, things that individuals generally do on their own, i.e., hoisting themselves by their own moral bootstraps (though on occasion it does happen). Instead, more generally, individual marketers must be aided in the process of developing the moral courage and determination to act upon what they believe to be the right course of action. Friends, mentors, and families may be part of this. They may require others to help them recognize ethically appropriate behavior. However, much of this points to the impor-tance of the organizational and societal contexts within which marketers live and work.

Accordingly, to foster ethical marketing at the individual level is to recog-nize the cognitive, practical, and motivational resources marketers must have and to take the preceding steps. However, it is also to recognize that these measures are unlikely in some cases, and impossible in others, to come from the individuals themselves. In general, they will require support from the organizations and societies of which these individuals are members. As others have urged, the answer to ethical problems at the individual level isn't simply one of trying harder (see Banaji et al., 2003). Individuals are responsible for their own conduct. But the larger contexts of their organizations and societies are significantly involved in making this assumption of responsibility possible.

The organizational level

Mindsets, schemas, norms, and even personal expectations do not arise without the connections, relations, and sources within which each individual lives. They arise from and are fed by praise, the expectations of others, financial rewards, promotions for those who act in certain ways, as well as censure from others. In short, they are supported by the organizations and institutions of which people are members (see Paine, 1994).

Accordingly, marketing organizations must consider their influence on the actions of their members and customers, and on the environment. This requires attention to structural as well as cultural issues within the organization. Regarding structural issues, organizations should articulate a set of ethical values and norms by which their members are to act. With an increasingly diverse membership, this exercise is all the more important. Such values and norms should be an integral part of the decisions that a marketing organization makes about its strategy as well as its particular actions. The previous chapters have suggested the kinds of values and norms that marketing organizations may (or must, in some cases) adopt. They have also sought to indicate ways in which those normative elements of marketing might be brought to bear on particular issues in marketing.

These structures must make room for an open discussion of moral issues. Indeed, without "institutionalized structures which accord a public character to moral concerns" individual marketers tend to experience moral lapses and failures as they go about their jobs. They are also more likely to experience moral stress (Waters and Bird, 1987: 18). Accordingly, an organization should encourage bringing the discussion of moral issues out of the closet so that marketing managers can openly discuss them. This requires that organizations educate their members regarding their values and norms. This is not a 15-minute or even an hour-long computer session once a year. Instead, such education must be aimed at continuously informing and shaping how people view themselves and their jobs. Training programs should "expose managers directly to the unconscious mechanisms that underlie biased decision making" (Banaji et al., 2003: 60). They must help them to see how these values and norms are to be applied in normal situations, as well as in any exceptional situations that might be anticipated. Organization members should know what rewards, incentives, and/or punishments are in place regarding their daily behavior and how they relate to the organization's values and norms. Hence, ethical marketing requires that evaluation and compensation systems be addressed so that they are not only fair but also supportive of the organization's values and norms.

When marketing organizations make marketing decisions regarding market research, product development, competitive intelligence, advertising, and all the other topics previously discussed in this book, they need to consider the ethical dimensions of the proposed actions and policies. Value risk assessments of where their organization might go astray should be developed. Do they develop, in effect, ethical impact statements of new business ventures? If they propose to enter into some new business area, do their business proposals include an assessment of its ethical climate (see Waters and Bird, 1987: 86)? Such ethical reports and policies must not be viewed as external to marketing and its strategic decision-making process, but rather part of the organization's use of the integrated marketing concept (see Robin and Reidenbach, 1987: 47).

What forms of accountability are built in to the organization? Does the organization see itself as accountable only to stockholders or also to other stakeholders? How are members within the organization to be held accountable? How are individuals to be treated who point out problems in the organization? If internal whistle-blowers are not protected, then bad news will be hidden or denied. The antidote to such poisonous situations requires an ethical culture of openness. Hence, does the organization have means to encourage the "outing" of bad news to the proper recipients? Are there ombudspersons or ethics directors available to whom people may come, without fear of retribution, to bring ethical problems? Some businesses may even build "devil's advocates" into decision-making situations to disrupt tendencies to groupthink. To what extent is the marketing behavior of individuals monitored to determine whether the structures are working? This will involve gathering data about ethically relevant decisions made and consequences experienced. Such data may be very revealing about biases, unintended consequences, and decision-making processes. Are there procedures within the organization that can detect when people do not comply with the law or with organizational ethical standards? When violations of these standards take place, are those involved penalized when appropriate, or counseled to change their ways? Is this done consistently across all employees, including top management?[11]

Finally, what kind of leadership do top management and executives offer? The engagement and importance of the top leadership in efforts to embed ethics in organizations cannot be overstated. Do they seek to engage others or do they simply direct others to act in various ways? Do they strongly support, in word and action, the professed values and norms of the organization? Or is their failure to see or to acknowledge ethical problems encouraged by the silence of others? Can organization members relate stories of exemplary moral behavior that present (or past) employees or executives have engaged in? Have important deals been rejected on moral grounds? Have people been penalized, or even let go, for moral failures? Have others been praised (and even rewarded) for their moral courage and imagination? Only if organizations can respond to these questions in a positive manner can we say that the organizations within which marketers work are playing their role in fostering ethical marketing.

Answers to the above questions and issues may take various forms. But unless there are concrete, substantive answers that respond to the spirit and intent of these points, ethical marketing will not be fostered, but hindered, at the organizational level. These answers need not take the form of rigid rules and procedures. Though structures, with their rules, procedures, reviews, and compliance aspects, are important, they may also lack the flexibility and sensitivity required to deal with actual moral issues (see Paine, 1994; Waters and Bird, 1987). These latter features of ethical marketing are captured by the notion of an ethical culture, which requires the values, customs, procedures, and stories whose importance has already been mentioned.

The societal level

Ethical marketing must also look at individuals and organizations within the social, economic, and political systems in which (and through which) they operate. They must do this at the local, national, and international levels. Too often marketing ethicists look only at individuals and marketing organizations when they examine the issue of fostering ethical marketing. Though important, such an approach is too narrow.

At each of these levels – the local, national, and international – organizations operate within various webs of laws, regulations, customs, popular pressures, non-governmental organizations, etc. These are part of what De George has called "background institutions" (De George, 1993). The right combination (and there may be many different forms that are "right") is essential for ethical marketing. Given that we are talking about marketing which takes place in a capitalist society, there are frequent appeals for self-regulation. This fits in with the general appeal with regard to social responsibility for voluntary measures.

However, this is misleading in several ways. First, when people speak of corporate social responsibility as being voluntary, they mean this in a legal sense. There are, however, any number of activities that are morally obligatory for marketers even if they are not legally obligatory. Consequently, those practices or policies of ethical marketing that are morally obligatory are not simply voluntary (even if legally voluntary) and may still, justifiably, be the object of popular demands or NGO actions.

Second, though we need to draw a distinction between the law and morality, we must also affirm their interconnection. If the law involves socially approved coercion, then with regard to certain immoral activities, social coercion is (and should be) approved. If the law does not address, for example, new forms of false advertising, dangerous products, deceptive promotions, or the invasion of privacy, then the law may not be doing what morality requires.

Laws may be necessary to capture morally important requirements. When a reasonable case has been made that a law is necessary to capture these moral requirements, marketing organizations ought not to resist, but should support, such measures. Too often they have dragged their feet.

Third, people's moral behavior requires support from the society in which they live and work. To encourage or foster moral behavior it is important that there are customs, understandings, and other (non-governmental) institutional reinforcement so that actual moral behavior is not undercut or made self-destructive by others. These background institutions and conditions are especially important for those who find it difficult to do what is morally required without external support or pressure. Hence, ethical marketing requires society's active protection on both formal and informal levels.

Another important societal condition is that of transparency. When the actions of individuals and organizations that are importantly affecting others in society can be hidden from their view, the situation is ripe for unethical behavior. Transparency may be accomplished, in various ways, through laws and regulations. However, the press and NGOs play an important role here by calling attention to the consequences of various marketing and corporate activities. Accordingly, when businesses engage in SLAPP suits they undercut these conditions for the ethics of marketing.[12] A very different and more positive response has been that of some marketers, such as Nike, Mattel, and Starbucks, who have, in recent years, moved to allow independent monitors to examine their successes or failures with their suppliers. Such initiatives are important steps towards ascertaining the nature and extent of marketers' fulfillment of their responsibilities.

Similarly it is also important to have professional associations that seek to identify ethical paths marketers should take, to illustrate them, and even to enforce them. And though the American Marketing Association has created a Statement of Ethics for marketers, previous arguments in this book have identified the shortcomings of this. In addition, the enforcement aspect of these professionally identified responsibilities is not something that associations such as the AMA have been inclined to undertake. It is a rare occasion when members are kicked out of such organizations. However, to be serious about their codes of ethics, they also need to be serious about monitoring and enforcing such codes.

The point of the preceding is that the ethical is not something regarding which a single person or organization can have an unerring insight. What is ethical must emerge out of discussions and dialogue (see chapter 2) with the multiple stakeholders involved. Just as the individuals within an organization must be held accountable, so too marketing organizations must themselves be held accountable in society. Traditionally their accountability has been to their stockholders. But we have seen in preceding chapters that this accountability extends much more broadly to their stakeholders. Recently the U.S. Federal Sentencing Guidelines were amended to make members of the governing boards of corporations responsible for their oversight of the business's compliance and ethics programs. The recognition that their responsibilities also extend to ethics programs is yet another societal and structural measure that helps to hold those who are essential to the governance of business organizations ethically responsible. Such laws and regulations address those aspects of the marketplace which permit, and in some cases encourage, unethical behavior. Other laws have been necessary to protect consumers who may lack knowledge of products or to deter others inclined to act as free riders or engage in moral hazard.

The international dimension

Finally, the international level remains a crucial arena in which the ethics of marketing is particularly challenged. Since marketing increasingly takes place on the global level, efforts to foster ethical marketing must take place on this level as well. Yet this is another significant area in which marketing ethics may suffer. In the international arena, since there is not a sovereign power or authority, individual nations and localities may play off against each other in ways reminiscent of the problem of the commons (Hardin, 1968). Marketing organizations may thereby see incentives to take unethical advantage of this or that locality. Contrariwise, they may believe that they must engage in certain acts to protect their own competitive situation.

Even though some companies try to lead the way here, they cannot do it all by themselves. In the international realm, we are constantly reminded that any successful marketing ethics has its feet rooted in real, practical conditions. Accordingly, international organizations (the World Bank, the World Trade Organization, the United Nations, the International Labour Organization) must play a role by setting ethical standards and monitoring their fulfillment. It is noteworthy, however, that only parts of the UN Global Compact relate to marketing. A related problem marketers face is to know which ethical standards to follow. Various organizations have identified a multiplicity of ethical standards. They do not all agree. One of the primary items on the international marketing ethics agenda must be an effort to arrive at compatible moral standards and expectations for marketers. Perhaps something along the lines of a Global Reporting Initiative that focuses on marketing is needed to provide general and consistent ethical guidelines for marketers.

The internet and large numbers of international non-governmental organizations will play a crucial role in helping to arrive at these standards as well as in revealing unsavory marketing practices and mobilizing customer behavior to support higher ethical standards. When marketers are aware that policies enacted in Nigeria, Ecuador, or Vietnam may quickly and globally be brought to the attention of customers, other NGOs, and governments, they will have a significant incentive to attend much more closely to both the legal and the ethical dimensions of those policies and actions. Though this situation may be perceived as a threat by some marketers, others will see opportunities here to work with NGOs and local groups to enhance the ethical acceptability of their marketing programs.

For both marketers and customers there are clearly advantages to developing international ethics standards. With regard to marketers such standards make for consistency, fewer conflicts, and greater congruence of expectations and perceptions (Rallapalli, 1999: 126). From the customer standpoint and that of those impacted by marketing activities, such codes have the advantage of offering a commitment by marketers to which they can be held. If they do not act in accord with such principles, they can be charged with hypocrisy, a more damning criticism than simply not following certain rules or guidelines which they don't accept.

The upshot is that ethical marketing requires a many-sided and multi-level approach. Many of these efforts are being made, but much more needs to be done. The fostering of ethical marketing is clearly still a work in progress.

V Conclusion

This chapter has considered the ethical implications of the extension of marketing within the international arena (e.g. to areas within India or China which have not previously been targeted by marketers) and within society itself to social and political issues. In the former case, it has portrayed the manner in which cross-cultural ethical issues could be approached and resolved. In the latter case, it has discussed the ethical presuppositions and consequences of social marketing. One of the ethical concerns that has been raised regards the importation of market assumptions and values into non-market relationships. With regard to political marketing, I considered the charge that this extension of marketing undercuts the democratic efforts of ordinary people to give voice to their concerns and replaces them with sophisticated propaganda approaches to persuade people without rationally appealing to them. In both of these cases, marketers need to take into account the consequences of their actions for the future of society before they lend their hand to these new forms of marketing. In some cases, they ought not to go forward with these extensions of marketing. In other cases, if they choose to go forward with them, they must seek ways to limit the negative effects of their actions.

Finally, I have briefly considered what might be involved in fostering ethical marketing. The view that ethical problems in marketing are merely those of a few "bad apples" is woefully oversimplified. Even the claim that marketers must adopt different mindsets is too easy. Individual initiative, through education, reflection, and determination, can address some of these problems. But, in general, the development of ethical marketing requires complex structures and cultures within marketing organizations as well as within local, national, and international society. Over recent decades, some progress has been made in fostering ethical marketing, but the threats and obstacles to it are also very real and very significant.

This chapter also concludes this book. Here and in the preceding chapters I have tried to provide an overview of marketing ethics, though it is far from a complete one. That would take a much longer book, most likely a series of books. I have tried to give the person unfamiliar with marketing some idea of what marketing encompasses, while at the same time focusing on the ethical issues that are part of marketing. For those not already familiar with marketing, my presentations of marketing itself will perhaps have been too abbreviated, but my focus has been on its ethical dimensions. And though even this discussion has necessarily been rather limited, my hope and intention is that readers of this book will come away with a sense that there are real and important questions here, and that they have gained some ideas about how to go about approaching them. One of the important messages that this discussion has sought to convey is that we should not be led into the mistaken view that, for ethics or morality to be significant, we must be able to give answers to which everyone will agree. The significance of ethics does not mean that it does not have its own limits, but those limits do not undermine its significance. However, my most important message has been that ethics is inextricably bound up with marketing. Separate the two and endless ethical and marketing problems arise. Acknowledge their interconnections, and we have the basis for responding to the ethical problems marketing faces.

Notes

1   I do not mean to imply that these issues only arise in "other societies" or countries outside the U.S. or Europe. There is plenty of bribery, corruption, and problems of gift-giving within these areas. I mention these issues here simply because they tend to arise in more dramatic forms for marketers when they arise in locations outside their own countries.

2   The claim regarding the source of U.S. corporate profits is not a new one. See Zikmund and d'Amico, 1993: 280. But also see Cooper and Madigan, 2005.

3   See *The Achieving Society* (see Lee, 1981: 59). But the importance of achievement (though perhaps of different sorts) is also clearly evident in China and Japan.

4   One can better appreciate, accordingly, that in this situation problems might arise if a uniform code of ethics is brought in.

5   In such a case, we should ask whether there is any intrinsic value or importance to the use of contracts. If there isn't then the non-Arab might be willing to budge on this issue, so long as the trust and commitment values were seen as congruent in this case. On the other hand, the Arab businessperson might be asked whether there is any other external sign of commitment and trust which each could exchange, other than (or in addition to) the handshake, that would not have intrinsic disvalue that he could accept.

6   See Fadiman's account of receiving and giving chickens in Kenya (Fadiman, 1986: 7–8).

7   In this section, I draw on work I have previously published in Brenkert, 2002.

8   Numerous authors have emphasized the importance of the distinct differences between different spheres of life. See Walzer, 1983; Jacobs, 1992.

9   Andreasen (1994: 111) does distinguish marketing from propaganda.

10 The case of Kasky v. Nike was very different in that it alleged that Nike's public messages regarding its products and places of production were commercial in nature and hence were subject to FTC standards regarding deception. Nike portrayed those messages as part of its own political speech and hence not subject to such oversight. Now surely commercial marketers can engage in free, political speech about a host of issues, for example immigration, tariffs, minimum wage. However, when their speech is designed to portray their products as not subject to concerns some have raised about their sourcing policies and thereby to remove this threat to their commercial sales, then such speech is plausibly commercial rather than political. This case was not settled by the U.S. Supreme Court. Instead, it was sent back to the lower court.

11 See LeClair et al., 1997, on the United States Sentencing Guidelines and various mechanisms associated with promoting ethical behavior.

12 SLAPP (Strategic Lawsuit Against Public Participation) suits are legal actions powerful businesses bring against organizations or groups of individuals to influence them to be quiet and not publicly to air any complaints about some corporate initiative.

AMA Statement of Ethics (adopted in 2004): Ethical Norms and Values for Marketers

Preamble

The American Marketing Association commits itself to promoting the highest standard of professional ethical norms and values for its members. Norms are established standards of conduct that are expected and maintained by society and/or professional organizations. Values represent the collective conception of what people find desirable, important and morally proper. Values serve as the criteria for evaluating the actions of others. Marketing practitioners must recognize that they not only serve their enterprises but also act as stewards of society in creating, facilitating and executing the efficient and effective transactions that are part of the greater economy. In this role, marketers should embrace the highest ethical norms of practicing professionals and the ethical values implied by their responsibility toward stakeholders (e.g., customers, employees, investors, channel members, regulators and the host community).

General Norms

1. Marketers must do no harm. This means doing work for which they are appropriately trained or experienced so that they can actively add value to their organizations and customers. It also means adhering to all applicable laws and regulations and embodying high ethical standards in the choices they make.
2. Marketers must foster trust in the marketing system. This means that products are appropriate for their intended and promoted uses. It requires

that marketing communications about goods and services are not intentionally deceptive or misleading. It suggests building relationships that provide for the equitable adjustment and/or redress of customer grievances. It implies striving for good faith and fair dealing so as to contribute toward the efficacy of the exchange process.

3. Marketers must embrace, communicate and practice the fundamental ethical values that will improve consumer confidence in the integrity of the marketing exchange system. These basic values are intentionally aspirational and include honesty, responsibility, fairness, respect, openness and citizenship.

Ethical Values

Honesty – to be truthful and forthright in our dealings with customers and stakeholders.

- We will tell the truth in all situations and at all times.
- We will offer products of value that do what we claim in our communications.
- We will stand behind our products if they fail to deliver their claimed benefits.
- We will honor our explicit and implicit commitments and promises.

Responsibility – to accept the consequences of our marketing decisions and strategies.

- We will make strenuous efforts to serve the needs of our customers.
- We will avoid using coercion with all stakeholders.
- We will acknowledge the social obligations to stakeholders that come with increased marketing and economic power.
- We will recognize our special commitments to economically vulnerable segments of the market such as children, the elderly and others who may be substantially disadvantaged.

Fairness – to try to balance justly the needs of the buyer with the interests of the seller.

- We will represent our products in a clear way in selling, advertising and other forms of communication; this includes the avoidance of false, misleading and deceptive promotion.

- We will reject manipulations and sales tactics that harm customer trust.
- We will not engage in price fixing, predatory pricing, price gouging or "bait-and-switch" tactics.
- We will not knowingly participate in material conflicts of interest.

Respect – to acknowledge the basic human dignity of all stakeholders.

- We will value individual differences even as we avoid stereotyping customers or depicting demographic groups (e.g., gender, race, sexual orientation) in a negative or dehumanizing way in our promotions.
- We will listen to the needs of our customers and make all reasonable efforts to monitor and improve their satisfaction on an ongoing basis.
- We will make a special effort to understand suppliers, intermediaries and distributors from other cultures.
- We will appropriately acknowledge the contributions of others, such as consultants, employees and coworkers, to our marketing endeavors.

Openness – to create transparency in our marketing operations.

- We will strive to communicate clearly with all our constituencies.
- We will accept constructive criticism from our customers and other stakeholders.
- We will explain significant product or service risks, component substitutions or other foreseeable eventualities that could affect customers or their perception of the purchase decision.
- We will fully disclose list prices and terms of financing as well as available price deals and adjustments.

Citizenship – to fulfill the economic, legal, philanthropic and societal responsibilities that serve stakeholders in a strategic manner.

- We will strive to protect the natural environment in the execution of marketing campaigns.
- We will give back to the community through volunteerism and charitable donations.
- We will work to contribute to the overall betterment of marketing and its reputation.
- We will encourage supply chain members to ensure that trade is fair for all participants, including producers in developing countries.

Implementation

Finally, we recognize that every industry sector and marketing subdiscipline (e.g., marketing research, e-commerce, direct selling, direct marketing, advertising) has its own specific ethical issues that require policies and commentary. An array of such codes can be accessed through links on the AMA Web site. We encourage all such groups to develop and/or refine their industry and discipline-specific codes of ethics to supplement these general norms and values.

Reprinted by permission of the American Marketing Association; <http://www.marketingpower.com/content435.php>

Appendix II
The Hunt–Vitell General Theory of Marketing Ethics

One of the best-known positive or descriptive accounts by marketers of ethical decision-making is that developed by Hunt and Vitell. Though this model, as represented in the figure below, has undergone an important revision, its essentials remain the same. Based upon a complex mixture of background conditions, individuals perceive ethical problems, alternatives, and potential consequences. They then engage in a twofold process, part of which is deontological and part teleological. Together, the product of these processes is an ethical judgment which results in intentions to behave accordingly and consequent behavior. The consequences of this behavior then act as a feedback mechanism.

There are several striking aspects of this model. First, its formulation relies heavily on normative ethical theories that focus on deontological and consequentialist views of moral decision-making. The authors readily acknowledge this point (Hunt and Vitell, 2006: 149). However, they have selectively drawn on ethical theory inasmuch as the authors do not consider or include in their model other normative ethical approaches to ethical decision-making that are non-principle-based and/or virtue-based. It is true that Hunt and Vitell mention virtues in their account, but on their view the virtues are portrayed as moderators of one's behavior, rather than as alternative normative bases through which ethical decisions are arrived at, as virtue theorists would argue. Second, the justification that Hunt and Vitell offer for this model is that empirical studies have shown that this is the way people actually make ethical decisions. Now this might well be disputed by Freudians or social psychologists, who point out the less than rational approach that many people take to ethical decision-making. In this manner, though Hunt and Vitell deny that their model is prescriptive of how people should make ethical decisions, there is, at the least, an implicit idealized model here of how people do make ethical decisions. It is rational and objective. The difference between this idealized model and a prescriptive model might well be the subject of interesting debate.

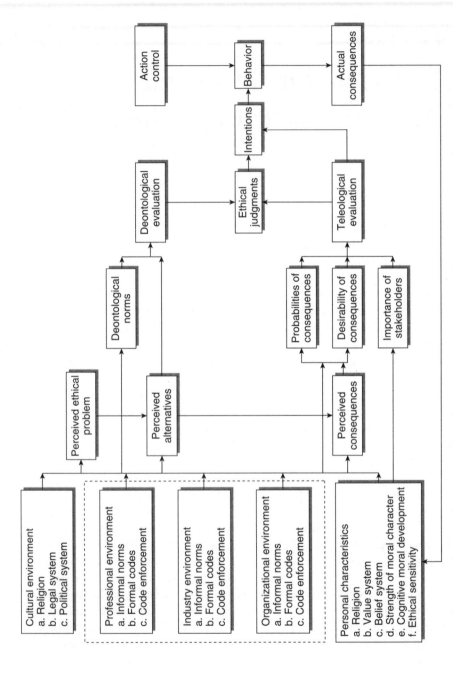

© Shelby D. Hunt and Scott J. Vitell, 1991. Reprinted by permission of the authors

Third, not withstanding the preceding point, the Hunt–Vitell model is not intended to tell people how they ought to make moral decisions. Accordingly, this model should not be used, according to its authors, by marketers who are seeking answers to what they ought or ought not to do in any of the countless marketing ethical problems they face.

Finally, it might be contended that the value of this model for marketers is that it can help tell marketing managers how to "control" the ethical behavior of members of their organizations.[1] It would be presumptuous of me to deny that some marketing managers might have gained knowledge from this model useful for that purpose. However, another perspective would be that marketing managers might also gain means of managing ethical questions and behavior in their organizations by using the normative framework developed in this book. Of course, in doing this it might be helpful to know how others actually do make moral decisions. But for this purpose, as I have suggested, the work of psychologists and social psychologists, as well as that of Hunt and Vitell, would be helpful.

Note

1   This point was suggested to me by an anonymous reviewer of this book.

Appendix III

SCIP Code of Ethics for Competitive Intelligence Professionals

- To continually strive to increase the recognition and respect of the profession.

- To comply with all applicable laws, domestic and international.

- To accurately disclose all relevant information, including one's identity and organization, prior to all interviews.

- To avoid conflicts of interest in fulfilling one's duties.

- To provide honest and realistic recommendations and conclusions in the execution of one's duties.

- To promote this code of ethics within one's company, with third-party contractors and within the entire profession.

- To faithfully adhere to and abide by one's company policies, objectives, and guidelines.

Reprinted by permission of the Society for Competitive Intelligence Professionals <www.scip.org>

Bibliography

Abratt, Russell and Diane Sacks. 1989. "Perceptions of the Societal Marketing Concept." *European Journal of Marketing*, 23(6): 25–33.

AMA (Committee on Definitions). 1960. *Marketing Definitions: A Glossary of Marketing Terms*. Chicago: American Marketing Association.

AMA. 2003. "News: JetBlue in Trouble with Customer Privacy." *Marketing Matters*, 2(16): 1–7.

Andreasen, Alan R. 1994. "Social Marketing: Its Definition and Domain." *Journal of Public Policy & Marketing*, 13(Spring): 108–14.

—— 1995. *Marketing Social Change*. San Francisco: Jossey-Bass.

—— 2001. *Ethics in Social Marketing*. Washington, DC: Georgetown University Press.

Ansberry, Clare. 1988. "For These M.B.A.s, Class Became Exercise in Corporate Espionage." *The Wall Street Journal*, March 22, p. 37.

Armstrong, Robert W., Bruce W. Stening, John K. Ryans, Larry Marks, and Michael Mayo. 1990. "International Marketing Ethics: Problems Encountered by Australian Firms." *European Journal of Marketing*, 24: 5–18.

Bagozzi, Richard P. 1975. "Marketing as Exchange." *Journal of Marketing*, 39(October): 32–9.

—— 1978. "Marketing as Exchange." *American Behavioral Scientist*, 21(March/April): 535–56.

Baier, Annette. 1985. "Doing Without Moral Theory?" In Annette Baier, *Postures of the Mind*. Minneapolis: University of Minneapolis Press, pp. 228–45.

Banaji, Mahzarin R., Max H. Bazerman, and Dolly Chugh. 2003. "How (Un)ethical Are You?" *Harvard Business Review*, 81(12): 56–64.

Banker, Steve. 1992. "The Ethics of Political Marketing Practices, The Rhetorical Perspective." *Journal of Business Ethics*, 11: 843–8.

Barney, J. B. and M. H. Hansen. 1994. "Trustworthiness as a Source of Competitive Advantage." *Strategic Management Journal*, 15: 175–90.

Barnhart, Clarence L. 1956. *The American College Dictionary*. New York: Random House.

Bartels, Robert. 1965. "Development of Marketing Thought: A Brief History." In George Schwartz (ed.), *Science in Marketing*. New York: John Wiley & Sons, pp. 20–6.

—— 1974. "The Identity Crisis in Marketing." *Journal of Marketing*, 38(October): 73–6.

Bell, Martin L. and C. William Emory. 1971. "The Faltering Marketing Concept." *Journal of Marketing*, 35: 37–42.

Berlin, Isaiah. 1991. "The Pursuit of the Ideal." In Isaiah Berlin, *The Crooked Timber of Humanity*, ed. Henry Hardy. New York: Alfred A. Knopf, pp. 1–19.

Bird, Frederick B. and James A. Waters. 1989. "The Moral Muteness of Managers." *California Management Review*, 32(1): 73–88.

Bok, Sissela. 1978. *Lying: Moral Choice in Public and Private Life*. New York: Vintage Books.

Brenkert, George G. 1998. "Trust, Morality and International Business." In Reinhard Bachmann and Christel Lane (eds.), *Trust in Inter-Organizational Relations*. Oxford: Oxford University Press. pp. 273–97.

—— 2002. "Ethical Challenges of Social Marketing." *Journal of Public Policy & Marketing*, 21(1): 14–25.

Bulmer, M. 1982. "The Merits and Demerits of Covert Participant Observation." In Martin Bulmer (ed.), *Social Research Ethics*. New York: Holmes & Meier, pp. 217–51.

Cady, John F. 1982. "Reasonable Rules and Rules of Reason: Vertical Restrictions on Distributors." *Journal of Marketing*, 46(Summer): 27–37.

Carr, Albert Z. 1968. "Is Business Bluffing Ethical?" *Harvard Business Review*, 46(1): 143–53.

Cespedes, Frank V. 1993. "Ethical Issues in Distribution." In N. C. Smith and J. A. Quelch (eds.), *Ethics in Marketing*. Homewood, IL: Irwin, pp. 473–90.

Claiborne, Keri. 1998. "The Effects of Manipulative Advertising on Society." <http://courses.dce.harvard.edu/~humae105/fall97/kclaiborne01.htm>.

Collins, James C. and Jerry Porras. 1994. *Built to Last: Successful Habits of Visionary Companies*. New York: Harper Business.

Cooper, James C. and Kathleen Madigan. 2005. "U.S.: Why Profits Are Defying Gravity." *Business Week Online* <http://www.businessweek.com/magazine/content/05_16/b3929033_mz010.htm>, accessed July 20, 2006.

Crane, Andrew and John Desmond. 2002. "Societal Marketing and Morality." *European Journal of Marketing*, 36(5/6): 548–70.

Cravens, David W. 1995. "Introduction to Special Issue." *Journal of the Academy of Marketing Science*, 23(4): 235.

Crock, Stan. 1996. "They Snoop to Conquer." *Business Week*, October 28, pp. 172–6.

De George, Richard. 1990. *Business Ethics*, 3rd edn. New York: Macmillan.

—— 1993. *Competing with Integrity in International Business*. New York: Oxford University Press.

Denzin, N. K. and K. Erikson 1982. "On the Ethics of Disguised Observation: An Exchange." In Martin Bulmer (ed.), *Social Research Ethics*. New York: Holmes & Meier, pp. 142–51.

Donaldson, Thomas. 1996. "Values in Tension." *Harvard Business Review*, 74(5): 44–56.

Donaldson, Thomas and Thomas W. Dunfee. 1999. *Ties that Bind*. Cambridge, MA: Harvard University Press.

Donath, Bob. 1999. "No, Really, the Marketing Concept Never Left." *Marketing News*, July 19, p. 10.

Drucker, Peter F. 1954. *The Practice of Management*. New York: Harper & Row.

Duke, Lynne. 2000. "Nike's Cutting-Edge Ad Sliced Both Ways." *Washington Post*, September 20, p. C01.

Ebejer, James M. and Michael J. Morden. 1988. "Paternalism in the Marketplace: Should a Salesman Be his Buyer's Keeper?" *Journal of Business Ethics*, 7: 337–9.

Fadiman, Jeffrey A. 1986. "A Traveler's Guide to Gifts and Bribes." *Harvard Business Review*, 64(4): 4–12.

Farhi, Paul. 2000. "A Repugnant Ad." *Washington Post*, September 19, p. A22.

Ferrell, O. C. and Larry G. Gresham. 1985. "A Contingency Framework for Understanding Ethical Decision Making in Marketing." *Journal of Marketing*, 49(Summer): 87–96.

Fitzpatrick, William M. 2003. "Uncovering Trade Secrets: The Legal and Ethical Conundrum of Creative Competitive Intelligence." *S.A.M. Advanced Management Journal*, 68(3): 4–13.

Fox, Karen F. A. and Philip Kotler. 1980. "The Marketing of Social Causes: The First 10 Years." *Journal of Marketing*, 44(Fall): 24–33.

Frankena, William. 1973. *Ethics*. Englewood Cliffs, NJ: Prentice Hall.

Fritzsche, David J. 1985. "Ethical Issues in Multinational Marketing." In Gene R. Laczniak and Patrick E. Murphy (eds.), *Marketing Ethics*. Lexington, MA: D. C. Heath, pp. 85–96.

Fritzsche, David J. and Helmut Becker. 1984. "Linking Management Behavior to Ethical Philosophy: An Empirical Investigation." *Academy of Management Journal*, 27(1): 166–75.

Fromm, Eric. 1955. *The Sane Society*. Greenwich, CT: Fawcett Publications.

Fukuyama, Francis. 1995. *Trust*. New York: The Free Press.

Gaski, John F. 1984. "The Theory of Power and Conflict in Channels of Distribution." *Journal of Marketing*, 48(Summer): 9–29.

—— 1999. "Does Marketing Ethics Really Have Anything to Say? A Critical Inventory of the Literature". *Journal of Business Ethics*, 18(3): 315–34.

Ghosh, Avijit and Sara McLafferty. 1986. "Shopping Behavior and Optimal Store Locations in Multipurpose Trip Environments." In Luca Pellegrini and Srinivas K. Reddy (eds.), *Marketing Channels*. Lexington, MA: D. C. Heath, pp. 157–70.

Gioia, Dennis A. 1992. "Pinto Fires and Personal Ethics: A Script Analysis of Missed Opportunities." *Journal of Business Ethics*, 11: 379–89.

Greenland, Leo. 1974. "Thinking Ahead: Advertisers Must Stop Conning Consumers." *Harvard Business Review*, 52(4): 18–20, 24, 28, 156.

Gupta, Omprakas K. and Anna S. Rominger. 1996. "Blind Man's Bluff: The Ethics of Quantity Surcharges." *Journal of Business Ethics*, 15(12): 1299–1313.

Hall, Edward Twitchell. 1983. *The Dance of Life: The Other Dimension of Time.* Garden City, NY: Anchor Press/Doubleday.

Hampshire, Stuart. 1989. *Innocence and Experience.* Cambridge, MA: Harvard University Press.

Hansen, Don R., Rick L. Crosser, and Doug Laufer. 1992. "Moral Ethics v. Tax Ethics: The Case of Transfer Pricing among Multinational Corporations." *Journal of Business Ethics*, 11(9): 679–86.

Hardin, Garritt. 1968. "The Tragedy of the Commons." *Science* (new series), 162: 1243–8.

Hirschman, Elizabeth C. 1983. "Aesthetics, Ideologies and the Limits of the Marketing Concept." *Journal of Marketing*, 47(Summer): 45–55.

——1986. "Humanistic Inquiry in Marketing Research: Philosophy, Method and Criteria." *Journal of Marketing Research*, 23: 237–49.

Hodges, Louis W. 1988. "Undercover, Masquerading, Surreptitious Taping." *Journal of Mass Media Ethics*, 3(2): 26–36.

Hofstede, Geert and Gert Jan Hofstede. 2005. *Cultures and Organizations.* New York: McGraw-Hill.

Holley, David. 1986. "A Moral Evaluation of Sales Practices." *Business and Professional Ethics Journal*, 5: 3–21.

Houston, Franklin S. 1986. "The Marketing Concept: What It Is and What It Is Not." *Journal of Marketing*, 50(April): 81–7.

Hunt, Shelby D. 1976. "The Nature and Scope of Marketing." *Journal of Marketing*, 40: 17–28.

Hunt, Shelby D. and Scott J. Vitel. 1986. "A General Theory of Marketing Ethics." *Journal of Macromarketing*, 6(Spring): 5–16.

——1993. "The General Theory of Marketing Ethics: A Retrospective and Revision." In N. Craig Smith and John A. Quelch (eds.), *Ethics in Marketing.* Homewood, IL: Irwin, pp. 775–82.

——2006. "The General Theory of Marketing Ethics: A Revision and Three Questions." *Journal of Macromarketing*, 26: 143–53.

Jackson, J. 1990. "Honesty in Marketing". *Journal of Applied Philosophy*, 7(1): 51–60.

Jacobs, Jane. 1992. *Systems of Survival.* New York: Random House.

Johansson, Johny K. 2004. *In Your Face.* Upper Saddle River, NJ: Financial Times/ Prentice Hall.

Jorgensen, D. L. 1989. Participant Observation, A Methodology for Human Studies. Newbury Park, CA: Sage Publications.

Kaldor, Andrew G. 1971. "Imbricative Marketing." *Journal of Marketing*, 35(April): 19–25.

Kaufmann, Patrick J., Gwendolyn K. Ortmeyer, and N. Craig Smith. 1991. "Fairness in Consumer Pricing." *Journal of Consumer Policy*, 14: 117–40.

Kavali, Stella, Nikolaos Tzokas, and Michael Saren. 2001. "Corporate Ethics: An Exploration of Contemporary Greece." *Journal of Business Ethics*, 30(1/1): 87–105.

Kimmel, Allan J. and N. Craig Smith. 2001. "Deception in Marketing Research: Ethical, Methodological, and Disciplinary Implications." *Psychology & Marketing*, 18(7): 663–89.

Kotler, Philip, 1972a. "A Generic Concept of Marketing." *Journal of Marketing*, 36(April): 46–54.

—— 1972b. "What Consumerism Means for Marketers." *Harvard Business Review*, 50(3): 48–57.

—— 1987. "Humanistic Marketing: Beyond the Marketing Concept." In A. Fuat Firat, Nikhilesh Dholakia, and Richard P. Bagozzi (eds.), *Philosophical and Radical Thought in Marketing*. Lexington, MA: Lexington Books, pp. 271–88.

—— 2000. *Marketing Management: The Millennium Edition*. Upper Saddle River, NJ: Prentice Hall.

Kotler, Philip and Sidney J. Levy. 1969a. "Broadening the Concept of Marketing." *Journal of Marketing*, 33(January): 10–15.

———— 1969b. "A New Form of Marketing Myopia: Rejoinder to Professor Luck." *Journal of Marketing*, 33(July): 55–7.

Kotler, Philip and Gerald Zaltman. 1971. "Social Marketing: An Approach to Planned Social Change." *Journal of Marketing*, 35(July): 3–12.

Laczniak, Gene R. 1983. "Framework for Analyzing Marketing Ethics." *Journal of Macromarketing*, 3(1): 7–18.

Laczniak, Gene R. and Patrick E. Murphy. 1993. *Ethical Marketing Decisions: The Higher Road*. Boston: Allyn & Bacon.

LeClair, Debbie Thorne, O. C. Ferrell, and Linda Ferrell. 1997. "Federal Sentencing Guidelines for Organizations: Legal, Ethical and Public Policy Issues for International Marketing." *Journal of Public Policy & Marketing*, 6(1): 26–37.

Lee, Dong-Jin and M. Joseph Sirgy. 1999. "The Effect of Moral Philosophy and Ethnocentrism on Quality-of-Life Orientation in International Marketing: A Cross-Cultural Comparison." *Journal of Business Ethics*, 18(1): 73–89.

Lee, Kam-Hon. 1981. "Ethical Beliefs in Marketing Management: A Cross-Cultural Study." *European Journal of Marketing*, 15(1): 58–67.

Levitt, Theodore. 1970. "The Morality(?) of Advertising." *Harvard Business Review*, 48(4): 84–92.

—— 1983. "The Globalization of Markets." *Harvard Business Review*, 61(3): 92–103.

—— 1986. *The Marketing Imagination*, 2nd edn. New York: The Free Press.

Luck, David J. 1969. "Broadening the Concept of Marketing – Too Far." *Journal of Marketing*, 33(July): 53–63.

—— 1974. "Social Marketing: Confusion Compounded." *Journal of Marketing*, 38(October): 70–2.

MacIntyre, Alasdair. 1984. *After Virtue*, 2nd edn. Notre Dame: University of Notre Dame Press.

McDonough, William A. 2000. "A Boat for Thoreau." In Joel Reichart and Patricia H. Werhane (eds.), *Environmental Challenges to Business*, Ruffin Series 2. Bowling Green, OH: Society for Business Ethics, pp. 115–33.

McDonough, William and Michael Braungart. 2002. *Cradle to Cradle.* New York: North Point Press.

McMurry, Robert N. 1961. "The Mystique of Super-Salesmanship." *Harvard Business Review,* 39(2): 113–22.

Maitland, Ian. 1997. "The Great Non-Debate over International Sweatshops." *British Academy of Management Annual Conference Proceedings* (September): 240–65.

Malhotra, Naresh K. 1992. "Shifting Perspective on the Shifting Paradigm in Marketing Research: A New Paradigm in Marketing Research." *Journal of the Academy of Marketing Science,* 20(4): 379–87.

Mayer, Caroline E. 2006. "Sugary Drinks to be Pulled from Schools." *Washington Post,* May 3, p. D01.

Mayo, Michael A. and Lawrence J. Marks. 1990. "An Empirical Investigation of a General Theory of Marketing Ethics." *Journal of the Academy of Marketing Science,* 18(2): 163–71.

Mehafdi, Messaoud. 2000. "The Ethics of International Transfer Pricing." *Journal of Business Ethics,* 28(4/2): 365–81.

Menezes, Melvyn A. J. 1993. "Ethical Issues in Product Policy." In N. Craig Smith and John A. Quelch (eds.), *Ethics in Marketing.* Homewood, IL: Irwin, pp. 283–301.

Messick, D., S. Bloom, J. P. Boldizar, and C. D. Samuelson. 1985. "Why We Are Fairer than Others." *Journal of Experimental Social Psychology,* 21: 480–500.

Messick, David M. and Max H. Bazerman. 1996. "Ethical Leadership and the Psychology of Decision Making." *Sloan Management Review,* 37(2): 9–22.

Mills, Mike. 1998. "By Any Means: You Might Owe Merchants a Bit More than You Bargained For." *Washington Post,* November 22, pp. C1, C4.

Mocwa, Michael. 1987. "Ethical Consciousness and the Competence of Product Management: Beyond Righteousness, Rituals and Rules." In A. Fuat Firat, Nikhilesh Dholakia, and Richard P. Bagozzi (eds.), *Philosophical and Radical Thought in Marketing.* Lexington, MA: Lexington Books, pp. 57–76.

Morello, Gabriele 1993. "The Hidden Dimensions of Marketing." *Journal of the Market Research Society,* 35(4): 293–313.

Morello, Gabriele and Patricia Van der Reis. 1990. "Attitudes towards Time in Different Cultures: African Time and European Time." In *Proceedings of the Third Symposium on Cross-Cultural Consumer and Business Studies.* University of Hawaii, Honolulu.

Mortished, Carl. 2001. "Shampoo Giants Tell Spies to Wash and Go." *Times of London,* September 1, <www.commondreams.org>.

Nagle, Thomas T. 1987. *The Strategy and Tactics of Pricing.* Englewood Cliffs, NJ: Prentice Hall.

Nickels, William G. 1974. "Conceptual Conflicts in Marketing." *Journal of Economics and Business,* 26(Winter): 140–3.

Noonan, John T. 1984. *Bribes.* New York: Macmillan.

Nussbaum, Martha C. 2000. *Women and Human Development.* Cambridge: Cambridge University Press.

Ortega, Bob and John R. Wilke. 1998. "Amid Probe, Anheuser Conquers Turf." *Wall Street Journal*, March 9, pp. B1, B4.

Ortmeyer, Gwendolyn K. 1993. "Ethical Issues in Pricing." In N. Craig Smith and John A. Quelch (eds.), *Ethics in Marketing*. Homewood, IL: Irwin, pp. 389–404.

O'Shaughnessy, Nicholas J. 2002. "Toward an Ethical Framework for Political Marketing." *Psychology & Marketing*, 19(12): 1079–94.

Paine, Lynn Sharp. 1991. Corporate Policy and the Ethics of Competitor Intelligence Gathering." *Journal of Business Ethics*, 10(6): 423–37.

——1994. "Managing for Organizational Integrity." *Harvard Business Review*, 72(2): 106–17.

Perkins, Ed. 2003. "How to Battle Deceptive Pricing." *The Record* (Bergen County, NJ), January 19, p. T02.

Pollay, Richard W. 1986. "The Distorted Mirror: Reflections on the Unintended Consequences of Advertising." *Journal of Marketing*, 50(April): 18–36.

Polonsky, Michael Jay, Pedro Quelhas Brito, Jorge Pinto, and Nicola Higgs-Kleyn. 2001. "Consumer Ethics in the European Union: A Comparison of Northern and Southern Views." *Journal of Business Ethics*, 31: 117–30.

Porter, Michael E. 1996. "What Is Strategy?" *Harvard Business Review*, 74(6): 61–78.

Prescott, John. 2001. "The Private Sector: Espionage, Ethics and 'Competitive Intelligence'." *Pittsburgh Post-Gazette*, October 9, 2 pp.

Preston, Ivan L. 1994. *The Tangled Web They Weave*. Madison: University of Wisconsin Press.

Putnam, Hilary. 1995. *Pragmatism: An Open Question*. Oxford: Blackwell.

Quelch, John A. and Aimee L. Stern. 1993. "Sorrell Ridge: Slotting Allowances." In N. C. Smith and J. A. Quelch (eds.), *Ethics in Marketing*. Homewood, IL: Irwin, pp. 491–506.

Rallapalli, 1999. "A Paradigm for Development and Promulgation of a Global Code of Marketing Ethics." *Journal of Business Ethics*, 18: 125–37.

Rawls, John. 1971. *A Theory of Justice*. Cambridge, MA: Harvard University Press.

——1989. *The Law of Peoples*. Cambridge, MA: Harvard University Press.

Ricks, David A. 1993. *Blunders in International Business*. Oxford: Blackwell.

Ries, Al and Jack Trout. 1986. *Marketing Warfare*. New York: McGraw-Hill.

Ritzer, George. 2000. *The McDonaldization of Society*. Thousand Oaks, CA: Pine Forge Press.

Robin, Donald P. 1979. "Useful Boundaries for Marketing." In O. C. Ferrell, Stephen W. Brown, and Charles W. Lamb, Jr. (eds.), *Conceptual and Theoretical Developments in Marketing*. Chicago: American Marketing Association, pp. 605–13.

Robin, Donald P. and R. Eric Reidenbach. 1987. "Social Responsibility, Ethics, and Marketing Strategy: Closing the Gap Between Concept and Application." *Journal of Marketing*, 51(1): 44–58.

——1993. "Searching for a Place to Stand: Toward a Workable Ethical Philosophy for Marketing." *Journal of Public Policy & Marketing*, 12(1): 97–106.

Salkever, Alex. 2004. "The Technology of Personalized Pitches." *Business Week Online*, June 22, <http://www.businessweek.com/technology/content/jun2004/tc20040622_4257_tc150.htm>, accessed June 25, 2004.

Schneider, Kenneth C. and Cynthia K. Holm. 1982. "Deceptive Practices in Marketing Research: The Consumer's Viewpoint." *California Management Review*, 24(3): 89–96.

Schollhammer, Hans. 1977. "Ethics in an International Business Context." *MSU Business Topics*, 25: 54–63.

Schudson, Michael. 2003. "Advertising: Hit or Myth?" Center for Media Literacy, <www.medialit.org/reading_room/article217.html>.

Schwartz, George. 1971. "Marketing: The Societal Concept." *University of Washington Business Review*, 31(Autumn): 31–8.

Shaw, William H. 1991. *Business Ethics*. Belmont, CA: Wadsworth.

Singhapakdi, Anusorn and Scott J. Vitell (eds.). 1999. "Special Issue on International Marketing Ethics." *Journal of Business Ethics*, 18(1): 1–2.

Solomon, Robert. 1992. *Ethics and Excellence*. New York: Oxford University Press.

Soule, Edward. 2003. *Morality & Markets*. Lanham, MD: Rowman & Littlefield.

——2005. *Embedding Ethics in Business and Higher Education*. Washington, DC: Business-Higher Education Forum.

Stafford, Marla Royne and Thomas F. Stafford. 1993. "Participant Observation and the Pursuit of Truth: Methodological and Ethical Considerations." *Journal of the Market Research Society*, 35: 63–76.

Stanton, William J., Michael J. Etzel, and Bruce J. Walker. 1994. *Fundamentals of Marketing*, 10th edn. New York: McGraw-Hill.

Sturdivant, Frederick D. 1968. "Better Deal for Ghetto Shoppers." *Harvard Business Review*, 46(2): 130–9.

Takala, Tuomo and Outi Uusitalo. 1996. "An Alternative View of Relationship Marketing: A Framework for Ethical Analysis." *European Journal of Marketing*, 30: 45–60.

Touche Ross. 1989. *Ethics in American Business* (January). Survey of US executive perceptions of ethics of foreign managers, p. 6.

Trawick, I. Fredrick, John E. Swan, Gail W. McGee, and David R. Rink. 1991. "Influence of Buyer Ethics and Salesperson Behavior on Intention to Choose a Supplier." *Journal of the Academy of Marketing Science*, 19(1): 17–23.

Turque, Bill, Deborah Rosenberg, and Todd Barrett. 1992. "Where the Food Isn't." *Newsweek*, February 24, pp. 36–7.

Tybout, Alice M. and Gerald Zaltman. 1974. "Ethics in Marketing Research: Their Practical Relevance." *Journal of Marketing Research*, 11(November): 357–68.

U.S. Environmental Protection Agency. 2006. "Municipal Solid Waste in the United States: 2005 Facts and Figures. Executive Summary." <www.epa.gov/osw>.

Velasquez, Manuel. 2004. "Is Corruption Always Corrupt?" In George G. Brenkert (ed.), *Corporate Integrity & Accountability*. Thousand Oaks: Sage Publications, pp. 148–65.

Waddock, Sandra. 2004. "Managing Responsibility: What Can Be Learned from the Quality Movement?" *California Management Review*, 47(1): 25–37.

Walzer, Michael. 1983. *Spheres of Justice*. New York: Basic Publishers.

—— 1994. *Thick and Thin*. Notre Dame: University of Notre Dame Press.

Warnock G. J. 1971. *The Object of Morality*. London: Methuen.

Waters, James A. and Frederick Bird. 1987. "The Moral Dimension of Organizational Culture." *Journal of Business Ethics*, 6(1): 15–22.

Webster, F. E. Jr. 1988. "The Rediscovery of the Marketing Concept." *Business Horizons*, 31(May/June): 29–39.

Wolf, Susan. 1992. "Two Levels of Pluralism." *Ethics*, 102(July): 785–98.

Zelek, Eugene F., Jr., Louis W. Stern, and Thomas W. Dunfee. 1980. "A Rule of Reason Decision Model after *Sylvania*." *California Law Review*, 68: 13–47.

Zikmund, William G. and Michael d'Amico. 1993. *Marketing*, 4th edn. Minneapolis: West Publishing.

Index